Migration and
Remittances from Mexico

Migration and Remittances from Mexico

Trends, Impacts, and New Challenges

Edited by
Alfredo Cuecuecha
and Carla Pederzini

LEXINGTON BOOKS
Lanham • Boulder • New York • Toronto • Plymouth, UK

Published by Lexington Books

A wholly owned subsidary of The Rowman & Littlefield Publishing Group, Inc.
4501 Forbes Boulevard, Suite 200, Lanham, Maryland 20706
www.lexingtonbooks.com

Estover Road, Plymouth PL6 7PY, United Kingdom

British Library Cataloguing in Publication Information Available

Library of Congress Cataloging-in-Publication Data

Migration and remittances from Mexico : trends, impacts, and new challenges / edited by
    Alfredo Cuecuecha and Carla Pederzini.
      p. cm.
    Includes bibliographical references and index.
    ISBN 978-0-7391-6979-7 (cloth : alk. paper) — ISBN 978-0-7391-6980-3 (electronic)
    1. Mexico—Emigration and immigration. 2. Migration, Internal—Mexico.
  3. Mexico—Emigration and immigration—Economic aspects. 4. Migration,
  Internal—Mexico—Economic aspects. 5. Emigrant remittances—Mexico. 6. Migrant
  remittances—Mexico. 7. Foreign workers, Mexican—United States. 8. Mexicans—
  United States. I. Cuecuecha, Alfredo. II. Pederzini, Carla.
    JV7401.M58 2012
    304.80972—dc23   2011039645

∞™ The paper used in this publication meets the minimum requirements of American
National Standard for Information Sciences—Permanence of Paper for Printed Library
Materials, ANSI/NISO Z39.48-1992.

Printed in the United States of America

Contents

Acknowledgements

Our work was possible thanks to the support of the Mexico–U.S. Binational Research Initiative on International Migration, which benefited from the generous contributions of Plácido Domingo, Fundación Manuel Arango, and the John D. and Catherine T. MacArthur Foundation. We were especially fortunate for the continual interest and enthusiasm of Enrique Gónzalez Torres, S.J., who has continually pursued the migration topic, and for the support and encouragement we received from Susan Martin, director of the Institute for the Study of International Migration (ISIM).

We are also grateful for the generosity and support of the Department of Economics at *Centro de Investigación y Docencia Económicas* (CIDE); the Department of Economics and *Programa para Estudios Migratorios* (PRAMI) at Universidad Iberoamericana, Ciudad de México; the Institute for the Study of International Migration (ISIM) at Georgetown University; and the United Nations Development Program (UNDP) at Mexico City, who sponsored the International Workshop on Migration and Remittances: Trends, Impacts and New Challenges. This book is a direct product of the International Workshop.

A particular thank you goes to Rocío Lavalle and Isabel Espinosa de los Reyes for their excellent editorial assistance. Similarly, we are grateful for the enthusiasm and dedication of the authors who helped create this book: first by participating in the International Workshop, and later on in the process of writing and editing this book.

Finally, we want to thank our editor at Lexington Books, Lenore Lautigar, and her editorial assistant, Amy King, for their kind and dedicated work helping us edit the final version of this book.

Introduction

Alfredo Cuecuecha and Carla Pederzini

Scientists have traced down the origins of all mankind to Homo sapiens, a species that evolved in Africa during a time of dramatic climate change, 200,000 years ago. The overwhelming consensus about their leaving Africa in search of more space and new habitats in one large wave between 100,000 and 50,000 years ago has been recently challenged by a new hypothesis that states that they left in smaller movements across many different regions. In either case, all humans living outside Africa stem from international migrants. Migration is one of the main forces that shaped the history of human kind. In a sense, we all are migrants.

Researchers from diverse study fields have tried to explain the forces determining migration and the consequences of migration for both sending and receiving countries. Among other fields, researchers from economics, sociology, geography, and international relations have contributed to this effort.

The study of migration in Mexico and Latin America has received increasing attention in recent years, both by researchers in Mexico and in the United States. This extraordinary interest arises from the fact that the United States is the country of the world with the largest foreign-born population (above 40 million in 2010), half of which originated in Latin-American countries—almost one-third in Mexico. One out of five Mexican males between 25 and 35 lives in the United States. According to the 2010 Population Census in the United States, Hispanics or Latinos have become the first minority, representing 60 percent of all the minority population and 16.3 percent of the total population.

The above figures imply that migration in the Americas is called to strongly influence the lives of most citizens in this region of the world in many different ways. However, precisely because of the nature of migration—i.e.

the movement of population—migration is one of the most elusive social study topics. In order to fully comprehend the migratory phenomenon, more empirical studies and improved data sets, which allow the validation of current migratory models or the development of new theories, are required. This book displays the main research studies presented at the International Workshop entitled "Migration and Remittances: Trends, Impacts and New Challenges" which took place in Mexico City in 2008, jointly organized by the *Centro de Investigación y Docencia Económicas* (CIDE), the *Universidad Iberoamericana* Mexico, and the Institute for the Study of International Migration (ISIM) at Georgetown University.

The workshop concentrated on three main topics: databases for the study of migration from Mexico and Latin America, internal migration in Mexico, and international migration and remittances. The book follows the same order, with a small change dividing research on international migration from research focused on remittances.

The first section presents efforts made to overcome the different challenges faced in measuring migration in Mexico. The second section presents studies focused in studying internal migration in Mexico. In the third section, we include studies which focus on various features of the migration process in Mexico and in Latin America. Finally, the fourth section focuses in studies that cover topics on remittances in Mexico and Latin America.

SECTION 1: DATABASES TO STUDY MIGRATION FROM MEXICO TO THE US

The three first chapters of the book intend to describe three different databases which can be used for the study of the internal and international migration from Mexico.

In chapter 1, Pérez-Paredes and Mera-Ceballos reveal the main capabilities of *Encuesta Nacional de Ocupación y Empleo* (ENOE), a nationally representative survey designed mainly for labor market purposes, to measure demographic dynamics of the Mexican population. In particular, the paper concentrates in showing how the survey can be used to measure out-migration and return migration flows between Mexico and the United States. The chapter describes the statistical adjustments needed to ensure that the information obtained from ENOE is as accurate as possible, as well as the measurements of the emigration flows from Mexico to the United States from 2005 to 2009.

In chapter 2, Teruel, Rubalcava, and Arenas describe the *Mexican Family Life Survey* (MxFLS) and the variety of purposes which can be achieved with it. The MxFLS is a longitudinal survey designed to collect information on Mexicans who have never left Mexico as well as of migrants before they migrate, at the moment the survey was carried out, while they were in the United States, and after they return to Mexico. The survey has been carried out in 2002 and 2005–2006, and a third wave is being carried out in 2010–2011. The survey is multipurpose, and as it accumulates more waves, the span of topics that can be studied increases. Currently, its modules contain information about the well-being of individuals, ranging from socioeconomic measures to objective and subjective measures of health, crime histories and victimization, marriage and migration histories, a detailed employment module, information about the assets and wealth of both the origin and destination household, and transfers to and from the migrants.

In chapter 3, Mora-Rivera explains the main features of the *Encuesta Nacional a Hogares Rurales de México* (ENHRUM), a national survey representative of communities between 500 and 2,499 inhabitants. Its detailed information allows the study of production, income, and migration of rural households. The survey has been carried out in 2002 and 2007 and also constitutes a panel data set. The first results of the survey show the importance of both international migration and internal migration for rural communities in Mexico. As more waves of ENHRUM are being planned the range of topics that can be studied with the survey will increase in the future.

SECTION 2: INTERNAL MIGRATION IN MEXICO

The two chapters included in this section are devoted to the study of internal migration in Mexico. Rivero-Fuentes explores the determinants of internal migration, while Soloaga and Lara-Ibarra look at its impact on the human development index

In chapter 4, Rivero-Fuentes, taking the case of interstate migration in Mexico in three different periods (1975–1980, 1985–1990, and 1995–2000), tests whether or not the level of past migration, past and recent trade, and administrative and infrastructure ties between states, help explain why migrants from different states of origin go to different destinations. It is the first study of internal migration in any country that tests the power of variables other than the ones implied by the neoclassical hypotheses in explaining migrants' destinations. Furthermore, by comparing the determinants of the distribution of interstate migrants in 1975–1980, 1985–1990, and 1995–2000, this chapter moves from ad hoc explanations to the recent changes in migration patterns in developing countries.

By suggesting that the long-term impact on the distribution of the population of a change from import-substitution to export-oriented development does not depend solely on the location of the new manufacturing centers, but also on the way trade between states is reorganized and on the changes in regional wage and unemployment inequalities, this research brings a new dimension to the study of internal migration in Mexico.

Soloaga and Lara-Ibarra (chapter 5), using the 2000 Mexican Census estimate the impact of migration on the Human Development Index (HDI).They estimate a counterfactual state-level HDI had no internal migration occurred. According to the authors, the overall impact on the HDI is small in magnitude. However, the small overall effect is the result of opposing effects of migration on the components of the index.

SECTION 3: INTERNATIONAL MIGRATION FROM MEXICO AND LATIN AMERICA

The topics covered by this section of the book range from gender differentials by educational level, labor determinants of migration and the evolution of H2 visas to measures of migration connections.

The first chapter of this section (Lowell and Pederzini) contributes to a better understanding of the nuances of how international mobility varies within the tertiary-educated population—it does so with a case study of migration from Mexico to the United States. The authors use Mexican and U.S. data sources to examine gender differentials in emigration for the year 2010, as well as to explore some simple first-order explanations for the forces that drive these differentials. Their analysis shows that highly educated Mexican female migrants do not close the labor force participation gap with males and, surprisingly, do relatively less well in the United States than women in Mexico. Even though no definitive conclusions are reached, it appears that highly educated Mexican women migrate primarily for family and not economic reasons; the authors speculate that assortative mating and Mexican marriage markets may explain some of the otherwise inexplicable gender differentials in emigration and labor markets that they find.

Rendón and Cuecuecha (chapter 7) use detailed descriptive evidence coming from census data, employment surveys, and panel data from Mexico and the United States to show that migration patterns between the two countries are not explained merely by wage differentials but also by job turnover, in particular, job to job transitions. According to the authors, this result indicates that a more dynamic labor market in Mexico could potentially reduce migration rates from Mexico to the United States.

In chapter 8, Trigueros-Legarreta analyzes the evolution of H-2 visas have since 1990 and the limitations imposed in the legislation, along with their effects on the living conditions of workers who are granted them. In particular, the author looks at violations of H-2 workers' rights by employers in the United States, and such workers' limited access to justice. The author lists a number of mechanisms that have been proposed in various forums in order to reduce the abuse of the workers in terms of labor and human rights.

In order to move beyond the single country studies of the past, Hiskey and Cordova (chapter 9) rely on recently released cross-national survey data that allows them to assess the range of migration connections across over 33,000 individuals living in myriad communities located in twenty-one Latin American and Caribbean countries with distinct migration histories. Such a wide range of countries offers the chance to assess not only the individual-level effect of migration connections but also to incorporate into that analysis the contextual effects associated with high and low aggregate migration levels. The authors put forth systematic, individual-based measures of migration connections as merely one more step in trying to answer the wide range of questions related to the impact of migration on those left behind.

SECTION 4: REMITTANCES TOWARD MEXICO AND LATIN AMERICA

This last section of the book focuses on the use and impact of remittances. Chapters 10 and 11 focus on Mexican migrants, while chapter 12 ends the book by using data from six Latin American countries to analyze the use of remittances.

In the first chapter of section 4, Orrenius, Zavodny, Cañas, and Coronado (chapter 10) present an overview of recent trends in Mexican remittances. They review the literature on the economic impacts of remittances to Mexico and summarize recent research findings on the effects of remittances on several aspects of economic development, including employment, unemployment, wages, wage inequality, and school enrollment rates. Based on Mexican state-level data from 2003–2007, the results discussed here indicate that remittances improve labor market conditions—formal employment rises and unemployment rates fall when remittances increase in high-migration states. Remittances also appear to shift the wage distribution to the right by reducing the fraction of workers in a state who earn the minimum wage or less. However, they do not find any remittance effects on school enrollment rates.

Guillermina Jasso (chapter 11) contributes to the understanding of transfers behavior by examining financial transfers among persons born in Mexico who are new legal immigrants in the United States. Data are drawn from the first round of the New Immigrant Survey (NIS), a longitudinal survey of immigrants admitted to U.S. legal permanent residence in 2003. To explore more deeply the idea of financial transfers as tickets to America, the author develops a new way to think about transfers involving legal permanent residents. Due to provisions of U.S. immigration law which require that most family and employment immigrants be sponsored, she is able to identify select pairs of new immigrants and their sponsors in which transfers are likely to be from sponsors to immigrants. The author identifies parent immigrants, a group exempt of numerical limitations, as the second largest class of new legal immigrants. About a fifth receive financial assistance from their adult children, and over half receive housing assistance in the United States after immigration. Approximately 59–60 percent receive either financial or housing assistance. Parents who are younger and healthier are less likely to receive financial assistance from their adult children—beyond sponsorship for immigration.

In chapter 12, Massey, Durand, and Pren draw upon data from the Mexican Migration Project and Latin American Migration Project to study the repatriation and use of migradollars in six Latin American nations. They find that across all countries, remittances are used primarily to diversify risks to household income by generating an alternative earnings stream, channeled mainly into consumption. The tendency to save and to use savings as a means of overcoming failures in capital and credit markets varies from setting to setting, even after background variables are controlled. They also document a paradox in that variables reducing the odds of remitting and saving and also lowering the quantities remitted and saved simultaneously act to increase the likelihood that whatever funds are repatriated are channeled more productively.

Chapter 1

International Migration Rates Based on the ENOE

Methodology and Main Results

Elsa Pérez Paredes and Sara Iveth Mera-Ceballos

The *Instituto Nacional de Estadística Geografía e Informática* (INEGI) is the agency responsible for organizing, regulating, coordinating, and creating the statistical infrastructure of the National System of Statistical and Geographical Information (SNIEG).[1] This system, made up of the body of data produced by public-sector institutions, aims to produce and communicate information of national interest that demonstrate the situation and the interdependence of economic, demographic, and social phenomena, as well as their relation with the physical environment and territorial space, in order to have a better understanding of them and to contribute to the design and monitoring of public programs and policies.

In order to fulfill its purpose, the system, as its main input, makes use of the traditional sources of demographic information (e.g., population censuses, vital statistics, demographic surveys), each one having a different subject matter, periodicity, coverage, disaggregation, quality, and opportunity.

Up until now, most studies have shown that the quality of each of these sources improves when new criteria and recommendations are incorporated, while the establishment of new homogeneous conceptual frameworks guarantees an adequate coverage of topics, avoiding duplication and gaps in the information. However, although the generation of data is at an advanced stage of consolidation, the exploitation of all the information available is still far from being optimum for a number of reasons.

The specific aim of the Demographic Rates project based on the ENOE is to make gross estimations of mortality, births, and international migration using information collected in the sociodemographic questionnaire in the ENOE and to at the same time attend the needs of the SNIEG to have indicators available that permit more opportune monitoring of the situation of demographic components and the study of the dynamics of the Mexican population. This chapter contains an overall description of the adjustment of the CELADE Demographic Survey Method (1979) proposed by the INEGI using the main results obtained from the first quarter of 2006 to the third quarter of 2009, in particular the results referring to *international migration*, the precision indicators in each case, and a brief description of the limitations faced and the analytical possibilities that exist.

AN ADJUSTMENT OF THE CELADE SURVEY METHOD

Demographers of the Latin American and Caribbean Demography Center (CELADE) designed a survey method which, given its characteristics, is classified as longitudinal cohort, based on a careful consideration of the data required for demographic indices calculation (person-years exposed to the risk of events demographic and the total of such events classified by age, sex, and other characteristics). The survey consists of repeated visits to a sample of households. In the first round, data on the characteristics of each household member are collected. On subsequent visits the dates when births, deaths, or changes in characteristics such as civil status occurred are recorded. Each person's history is followed until his or her death or emigration; a person gets into the household sample by birth or immigration. On the basis of this data it is possible to estimate the person-years exposed to the risk of giving birth or dying, both by subgroup and for the total sample, and to relate them to data on the corresponding births and deaths in order to obtain crude or specific rates. The method makes use of the circumstance that a person observation over a period of time represents an experience that has statistical value. Considered in isolation, it apparently makes a valuable contribution.

Originally the CELADE's method used as its main input not expanded totals (registers) observed between visits and considered a sample of up to 35,000 persons as valid in order to make annual estimates without worrying about the total number of the target population from which the sample was selected. On the other hand, it recommends ensuring the representativeness of the events as the breakdown and level of precision for the analysis increases, in such a way that the less common phenomena can be seen to have occurred often enough in each cutoff point.

The methodology proposed by the INEGI is a variation of the CELADE method, where the information analyzed comes from a survey designed mainly to detect occupation levels, though also, secondarily, demographic data; for this reason, with the exception of births, the survey does not register the dates of the demographic events. The INEGI's estimation is made considering the pondered events broken down geographically at national level and by migratory regions. Finally, the sample common to each period is maximally 80% and falls as the time increases.

CHARACTERISTICS OF THE ENOE

Today, the National Survey of Occupation and Employment (ENOE) is the largest continuous survey of households to be applied in Mexico. Its implementation in January 2005 marked the end of a model of data collection and processing in use for twenty years which corresponded to the National Survey of Urban Employment (ENEU), and then the National Employment Survey (ENE), into which the ENEU was integrated. The general objectives of the ENOE include ensure that the country can count nationally representative statistical information on the occupational characteristics of the population, as well as providing sociodemographic statistical information that permits us to complement the in-depth analysis of the occupational characteristics of the Mexican population. In particular, it aims to collect data on the start and end of jobs and the context in which these events took place. The target population is those individuals who have reached their fourteenth birthday or more on the interview date. The information of interest is collected in a sample which is probabilistic panel-type, multiphase stratified, and by area, where dwellings are the final selection unit and the households within them are the observation units.

The sample includes approximately 120,000 dwellings in which information on just over 400,000 individuals was collected. The period of data collection is quarterly, and in general each dwelling in the sample is visited on five consecutive occasions. There are two data-collection instruments: the first is the Sociodemographic Questionnaire (CS), which registers the main sociodemographic characteristics of the households in the dwelling selected. The full questionnaire is applied to every household member on the first visit; subsequent visits are for updating information only. When one or more new household members are identified, the full questions battery is applied to them. Second is the basic and augmented Occupation and Employment Questionnaire (COE I and COE II), which, as the name indicates, serves to identify the detailed occupational and employment situation of those interviewed. The basic reference periods in the survey are those used to determine the condition of the persons regarding occupation. These periods can be extended more than a month before the application date of the CS. Although the COE I information is the most important for the aims of the survey, in order determine the household members who are habitual residents and consequently must respond the questionnaire, the survey established a three-month period before and after the interview for setting residents.

PROCEDURE FOR CALCULATING INTERNATIONAL MIGRATION RATES

The estimations of *demographic rates based on ENOE information* depend only on the data obtained from the Sociodemographic Questionnaire, so when we refer to the databases it should be understood that the information from COE I and COE II is not included. On the other hand, although data collection for the survey was carried out from the first quarter of 2005 onward and the databases are available, the conceptual and operational differences between ENE and ENOE should be taken into account, as well as the fact that the validation criteria for the information collected were subject to modifications and adjustments over the whole of the first year. The exploration of this early data gave inconsistencies in the variables of interest, so we decided not to take into account information of 2005; the series starts from the first quarter of 2006, and each quarter incorporates new data. Although the original project contemplated the gross rates estimation of birth, mortality, immigration, and emigration, this article only refers to the results on international migration, broken down geographically for total national and three locality sizes[2] for quarterly and annual periods. In this report we present quarterly estimates up to the third quarter of 2009 and annual ones up to the fourth quarter of 2008. Due to questions of similarity in procedures, we will describe the procedure followed to obtain quarterly estimations and give the relevant explanations on the modifications when dealing with the calculations for each year.

COMPARISON OF CONSECUTIVE DATABASES

To calculate the gross rates using the method established in the first section of this document, it was necessary to compare the databases of consecutive quarters in pairs for quarterly estimates and in groups of five for annual estimates. To ensure the correct tracking of all cases, it is necessary determine the best way to identify data of each households members in each of the quarterly database. Consequently a *single identification code* is established for each register on the database; when the registers are compared period by period, we can determinate the number of entries due to birth or immigration or exits due to death or emigration could be carried out, with the guarantee that there was no duplication or omission of common registers in each interview.

The *single identification code* is formed by certain variables, including geographical identification, operational control, and household and individual identifiers, making the identifier is a new string variable. The variables considered are self-represented city, state, control, selected dwelling, household number, relocated household, and row number.

Selection of the Common Sample

Once the single code for all the registers in each of the databases is constructed, they are joined and then the process of selecting useful cases begins—and, on the basis of these, the count of events of interest. We define as useful cases all those that belong to 80% of the registers in households that coincide between quarters and which also have a full interview on both databases. Thus, all the registers that fulfill this condition are identified as the common sample.

RECALIBRATION OF EXPANSION FACTORS

These data are obtained from a survey, and for this reason all the estimates made from them should have the associated precision measurements. For this, it is necessary to define the weighting factors again. Although each database has its own factor which expands the sample to a population total at the date at the midpoint of the quarter being collected, it is not strictly appropriate to use any of these factors to estimate the quarterly rates, as they are located time-wise *on the mean date of each transition period* and do not coincide with any of those available. In addition, if we were to use the factors already included in the databases, we would be representing no more than 80% of the total national population—thus, a new set of weighting factors which expand the total national population on the mean date of the interquarterly period are built which also maintain the structure by state, municipality, self-represented city, locality, and locality size. This process is summarized when the registers (of the common sample) are ordered on the basis of the values of the variables: state, municipality, self-represented city, locality, and locality size, and later, when the new factor is calculated in the way:

$$facCal = \frac{n}{n^*} fac \text{ For the number of individuals belonging to the common sample}$$

$$0 \text{ For the individuals that are not in the common sample}$$

Figure 1.1.

where

n = Total number of individuals per self-represented city, locality size, and state on the mean date of the interquarterly period

n^* = Weighted number of individuals per self-represented city, locality size, and state of the common 80% — that is, that appear in the common sample

fac = Original expansion factor based on the compared second quarter

SELECTION OF SUBPOPULATIONS
(EVENT COUNT)

The sociodemographic questionnaire contains the data required to obtain the numerator and denominator for calculating each rate: residence condition, reason for definitive absence, destination of those definitively absent from the household, reason for new residence, and places of origin of new household residents.

The demographic events count in the common sample is used to define the numerator for each rate. Thus the changes in the situation of each person from one interview to another must be identified by comparing the residence condition at each moment, the reason for absence, and the place of origin or new residence, as well as the place of origin or destination, as appropriate. Regarding the residence condition, the quarterly registers are classified three ways: as residents, as new residents, and as definitely absent. Consequently, it is possible for a register to appear as a resident or new resident in one quarter and in the next still be resident or be registered as definitely absent. On the other hand, if a register is identified as absent in one quarter, in the next interview it has no correspondence and therefore no longer belongs to the common sample. It is important to mention that the registers of the second reference interview marked as new resident in the household are the only ones that have no coincidence with any register in the previous interview and still form part of the common sample.

Once the possibilities of transition from one quarter to the next are clear, the criteria considered for the classification of events are established and are described as follows:

Birth

No information in the previous interview, new resident in the household in the second interview having been "born," age zero, and date of birth in the quarterly reference period.

Death

Resident or new resident in the first interview and definitively absent from the household in the second, having "died."

International Immigrant

No information in the first interview, new resident in the household in the second interview for any reason other than "born" or "was omitted" and place of origin "another country."

International Emigrant

Resident or new resident in the first interview and definitively absent from the household except "died" and with destination "another country."

LIFE SPAN

The denominator of the ENOE demographic rates is the sum of the time lived by the population exposed to the risk of experiencing one of the demographic events of interest with respect to the aims of this project. The method proposed by CELADE obtained the date of each birth, death, emigration, or immigration so that the accumulation of the time lived can be precisely obtained by identifying each one. However, the ENOE only obtains dates of birth to validate age and identify the target population of the occupation and employment studies.

So, to calculate the time lived of all those observed we first have to assign the time lived to each type of person in the sample: (I) those whose residence condition remains without change between one interview and the next and (II) those people whose residence conditions change either because they were taken out of the sample or because they became a member of one of the households observed. For the former, the assignment of time lived is immediate, as the full periods subsist and each one contributes a complete quarter. On the other hand, given that it is impossible to define the exact moment in which type II persons leave or enter the panel, it is necessary to establish a supposition with respect to the uniformity of the occurrence of the events within the period, which in quantitative terms means that each person who entered or left the sample for whatever cause remained exposed to the risk for half of the quarter.

CALCULATION OF THE GROSS RATE

The general form of the quarterly rates calculated corresponding to the inter-quarterly period (t_0, t_1) is the following:

$$Rate_{(t_0,t_1)} = \frac{Events\ registered_{(t_0,t_1)}}{Lifespan_{(t_0,t_1)}}\ 1000$$

Figure 1.2.

Where the numerator is the total of events associated with each rate: births (TBN), deaths (TBM), international immigrants (TBII), and international emigrants (TBEI). And with the denominator composed as follows,

$$Lifespan_{(t_0,t_1)} = Lifespan^{PC}_{(t_0,t_1)} + Lifespan^{N}_{(t_0,t_1)} + Lifespan^{D}_{(t_0,t_1)}$$

$$+ Lifespan^{II}_{(t_0,t_1)} + Lifespan^{EI}_{(t_0,t_1)}$$

Figure 1.3.

STATISTICAL PRECISION

Statistical precision for each of the estimates becomes indispensable due to the fact that despite having established representativeness for the total population, these are obtained from the observation of only a fraction of the total number of individuals. We should say in passing that the precisions per se are not support for the inference on the total. However, they are important, as they are the indicator which refers to the reliability of this inference. Thus, although the information on international migration shows precise data, as with all information coming from surveys, the estimates should be treated as exact with their respective range of variation (confidence interval).

Given that this study is an exercise in derived statistics and with the intention of maintaining the homogeneity of the methodologies that use the ENOE as their main input, the estimate of the confidence intervals respects the methodology implemented in the precision of occupation and employment indicators, which means that due to the sample design of the survey, the method for estimating the sampling errors *a posteriori* of the demographic rates is that of the last conglomerates and that for ratio for estimators takes the form of the Taylor expansion.

GEOGRAPHICAL DISAGGREGATION

The estimates which are the object of this article have representativeness for the national total and for three sizes of locality: rural localities (fewer than 2,500 inhabitants), regional population centers (2,500 to 14,900 inhabitants), and urban localities (15,000 or more inhabitants). The rates with the most geographical disaggregation—that is, by state—have until now not been consolidated as variables due to the high level of variation which they show derived from the low frequency of the events of interest that they are made up of. So, despite the feasibility of obtaining them, we have not considered it appropriate to publish them due to the resulting lack of statistical support.

CONSIDERATIONS AND ASSUMPTIONS

Due to the range of the details and tests carried out to consolidate the methodology used in the estimates presented in this document, we will not go into them fully, but we should mention the main observations, reflections on the information, and suppositions that have emerged during the project. The great majority of the studies that make use of information sources such as surveys are faced with a scarcity of detail in the recording of demographic events, either because of deficiencies in the instruments or even due to the nature of the event of interest itself. This obliges us to establish a series of suppositions that permit the application of the proposed methodology. In this case, the strongest assumptions include the uniformity of the occurrence of events within each period and the independence of the population exposed in each transition—even when there is a percentage of coincident population seen between each quarter, this percentage reduces as the time increases.

On the other hand, among the methodological considerations which must be taken into account in this report is the non-inclusion in the estimates of the moved households, as up to now the lack of information on the reason for the change in status of these households and above all, their destination or origin does not permit us classify and include them correctly in the analysis of our common sample. Thus, these units should be excluded on the basis of a strong supposition which suggests that the percentage of this type of household, the most extreme cases of which are migrations of whole households, is not sufficiently for a significant change in level or trend estimates.

With respect to the quality of the information, we should also consider that the projects' input data come from a survey which, although it is one of the largest in Mexico and has ISO 9001–2000 certification, given the nature of the collection procedure, has a bias in the estimates generated which increases with the presence of other factors such as failure to reply, the exhaustion of the sample framework and the evolution of the phenomena detected.

LIMITATIONS FOR GEOGRAPHICAL DISAGGREGATION AND DUE TO SOCIO-DEMOGRAPHIC CHARACTERISTICS

Throughout this report we have mentioned on more than one occasion that the estimates of international migration according to time period are only available for some cases of geographical disaggregation. The insistence on this situation is because, having a solid source of information such as the ENOE and taking into account that on this basis a considerable number of indicators of occupation and employment are generated, it is often tempting to try to obtain detailed indicators for each and every one of the variables that are found in the survey questionnaires. However, in the case of *Demographic Rates*, this is not necessarily so, as we are dealing with estimates derived from an instrument created for ends different from those of the project, generated from data coming from questions of on operational type included in the questionnaire to verify the permanence of the target population for studies of occupation. So, although it is possible to generate precise rates and sums associated with practically all the sociodemographic variables contained in the questionnaires, very few of them can be considered statistically valid, which is why the information offered in the project is limited to large geographical groupings (national or locality size), time period (yearly, or two- or three-year periods), and sociodemographic variables (age and sex structure).

OTHER LINES OF ANALYSIS

Despite the limitations of the information, the fact that there is a series of fourteen observations permits us to propose new options for analysis among which we can mention the following: tracking the common panel over five interviews in order to identify return migration. The general characterization of migration: on the one hand, on the household level, the modifications and restructuring that the group undergoes due to the loss of members is identified, and also, by observing registers for three consecutive years, the estimation of the age and sex structure becomes possible, and even the sociodemographic characterization of the migrant population. Methodologically this has no important variations, as well as the fact that the database contains all the variables required. However, new difficulties are due to the quality of the data to be associated and the number of registers that have to be integrated into a single database, because as the quantity of databases to be compared grows, the reprocessing time also increases.

CONCLUSION

It has recently become clear as an overall symptom in the world population that of the three main components of demographic growth, it is migration which stands out due to the impact it has on age and sex composition as well as on the configuration of the population in a given territory. As Mexico is a country with an important internal and international migratory tradition, the effect it has is reflected in economic and social terms. For this reason there is great interest in finding sources and methods that permit us to measure and quantify migratory flows reliably, efficiently, and, above all, continuously, because although it is true that population censuses provide a good measurement of net migration in a particular period, the suitability of the data is open to doubt as they are retrospective in nature—and although there are methodologies that use them to make reliable short and medium term projections, in the final resort the supposed effects are fixed to a given period and we lose sight of the changes migratory flows undergo as a result of large–scale social or economic phenomena.

The information obtained from this project is far from ideal for a full characterization of the phenomenon of migration in Mexico due to the limitations already described. However, it is a good option as the data in themselves provide elements that in the first place confirm the seasonality of the phenomena over the course of the year and the predominance of a largely male migrant population. Second is the fact that the rates indicate that the population lost by our country due to international migration is significant, even considering that the intensity of the phenomenon shows a downward trend in 2008–2009 (in comparison to 2006).

On the other hand, with respect to geographical disaggregation, the possibility of making estimates according to locality size shows that it is the

Chapter 1

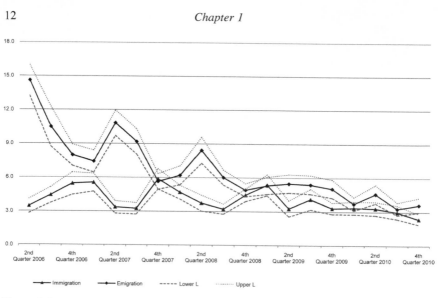

Figure 1.4.

rural sphere where international migration occurs with greatest intensity, as it is the one most closely linked to the seasonal pattern observed in the national total.

Finally, we have noticed the fact that during the last three quarters both emigration and immigration patterns have behaved quite differently to the rest of the series, which in consequence partially disrupts its seasonal character. On the one hand, the levels of international emigration have stayed practically constant, while immigration levels is still in the same range, the effect of which is a net balance that we could describe as "discreet" over the last quarters and which could point toward a temporary slowing down of migration flows from and to other countries.

Although these changes could be associated with the world economic recession and with the toughening of migration policies, it has meant we have had to revise the methodology in order to detect areas of opportunity for improving estimates, as we are aware of outstanding tasks and also of the potential for obtaining more detailed information on migration from the sociodemographic information in the ENOE. This is why we are confident that the growth of the historical series will provide us elements to define new strategies to exploit it and an important vein to generate opportune and reliable estimates which attend to the needs of both the public and academic sectors.

Table 1.1.   Gross Quarterly International Migration Rates and Net Migratory Balance, 2006–2010

Period	Immigration	Emigration	Net Migratory Balance
2nd quarter 2006	3.4	14.6	−11.1
3rd quarter 2006	4.4	10.5	−6.0
4th quarter 2006	5.4	8.0	−2.5
1st quarter 2007	5.5	7.4	−1.9
From the second quarter 2006 to the first quarter 2007	4.7	10.1	−5.4
2nd quarter 2007	3.4	10.8	−7.5
3rd quarter 2007	3.2	9.2	−5.9
4th quarter 2007	5.9	5.6	0.2
1st quarter 2008	4.7	6.2	−1.5
From the second quarter 2007 to the first quarter 2008	4.3	8.0	−3.7
2nd quarter 2008	3.7	8.4	−4.7
3rd quarter 2008	3.2	6.0	−2.8
4th quarter 2008	4.5	4.9	−0.4
1st quarter 2009	5.3	5.3	0.0
From the second quarter 2008 to the first quarter 2009	4.2	6.2	−2.0
2nd quarter 2009	3.3	5.5	−2.2
3rd quarter 2009	4.1	5.4	−1.3
4th quarter 2009	3.3	5.0	−1.7
1st quarter 2010	3.4	3.7	−0.4
From the second quarter 2009 to the first quarter 2010	3.5	4.9	−1.4
2nd quarter 2010	3.3	4.6	−1.3
3rd quarter 2010	3.0	3.3	−0.3
4th quarter 2010	2.4	3.6	−1.2

Source: INEGI. Estimates based on National Survey on Occupation and Employment, 2006-2010.
Note: Estimate per 1000 habitual residents in Mexico.

Below are some of the historical series (Table 1.1 and Figure 1.4) of the most important project results presented in this document and which are today common knowledge.[3]

NOTES

1. Special acknowledgments to Víctor García Vilchis and Alejandro Mozo Cruz for all their support and contributions to this work.

2. Three locality sizes are used: localities with fewer than 2,500 inhabitants, localities with up to 14,999 inhabitants, and last localities taking care of with 15,000 inhabitants and more.

3. For more tables containing precision measurements for several quarterly estimates, see the appendix to Chapter 1. The appendix, also available at http://isim.georgetown.edu.

Chapter 2

Migration in the Mexican Family Life Survey

Graciela Teruel, Luis Rubalcava,
and Erika Arenas

Research on migration between Mexico and the United States has been abundant for many reasons, one of the most important being that migration flows from Mexico to the United States has been very important and increasing in the last century.[1] Today, Mexicans living in the United States constitute the largest immigrant group in the world (Pew Hispanic Center, 2009).

For the United States, Mexican migration is of particular concern. Over the past 15 years, this migration flow has grown to levels comparable to the Great Migrations a century ago (Hanson, 2006) becoming an important contributor to U.S. population growth (Kent & Mather, 2002; Fry, 2008). While in 1960 Mexico was listed as the seventh source country of immigrants in the United States, since the 1970s and up until now, a surge in migration has situated Mexico as the primary source of immigrants (Lowell, Pederzini, Villareal, and Passel, 2006). In 2008, Mexicans comprised 12.7 million people, or 32 percent of the U.S. immigrant population and about 4 percent of the total U.S. population[2] (Pew Hispanic Center, 2009).

From Mexico's perspective, emigration to the United States is also of great significance. The most recent estimates suggest that today one in every ten Mexicans lives and works in the United States (Pew Hispanic Center, 2009). According to projections estimated by the National Council of Population in Mexico (CONAPO, 2004), between 1996 and 2010 migration to the United States will reduce Mexican population growth rates between the ages 15 to 44 to about 0.5 percent and 0.35 percent for males and females, respectively. Even though Mexican migration to the United States has slowed since 2006, projections made by the US Census Bureau, CONAPO, and the United Nations (UN) still forecast high outflow migration rates from Mexico until 2050 (Lowell, Pederzini, Villareal, and Passel, 2006). Even in the middle of the current global economic and financial crisis migration flows have ebbed and have been considered to be driven by deep structural forces not likely to disappear in the near future (Fussell and Massey, 2004; Palloni, Massey, Ceballos, Espinosa and Spittel, 2001; Massey and Zenteno, 1999; Massey and Espinoza, 1997).

Research on international migration in general, and in particular in the Mexico–United States case, is commonly based on data from population censuses and registers (e.g., migrants' admissions and departures), and sample surveys (Massey & Capoferro, 2004; Bilsborrow et al., 1997). The purpose of this paper is to present a relatively new source of information, coming from a Mexican survey of households that constitutes an important data source for the study of Mexican migration to the United States. We start with a short description of different data sources that are typically used in studies of Mexico–United States migration and we then proceed to explain the design of the migration modules and migration protocols of the Mexican Family Life Survey. We present some preliminary findings using the new dataset collected and conclude in the final section.

MIGRATION DATA SOURCES

Censuses

Data on movements between Mexico and the United States was first available from population censuses. Information from these sources allow researchers to identify international migrants by including questions about place of birth, year of arrival, and place of residence within the last five years. In the United States, in particular, the census includes questions on place of birth and year of arrival, both of which have been used to estimate stocks and flows of migrants. Likewise, information from the Mexican censuses has been used to estimate how many individuals have left the country. Thus information from censuses is useful to characterize the sociodemographic and geographic features of the migrant populations.

These data sources have limitations if one is studying the causes and consequences of migration. Among the limitations pointed out in the literature, four are worth mentioning: (1) population censuses do not collect information prior to migration, (2) the data do not adequately accounts for temporal or circular migration, (3) the data might be subject to selective out and in migration in sending and receiving countries respectively (Massey & Capoferro, 2004; Redstone & Massey, 2004; Rallu, 2004), and (4) in the case of receiving countries, the legal status of the migrant is not present. In Mexico, the Census has been used to estimate and characterize migrant flows (Hill & Wong 2005).

Population Registers

These include information on entries and departures. Neither in Mexico nor in the United States is information on entries or exits captured accurately. For example, the Ministry of the Exterior in Mexico has information from a sample of Mexicans living in the United States who willingly approach the consulates to obtain a Mexican identification card (Matrícula Consular), or a passport. However, there are Mexicans in the United States who do not hold either a passport or a Matrícula Consular. It is estimated that a high percentage of illegal migrants in high migration destinations in the United States do obtain this kind of identification (close to 80 percent). In the United States, information on new legal immigrants registered by the US Immigration and Naturalization Service (INS) has been used as the basis of a new multicohort prospective-retrospective panel survey called the New Immigrant Survey (NIS). The NIS focuses heavily on the consequences of migration once the mover has settled in the receiving society. This survey provides a rich set of data for the study of immigrant assimilation on a broad range of outcomes (e.g., wages, education, health status) (Jasso, Massey, Rosenzweig & Smith 2000). However, it holds information on legal migrants only, which clearly represents a drawback for the study of Mexico–U.S. migration, as most of the migrants coming into the United States are illegal.

Household Surveys

These are probably the largest source of information that exists today for the study of Mexico–U.S. migration. There have been different designs and implementations. For example, some studies have only specific geographical representation, as they have focused on migrants in specific locations within the United States. An example of this are the *Longitudinal Immigrant Student Adaptation Study* of children of immigrants who have recently arrived in the Boston and San Francisco areas (Suárez-Orozco & Suárez-Orozco, 2001), the *Children of Immigrants Longitudinal Study* (Portes & Rumbaut, 2008), and the *National Latino Survey* (Pew Hispanic Center). These datasets have been primarily used to examine processes for immigrant assimilation, however external validity of the results are still an issue.

In Mexico, there are national population surveys collected mainly by the National Statistics Office (*Instituto Nacional de Estadística, Geografía e Informática*, INEGI) that include migration modules specifically designed to capture emigration from Mexico (and largely to the United States). Examples of these are the Survey of Demographic Dynamics (*Encuesta Nacional de la Dinámica Demográfica*, ENADID) and the National Survey of Employment

(*Encuesta Nacional de Empleo*, ENE). The ENADID is a cross-sectional household survey whose main purpose is to collect social and demographic information on the Mexican population. The ENADID has been fielded three times: in 1992, 1997, and 2006. The 1992 and 1997 surveys included a section of international migration that asked whether any household member had lived in a foreign country within the last five years prior to the interview. For those household members with migration experience within the five years interval, interviewers recorded sociodemographic characteristics, date on emigration, country of destination, country of present residence as well as month and year of return. In 2006, the ENADID also asked questions regarding migrant legal status in the United States, and motivation for migration.

Although the ENE's main purpose is to collect data about labor market characteristics of the Mexican population, in 2002 INEGI added a brief migration module similar to the ENADID's 2006 module in order to update estimates of documented and undocumented migration flows. The advantage of the ENE is that it is a continuous, rotating panel with representation at the national and urban–rural levels. Both the ENADID and the ENE 2002 allow the counting emigration events in spite of the fact that migrants are not present. However, these data suffer from two problems for the study of migration. First is that they are likely to capture selective migration, since they do not incorporate households all of whose members have migrated and/or households that disintegrate between the migration event and the date of the survey interview (Wong, Resano, & Martínez, 2006). Second, the information collected in them is not enough to analyze in depth the determinants and consequences of migration, since they include very few migration questions.

There are other surveys that have been specifically designed to study international migration. One example is the Survey of Migration on the Northern Border of Mexico (*Encuesta sobre Migración en la Frontera Norte de México*, EMIF-N). The survey counts flows of migrants in the Northern border. This data has been collected annually since 1993 and covers eight border communities that concentrate about 94 percent of the entry and exit flows from and into the United States. Individuals are sampled in key transit zones, such as bus stations, airports, railroad stations, and the border itself (EMIF 2005). Three types of migrants can be identified: (1) returning migrants, (2) intending migrants, and (3) migrants sent back by the Border Patrol. The EMIF-N inquires into sociodemographic characteristics, labor history, and reasons for emigrating; collects data on community of origin and place of destination; and collects data about the crossing, social networks in the United States, and the type of documentation held to cross and work in the United States. The data collected in the EMIF-N is better suited to study some aspects of the migration processes, such as estimation of flows of documented and undocumented migrants, and differences in the conditions and characteristics of first emigrants compared to experienced emigrants. The periodicity of the survey allows for the study of changes in the characteristics of migrant flows, changes in the origins and destinations of migrants, and changes in crossing areas. However, the representativeness of the survey is not well established (Rendall, Aguila, Basurto-Dávila & Handcock, 2009).

Other surveys of this type are those in which the interviews to migrants are carried out in their home country once they have returned. An example of this is The *Mexican Health and Aging Study* (MHAS). MHAS is a panel study of health and aging in Mexico, nationally representative of Mexicans born prior to 1951. This study captures the impact of migration in two different ways. First, through the collection of retrospective data on the migration experience, directly provided by the respondent; and second, by assessing the impact of transfers received by respondents from their children that have migrated to the United States. Unquestionably, this project provides important information about the process of how migration of the younger cohorts shapes the welfare of older cohorts in Mexico today, and about the effect of previous migration experience of return migrants in later stages of life. Although MHAS collects retrospective data on migration which allows capturing circular and temporal migrants, the survey lacks information on migrants who settled in the United States and did not come back, especially those who do not have elderly parents living in Mexico.

A more integrated approach has been that of collecting information of migrants both at origin and destination locations.[3] International migration analyses have greatly benefited from these new specialized "both-way" surveys, which are more appropriate for analyzing the migration process. Even though efforts have been made to include all different types of migrants in these studies, the data usually continues to suffer from selectivity biases. Moreover, most of these specialized surveys lack representativeness at the national level, and most of the time the information collected is cross-sectional. The most well known study of this type concerning Mexico–U.S. migration is the *Mexican Migration Project* (MMP) (Massey, 1987). The MMP combines ethnographic and random sampling methods to gather data from sending communities of approximately 200 households, and relies on snowball sampling to collect information of about ten to twenty households of community members living in the United States. MMP includes information about 118 "binational communities" and has contributed greatly to our understanding of Mexican migration to the United States. Researchers have used these data to describe trends in Mexican migration (e.g., Cerruti & Massey, 2004), to investigate differences between documented and undocumented migrants and to analyze the process of undocumented crossing (e.g., Singer & Massey, 1998; Orrenius, 2004), to examine the use of remittances (e.g., Durand, Kandel, Parrado & Massey, 1996; Parrado, 2004), and to test several migration theories (Massey & Espinosa, 1997). Evidence using the MMP data shows considerable support for network theories and cumulative causation (Fussell & Massey, 2004; Massey & Espinosa, 1997; Massey, Ceballos, Espinosa, & Spittel, 2001; Cerruti & Massey, 2001). MMP has several advantages over other study designs. First, the survey oversamples regions with international migrants to the United States. Second, the survey's main focus is on international migration. Third, in the sending regions households with migrants and nonmigrants are included in the sample, which allows for the exploration of determinants of migration by comparing groups who migrate with those who do not. MPP is not drawn from a probability random sample of the Mexican population, so its representativeness of settlers to the United States is not well captured.

The Mexican Family Life Survey

The MxFLS is a prospective panel survey of individuals, households, and families; it is nationally representative and multithematic, with participants being interviewed in waves approximately every three to four years. The MxFLS includes socioeconomic, demographic, and health information of every household member. The first round of the study (MxFLS-1) was conducted in 2002 and was representative of the population at that time,[4] while the second was fielded in 2005–2006. The third round (MxFLS-3), is taking place over the period 2009–2011.

The MxFLS is a population based survey which was designed to interview all baseline respondents. Embedded in the design was the fact that those who moved within Mexico or into the United States would be tracked and interviewed. The decision to track migrants to the United States was considered with the intention of minimizing attrition rates in the sample, given the increasing and high migration rates observed in Mexico in recent years (Leite, Ramos, & Gaspar, 2003). Protocols were carefully implemented since the baseline needs to be able to follow movers in future waves. A recontact module was included which contained information (name, addresses, or telephone numbers) of relatives, friends, neighbors, or any other person who could—in case of a move—provide information of the whereabouts of the migrant.

The decision to follow international movers was taken given the high migration rates to the United States found from baseline to wave 1: 3 percent of the complete sample and close to 10 percent of the population between 15 and 29 years old (See Rubalcava et al., 2007) Within a context of high migration rates to the United States, tracking and interviewing international migrants reduces systematic biases in the sample—i.e., as long as migrants are different from those who stay, the larger the sample that gets lost in a panel the more biases will be introduced in any analysis (Thomas, Frankenberg & Smith, 2000). Thus, by including international movers, attrition rates are minimized and the sample remains representative of the Mexican population of 2002.

The MxFLS comprises a representative sample of Mexicans that have migrated to the United States since 2002. For example, if one uses information from 2002 to 2005 to analyze migration to the United States, we have a sample of people selected from a sampling frame of the Mexican population of 2002 who were interviewed in Mexico in 2002 but by 2005 had moved to the United States. The sample includes migrants of all ages, irrespective of their legal status. Migrants who decide to return to Mexico are interviewed in Mexico and those who decide to stay in the United States are followed and interviewed in the United States. The design to follow and interview respondents in the MxFLS is such that it is also easy to capture migrants who return. In this way, in the MxFLS we have information of Mexicans in Mexico; Mexicans in the United States; Mexicans who left for the United States and returned.

A panel of these characteristics offers unparalleled opportunities to link post-migration information with pre-migration data. The data thus collected represents an invaluable source of information for the study of migrant selectivity in that it allows comparisons of U.S. migrants with respect to other groups such as settlers, return migrants, internal migrants, and non-migrants. Selectivity of those who migrate can be dealt with using pre-migration information collected in the baseline.

As more waves are collected, the data will allow researchers to examine the effect of migration over the life cycle, as well as the impact of migration on sending and receiving communities. It offers a great opportunity to examine the relationships between migrants and their origin household over time. Because of its multithematic nature, the data makes it possible to analyze the effect of migration on health; on education; on cognitive ability; on employment and other dimensions of welfare of members who stay as we are using a dynamic framework. It is also possible to see the consequences on these dimensions of those who migrate to the United States.

Tracking Migrants in the United States

Is it possible to track migrants when they move to another country? To our knowledge, only few surveys are designed to interview respondents across the borders. One such example is the *Los Angeles Family and Neighborhoods Survey* (LA FANS). This is a longitudinal study of families and neighborhoods in Los Angeles County. The LA FANS is useful for the study of the effects of neighborhoods and families on children's development; residential mobility, and neighborhood change. It can be used to study immigrant well-being and social ties. In this case, the strategy is to apply telephone interviews to all those movers that leave the country (Sastry, Ghosh-Dastidar, Adams & Pebley, 2003). Rates from the first recontact for LA FANS are not yet public.

Another study that has collected longitudinal data across borders, this time in the context of migration from Turkey to Germany in the 1980s, is the *Survey of Return migrants*. Specifically, in 1984 an economic recession prompted the German government to offer financial incentives to Turkish immigrants to return to their country of origin. Among those who applied for the government support, 1,200 were selected randomly and surveyed before leaving Germany; afterward, in 1986 and 1988, 800 were traced and reinterviewed in Turkey (Dustmann & Kirchkamp, 2001).

The MxFLS is thus one of the few population based surveys that follows participants across borders. Among its strengths for analyzing migration are the following. First, it collects information across the largest migration border in the world (Mexico–United States migration). Second, the MxFLS collects information of both legal and illegal migrants. Third, it collects information prior to the migration event. Fourth, it follows individuals back and forth from and to Mexico and inside the United States. Fifth, it is embedded in a nationally representative survey of Mexicans in 2002. Sixth, it contains a wealth of information about the well-being of individuals, ranging from general socioeconomic characteristics to objective and subjective measures of health, from crime histories and victimization to marriage and migration histories, from a very detailed employment module to information about the assets and wealth of both the origin and destination household, transfers to and from the migrants being among the most important.

Recontact Rates to the United States

Between 2002 and 2005, about 3 percent of the MxFLS baseline respondents moved to the United States. Among those living in the United States during the MxFLS-2 data collection fieldwork, our team was able to locate and interview 91 percent of them. In the following section, we describe the protocols implemented by the MxFLS team to track and interview international movers.

Who Is an International Migrant?

Our first concern was to construct a useful definition of a migrant. We defined a Mexico–U.S. migrant as anyone who was living in the United States when the second wave was conducted and who (1) had lived there for at least one year or (2) declared to have the intention to stay in the United States for at least one year. Any participant who had been living in the United States for three months at the moment of the survey, but who said that he or she would return to live to Mexico in less than nine months, was not considered a migrant. In these cases, the battery of questionnaires pertaining to the MxFLS in Mexico was applied to them.[5]

Our definition includes people who work for less than one year in the United States, return to visit their families in Mexico or attend business at home, and then return to the United States to work. Individuals who were in the United States between waves for more than one year, but were living in Mexico when the MxFLS-2 was fielded are also considered international migrants, but the questionnaires applied to this group were the ones applied to respondents living in Mexico.

According to Table 2.1, from 2002 to 2005, 854 individuals in our sample were living in the United States in 2005, 3 were living outside Mexico in a country different from the United States, and forty-six were migrants who moved between the two waves and who were living in Mexico in 2005.

It is worth pointing out that from 2002 to 2005 it was not possible to relocate approximately 1,700 individuals. When we visited them in their original location, we found they were not living there anymore. Most of these cases are people who in 2002 lived in a rented dwelling. Leaving

Table 2.1.　International Migrants, MxFLS 2002–2005

	N	%
Migrants living in the United States in 2005	854	94.6
Migrants living in another country in 2005	3	0.3
Migrants to the United States living in Mexico in 2005	46	5.1
Total	903	100.0

Source: MxFLS-1, MxFLS2-MigUS, MxFLS-2 Book3a and Proxy

Table 2.2.   Migrants Living in the United States During MxFLS-2

Migrants	N	%
International	903	37.0
Domestic	1,550	63.0
Total	2,453	100.0

Source: Authors' own calculations using MxFLS-1 and MxFLS-2
Note: We consider as domestic migrants: a) All respondents interviewed in a different locality in 2005, and b) respondents who move for more than one year in the retrospective history of migration. Respondents who moved within a metropolitan area are not considered migrants.

this subsample aside, among movers 37 percent of total movers are international.

In the following sections, we describe the protocols we used to locate and interview the 854 Mexicans who moved from 2002 to 2005 to the United States and who were living there during the fieldwork of the second wave of the MxFLS.

Fieldwork Protocols

The first stage of the process consisted of the identification of US migrants. Throughout the course of the MxFLS-2 general fieldwork, interviewers asked information about the current location of every household member listed in the household roster of MxFLS-1. When a member moved (left the original household), we inquired about his or her whereabouts, first by asking someone in the original household and then by asking someone the migrant had indicated in MxFLS-1 as a contact person who could—in case of a move— provide information about its his or her new location. Respondents provided the information necessary to find the missing participant, specifically the migrant's new place of residence and a telephone number where he or she could be reached. In cases where the whole household moved, respondent's friends and relatives—listed in the re-contact information—or even neighbors, provided the location information of the absent household.

At this stage, the team responsible for conducting the massive fieldwork in Mexico was also in charge of the identification of movers and the collection of their location information. However, they had little success in gathering this data for the migrants in the United States. We then had to form a smaller team of more qualified people in Mexico and train them specifically in how to convince the respondents and how to provide the necessary trust.

The new organization allowed perfect communication between the Mexican and U.S. squads, which proved to be fundamental in the success of the operation for several reasons. First, once a telephone number was collected in Mexico, this was promptly submitted to the interviewers in the United States in order to verify its existence and contact the migrant. This procedure permitted revisiting migrants' relatives in Mexico more than once—without incurring additional costs—in order to obtain another telephone number (when necessary), and to ask their support in those cases in which migrants were hesitant to participate. Second, the interviewers in the United States developed *ad hoc* strategies to approach respondents depending on information provided by the family in Mexico and depending on their circumstances. For example, migrant respondents who experienced union dissolution between waves were particularly distrustful to disclose any information and to give us the interview if they found out that their ex-partner provided us with their location information. In these cases, our *ad hoc* strategy was to find another relative of the migrant in Mexico and to establish a trustful relationship with them in order to contact the migrant further on. This fieldwork had to be done in parallel to be able to verify in real time the information that was provided.

The original plan of MxFLS-2 was to interview U.S. migrants by telephone, based on the experience and positive results of a pilot study conducted in Northern California before MxFLS-1 was carried out. The decision to conduct the interviews by telephone was mainly budget-related, but we were also concerned about response rates given that most of our sample is undocumented. The telephone interview lasted approximately thirty minutes. It included several questions that tried first to establish trust and then to capture the well-being of these individuals in the United States covering health-related questions, employment, expectations, and earnings. We also included some specific migration questions related to getting across the border.

If in the course of tracking U.S. migrants returned to Mexico, interviews were carried out in their new location in Mexico. When migrants were difficult to reach, proxy interviews were conducted through their closest relative in Mexico or in the United States (e.g., spouse, parent, or sibling).

Before conducting the interviews in the United States, three actions were taken to facilitate the contact. First, a complete profile of the migrant was created; it contained all demographic and health information collected in 2002. In addition, we included information about the names of the people in the original household, the name of the person providing us the information about their location in the United States, and a complete history of the results of previous attempts to contact the migrant. Second, interviewers reminded migrants about their participation in MxFLS-1 in 2002, about the participation of their relatives in Mexico in MxFLS-2, and if the migrant requested it, we mentioned the names of the informants in Mexico who had provided the data to find them. Finally, we sent a monetary gratification by post to all participants in the United States after the interview was conducted, as a token of our appreciation.

As the fieldwork in the United States advanced, we had to modify our protocols to accommodate difficult cases. For example, in those cases in which families were not able to provide a telephone number in the United States because they truly did not know it, we implemented a twofold strategy. First we requested them to ask their migrant to call our interviewers in the United States. We left a card with our contact information. Second, we periodically made follow-up phone calls to the household in Mexico to update any information on the migrant. We kept contact with their family in Mexico. These strategies required great flexibility from our interviewers, since they had to answer calls when the migrant called back. In some cases, interviews took place in the middle of the night, after the migrant finished his or her shift at work, during weekends, or very early in the morning due to time changes between the different locations where he or she was to be found. Both of these strategies yielded positive outcomes.

In Mexico, to encourage participation we provided migrants' families with letters of gratitude, and in some cases with in-kind food baskets (*despensas*) or, in more extreme cases, monetary incentives. But most important of all was the ability of the interviewers to gain the migrant's families' trust so they could be confident that the information they were providing would not put any of their migrants in the United States at risk. This was not easy, given that most of them were both first-time movers and undocumented migrants. Crucial in this process was the participation of well-trained interviewers with high human capital, able to convey the purpose of the survey to migrants' households and the migrants themselves.

For households for which we did not have a telephone number in Mexico, it took several visits to get the information (up to five visits in the most difficult cases). However, this process was necessary and proved central to achieving high success rates. The combination of visits allowed fieldworkers to establish the required trust.

In the United States, for cases in which our normal procedures did not yield a positive response in terms of interviewing migrants by phone, we followed an alternative procedure which consisted of interviewing the migrants face-to-face. To do this for those who did not have a telephone number, we first had to locate migrants using information from their social networks. To reach migrants through their networks, we followed three steps. First, we identified the networks, with our own data, as specific flows with high intensity of migration from the same origin in Mexico to the same U.S. destination (e.g., we identified the fact that individuals from a town in Guanajuato consistently migrated to a town in Texas). Second, we asked for permission from the family in Mexico to contact their migrants through these networks, especially in those cases in which the family was willing to participate but lacked complete information to locate their relative in the United States. Finally, we obtained the relevant information from the network to locate and interview the migrant. In these cases, interviewers were sent in person to the destination areas. In total, face to face interviews were carried out with 10 percent of our sample and we covered different states including California, Nevada, Utah, Illinois, Indiana, North Carolina, Tennessee, Alabama, Oklahoma, Texas and Arizona.

Table 2.3 shows the distribution of migrants in terms of how we tracked and interviewed them. From 854 respondents that were identified as U.S. migrants, 73 percent were interviewed in the United States, 18 percent in Mexico, and 9 percent refused to participate in the survey. Among those who were interviewed, about 20 percent were surveyed by proxy while 80 percent provided the information directly to us. During the tracking process, about 7 percent of the migrants returned to Mexico and were surveyed face-to-face at their addresses in Mexico, 2 percent refused to participate in the United States, and 7 percent of the households in Mexico refused to provide information about the U.S. migrant.

To sum up, two types of strategies were implemented during the fieldwork, those oriented toward providing interviewers with complete and updated information on the cases in order to maximize the probability of success, and those aimed at encouraging people to participate. Those in the latter category consisted of (1) providing food baskets or monetary incentives to the households in Mexico, (2) visiting households in Mexico several times to build the trust necessary to obtain the information, (3) calling several times and at different hours to migrants living in the United States, in order to carry out

Table 2.3. Migrants Living in the United States During MxFLS-2

Interview Status	Location	N	%
By telephone	U.S.	516	60.4%
Face-to-face	U.S.	85	10.0%
Proxy by telephone	U.S.	15	1.8%
Proxy face-to-face	U.S.	4	0.5%
Face-to-face	MEX	64	7.5%
Proxy face-to-face	MEX	90	10.5%
Refusals	U.S.	17	2.0%
Refusals	MEX	63	7.4%
Total		854	100.0%

Source: MxFLS2-MigUS Fieldwork information

the interview, and (4) relying on social networks to find the migrants that we were unable to track by telephone.

U.S. MIGRANT SAMPLE

Descriptive Statistics

Table 2.4 shows weighted descriptive statistics of our sample of U.S. migrants. Our analytical sample comprises 854 MxFLS-1 respondents who moved to the United States between 2002 and 2005. In 2002, our sample of migrants were on average 21 years old, about 64 percent male, 27 percent were married or in a union, 42 percent were from rural areas, with a household

Table 2.4.   Descriptive Statistics (N = 854)[a]

	Mean	*S.E.*
Respondents' Demographic Characteristics		
Age	21.1	*(12.1)*
Male	0.6	*(0.5)*
Marital Status	0.3	*(0.4)*
Rural	0.4	*(0.5)*
Household Size	6.0	*(2.3)*
Log Per Capita Expenditure	6.6	*(1.0)*
Interviewers' Characteristics		
Male Interviewer	0.4	*(0.5)*
Fieldwork strategies implemented in Mexico		
=1 HH received Monetary Incentives	0.2	*(0.4)*
=1 HH received *Despensa*	0.5	*(0.5)*
=1 HH received follow-up calls	0.2	*(0.4)*
Cumulative Visits to the household	2.4	*(1.6)*
Cumulative Monetary Incentives	30.1	*(72.6)*
Cumulative *Despensas*	0.6	*(0.9)*
Cumulative follow-up Calls	0.4	*(0.9)*
Fieldwork strategies implemented in the U.S.		
=1 Migrant Visited	0.1	*(0.3)*
Cumulative Visits to the migrant	0.1	*(0.3)*
Cumulative Phone calls	4.1	*(2.4)*

Source: MxFLS-1, MxFLS2-MigUS, MxFLS2-MigUS Fieldwork data
[a] Estimates are weighted

size in Mexico of 6 members, and a log per-capita expenditure of 6.6. For this sample migrants or their family were visited, called, or interviewed by a male interviewer in about 45 percent of the cases. This table also shows means and standard errors for all the measures corresponding to the fieldwork strategies. In Mexico, households were visited on average twice, called 0.4 times, and received on average 30 pesos and 1 food basket. It is important to mention that the 854 migrants are linked to 510 households. Of those households, 45 percent received food baskets, 20 percent received monetary incentives, and 25 percent received follow-up calls. In the United States interviewers called on average each migrant about four times and only about 10 percent of the sample was visited in person by field-trackers in the United States.

Preliminary Findings

The U.S. Migrants module of the MxFLS (MxFLS-MigUS) includes representative information on Mexican migration to the United States that occurred from 2002 to 2005. While this data is not representative of Mexican migrants that moved prior to 2002, it is an accurate source for explaining the most recent migration patterns.

Sociodemographic Information

Table 2.5 shows the demographic composition of U.S. migrants in our sample; it indicates that men are more likely to migrate than women—about 62 percent of the individuals that migrated to the United States were males. Migrants from urban areas are younger and less educated than migrants from rural areas. However, in both cases the average age is about 25 years old. While movers from urban areas are more likely to have finished middle school, movers from rural areas are more likely to have finished elementary school. Our data is consistent with prior evidence (Cerruti & Massey, 2004).

MxFLS-MigUS provides the usual information required to understand the process of international migration such as year of first trip, year of latest entry, total number of trips made, total U.S. experience, birthplace of parents, English proficiency, and migrant networks. Table 2.5 shows that 81 percent of the urban migrants reported their move as their first trip to the United States, compared to 73 percent of respondents from rural areas.

Legal status was asked directly for the first hundred cases, but we observed that after this question was asked, some respondents were not willing to finish the survey, so we decided to drop it in light of our interest in building the necessary trust with respondents for following waves. However, in cases

Table 2.5.   US Migrants Who were Interviewed in 2005

	Urban	Rural
% Male	62%	62%
Age distribution		
01–09	6%	8%
10–14	12%	7%
15–24	39%	44%
25–34	22%	22%
35–44	12%	10%
45–54	5%	6%
55–64	2%	1%
65 or more	1%	1%
Years of schooling		
1–6	34%	48%
7–9	36%	39%
10–12	22%	12%
>12	8%	1%
First trip to the United States	81%	73%
Health assessment	85%	86%
N	292	482

Source: Mexican Family Life Survey - US MIG 2005

where respondents were open about their legal status during the interview, the interviewers recorded this information in the questionnaire. Our sample includes 12 percent documented migrants, about 65 percent undocumented, and 23 percent whose status we did not know.

Origin and Destination

Table 2.6 reveals the distribution of the migrants by sending region in Mexico, the most important being western Mexico, which sent around 58 percent of the migrants. Within this region, Michoacán was the main sender (20 percent), followed by Durango (16 percent) and Guanajuato (11 percent). The main destinations of Mexican migrants in our sample are California (31 percent), Texas (15 percent), and Illinois (8 percent). Nonetheless, Mexican migrants have spread all over the United States, as can be seen in Table 2.7, which is consistent with other research (Hernández-León & Zuñiga, 2005).

Table 2.6. 2002–2005 Mexican Migrants by Origin

Region	Urban	Rural	N
Northwest[a]	9.2%	7.9%	65
East[b]	18.8%	4.8%	78
Occident[c]	41.4%	60.8%	414
Center[d]	17.1%	13.1%	113
South[e]	13.4%	13.5%	104
Total	100.0%	100.0%	774

Source: Mexican Family Life Survey - US MIG 2005
[a] Northwest: Baja California Sur, Sinaloa, Sonora
[b] East: Coahuila, Nuevo León, Veracruz
[c] Occident: Jalisco, Michoacán, Guanajuato, Durango
[d] Center: D.F., Estado de México, Morelos, Puebla
[e] South: Oaxaca and Yucatán

Table 2.7. 2002–2005 Mexican Migrants by US Region

Region	Urban	Rural	N
Northeast[a]	6.6%	5.2%	44
Southeast[b]	27.6%	30.1%	225
Midwest[c]	11.4%	16.2%	111
Southwest[d]	10.7%	6.4%	62
West[e]	43.8%	42.1%	330
Total	100.0%	100.0%	772

Source: Mexican Family Life Survey - US MIG 2005
[a] Connecticut, New York, New Jersey, Pennsylvania, Delaware, Maryland
[b] Alabama, Florida, Georgia, Arkansas, North Carolina, South Carolina, Tennessee, Virginia, Kentucky, Texas
[c] Minnesota, Iowa, Indiana, Ohio, Kansas, Missouri, Wisconsin, Illinois
[d] Arizona, New Mexico, Oklahoma
[e] Colorado, Utah, Montana, Nevada, Oregon, Washington, California

Table 2.8 provides information of the destinations of migrants according to the sending region in Mexico. The data shows that migrants from the northwest region of Mexico are more likely to go to the West and Southwest. About 60 percent of respondents in the northwest region of Mexico are from Sinaloa and 35 percent are from Sonora; their main destinations in the United States are California and Arizona, respectively. The east region of Mexico is represented mainly by migrants from Nuevo León and Coahuila in 40 percent and 30 percent, respectively, and in both cases their main destination is Texas. Most of the migrants from the Occident of Mexico are from Michoacán and Durango, which comprise 40 percent and 30 percent of the respondents of that region, respectively, and their main destinations are California and Texas, respectively, as well as Illinois in both cases. About 50 percent of migrants from the central region of Mexico come from Morelos who are spread substantially across many regions of the United States. Finally, the

Table 2.8. 2002–2005 Mexican Migrants by Origin and Destination

U.S. Region[b]	Region in Mexico[a]				
	Northwest	East	Occident	Center	South
Urban origin					
Northeast	0%	7%	2%	21%	5%
Southeast	11%	56%	21%	29%	18%
Midwest	0%	16%	13%	17%	0%
Southwest	37%	7%	11%	8%	0%
West	52%	13%	53%	25%	77%
	100%	100%	100%	100%	100%
N	27	55	121	48	22
Rural Origin					
Northeast	0%	0%	3%	19%	8%
Southeast	5%	78%	31%	29%	23%
Midwest	0%	9%	23%	6%	6%
Southwest	26%	0%	5%	6%	2%
West	68%	13%	37%	40%	62%
	100%	100%	100%	100%	100%
N	38	23	293	63	64

Source: Mexican Family Life Survey - US MIG 2005

[a] Northwest: Baja California Sur, Sinaloa, Sonora; East: Coahuila, Nuevo León, Veracruz; Occident: Jalisco, Michoacán, Guanajuato, Durango; Center: D.F., Estado de México, Morelos, Puebla; South: Oaxaca, Yucatán

[b] Northeast: Connecticut, New York, New Jersey, Pennsylvania, Delaware, Maryland; Southeast: Alabama, Florida, Georgia, Arkansas, North Carolina, South Carolina, Tennessee, Virginia, Kentucky, Texas; Midwest: Minnesota, Iowa, Indiana, Ohio, Kansas, Missouri, Wisconsin, Illinois; Southwest: Arizona, New Mexico, Oklahoma; West: Colorado, Utah, Montana, Nevada, Oregon, Washington, California

south of Mexico is composed mainly of migrants from Oaxaca, whose main destination is California.

Employment Sector

The sectors that demand the highest number of recent Mexican immigrants are the Construction and the Service (Restaurant) Sectors. Table 2.9 shows that among the urban immigrants that were employed in 2005, about 22 percent were employed in the Construction sector and earned on average USD $1,754; 21 percent were employed in the Restaurant Sector and earned on average USD $1,335; and 11.6 percent were employed in other activities within the Service Sector[6] and earned on average

Table 2.9.   Employment Distribution and Average Earnings of Mexican Migrants to the United States from 2002 and 2005 by Origin

	Urban	Rural	Earnings[a] Urban	Rural
Construction	22.4%	26.4%	1,754	1,639
			(725)	(648)
Restaurant	21.1%	13.9%	1,335	1,020
			(507)	(392)
Agriculture & Livestock	8.6%	17.6%	1,331	1,146
			(754)	(404)
Other Services	11.6%	10.0%	1,031	1,237
			(688)	(785)
Manufactures	8.2%	6.6%	1,689	1,151
			(571)	(568)
Not employed	13.4%	11.7%		
Other sectors	14.7%	13.7%		
Total	100.0%	100.0%		
N	232	409		

Source: Mexican Family Life Survey - US MIG 2005
[a] Standard deviation in parenthesis

USD $1,031. Of the immigrants that moved from rural areas to the United States, 26 percent were employed in the construction sector and earned on average USD $1,639; 17 percent were employed in Agriculture and Livestock and earned USD $1,331; and 14 percent were employed in the Restaurant Sector. Table 2.9 also shows an unemployment rate of about 20 percent among immigrants—13 percent for migrants of urban origin and 12 percent for migrants of rural origins.

Table 2.10 links the previous experience of migrants in 2002 with their occupation in 2005. The table shows that 31 percent of the migrants employed in the Construction sector in the United States were unemployed in 2002; 28 percent used to work in the Agriculture and Livestock sector in 2002, whereas only 14 percent used to work in the Construction sector.

Among the migrants employed in the Restaurant and Agriculture & Livestock sector in the United States about 50 percent were unemployed in Mexico in 2002; and about 20 percent were working in the Agriculture and Livestock sector. Furthermore the data shows that 92 percent of the unemployed migrants in 2005 were also unemployed in 2002.

Table 2.10. Employment Sector in 2002 and 2005 of Mexican Adult Migrants

Sector 2002	Sector 2005				
	Construction	Restaurant	Agriculture and Livestock	Not Employed	Other Sectors in 2005
Agriculture & Livestock	28%	21%	20%	1%	15%
Construction	14%	3%	3%	0%	4%
Manufactures: Food	5%	4%	11%	1%	2%
Wholesale trade	6%	9%	5%	3%	6%
Other sectors in 2002	16%	16%	12%	4%	26%
Not employed	31%	47%	49%	92%	48%
	100%	100%	100%	100%	100%
N	160	106	92	170	235

Source: Mexican Family Life Survey - US MIG 2005 and MxFLS-1

Here we presented general information on the sample and found the socio-demographic information derived from the MxFLS-MigUS data consistent with other data sources. Our data also sheds light on new destinations of migrants, salaries, employment status, previous employment, and preferred sectors of employment, broken down by sex, age and rural/urban stratification, irrespective of legal status.

Conclusion

There has been a surge in the world's international migration, and the increase in Mexican migration to the United States is an example of this worldwide trend. In this case, historical trends have been dramatically modified both by the sheer scale of the new migration and the new behaviors displayed, expressed in new destinations and routes and novel interactions with the local host societies.

Although a more refined knowledge about this elusive population right at the moment of movement and during its migration process is desirable for the researcher and the policymaker as studying by means of traditional instruments becomes difficult or inefficient because they avoid contact with traditional instruments of measurement. In addition, core design problems persist that contribute to the opaqueness of this population: who constitutes a migrant, how to find them, where they are, to what extent they make use of health and education services in the United States, and what their contribution to the host society and to their town is, and on a different level, to their country.

We presented a panel study design that effectively tracked and interviewed migrants when they crossed national boundaries, with a success rate of 91 percent. This was accomplished by a combination of heavy use of social and human capital and telecommunication technologies such as small portable computers to share information instantly with teams across borders, satellite telephone communications to contact families across borders, and a careful design of communication between teams across borders.

Thus, we avoid some usual constrictions (small sample size, locating migrants in the host country, and keeping levels of attrition low) and provide a new panel dataset to study these populations, equipped with important demographic and socioeconomic information at the individual level for each household in the sample.

With MxFLS-MigUS it will be possible to study the selectivity of the emigration of immigrants, in particular the case of return migrants. It will contribute to providing an accurate picture of the relationships between sending and receiving communities at the household and community levels. This design is intended to provide an empirical methodology to analyze the mechanisms and processes that underlie transnational communities using a dynamic perspective. MxFLS-MigUS will allow researchers to analyze processes of migration considering both the sending and receiving society.

NOTES

1. Financial support from was received from the National Institute of Health through NICHD R01HD047522 and NIA R01 AG030668–01 and from the Ford Foundation.

2. As of 2002, the U.S. Census reported a total population of 288.6 million (http://www.census.gov/statab/hist/HS-01.pdf).

3. See Rallu 2004 for a review of projects that use this design.

4. It included approximately 8,400 households and 35,000 individuals distributed in sixteen states and 150 communities of Mexico.

5. This definition is consistent with one suggested by the UN Statistical Commission (UN 1998): to facilitate comparability between datasets collected on international migrants, particularly when undocumented migration occurs.

6. Other services includes: Babysitter, Domestic Service, Janitor, Sales Attendant, Mechanic, Plumber, Driver, Loader, Electrician, Car Washer, Hair Dresser, Gardener. All figures are monthly wage income. All figures are monthly wage income.

Chapter 3

The Mexican National Rural Household Survey and Rural Migration

José Jorge Mora-Rivera

In developing countries, rural households diversify their sources of income through an extensive range of productive activities. They assign part of their endowments of labor, land, and capital to different activities—for example, agricultural and livestock production, self-employment activities, and salaried activities (within and outside the community)—and also increasingly decide to participate in activities which involve migration. Agriculture is one of the main activities for the majority of rural homes in Mexico. Although it yields little and is not an important source of income, most rural households decide to participate in this activity. The decisions on participating in activities outside agriculture are taken on a household level, mainly due to the fact that the profits of activities outside agriculture are often better than those of agriculture itself for which reason, the households find it attractive to participate in these activities as a measure to diversify their family income.

However, the participation of households in local non-agricultural activities is restricted by various factors. In rural Mexico, the land renting and labor markets are not developed, they are segmented or simply do not exist (Mora, 2007). This is due, among other things, to the lack of information and the high costs of travel. To the above we should add the direct public support for agricultural production, which affects households' decisions to participate in other activities which provide income. Thus, government support explains why rural households do not abandon agricultural production, which restricts the allocation of labor to non-agricultural activities. Moreover, in rural communities in developing countries, non-agricultural activities are affected by the lack of local credit markets and irrigation. In this situation, part of the rural population has to emigrate in order to obtain an additional source of

37

income which is not correlated to the uncertainly and the risk involved in local productive activities (Stark, 1991; Taylor, 1999).

The Mexican rural sector, given its social, cultural, and economic characteristics, is one of the most vulnerable to political decisions, represents a little over 25 percent of the total population[1] of Mexico and is an important source of expulsion of labor to the United States and the big cities in Mexico, which is why it is important to know the detailed characteristics and economic behavior, as well as the impact of policy decisions on the Mexican rural population. In order to understand this behavior it is necessary, among other things, to carry out serious and thorough quantitative research which will permit us to evaluate the impact of agricultural reform and other socioeconomic aspects closely related to this sector of the population. However, there is a factor limiting these studies: the lack of information.

Given the scenario above, the Studies of Economic Change and the Sustainability of Mexican Agriculture (PRECESAM) of the Colegio de México and the Rural Economies of the Americas and Pacific Rim (REAP) of the University of California at Davis took on the task of collecting this information by means of a representative national survey: the Mexican National Rural Household Survey (in Spanish *Encuesta Nacional a Hogares Rurales de* México, ENHRUM hereafter). The ENHRUM was funded by CON-ACYT, the Ford Foundation, the William and Flora Hewlett Foundation, and UC-MEXUS.

The survey is multithematic, as it gathers information from households on a variety of topics such as sociodemography, education, migration, income and expenditure, economic activities with emphasis on agriculture and livestock production, economic and social geography (where people buy and sell, where work, and migrate to), and work history.

The first edition was carried out in 2003 and took the year 2002 as its unit of analysis. Given the importance of the studies done on the basis of it, a second round was carried out in the months of January to March 2008, with the aim of making a panel-type data base. Thus, the ENHRUM II constitutes a joint effort by the participant institutions to offer detailed information on the Mexican rural sector and the changes it has undergone over this period.

The ENHRUM sample design is complex—that is, stratified, multistage, and by conglomerates—and was elaborated in such a way that the information obtained in the survey is representative nationally (Chávez Alvarado, 2007). The aim of this chapter is to describe the survey methodology and to present the main national level results with respect to the phenomenon of migration based on the data thrown up by the survey. The structure of the document is the following. In the second section the basic objectives of the survey are presented. The third section refers to coverage and survey periods. The main results of the survey which describe the population studied from the demographic and economic point of view are presented in the fourth section. In the last section some final thoughts are presented.

THE OBJECTIVES OF THE ENHRUM

The ENHRUM has two components: the Community Survey and the Household Survey. The basic instrument of the Household Survey is a household questionnaire, which in the second round is made up of fifteen sections. (See the Appendix to Chapter 2 for a description of the sections that make up each round of the survey.)

The overall objective of the ENHRUM was to gather socioeconomic information, nationally representative of the Mexican rural sector in villages of 500 to 2,499 inhabitants; this information would be useful to draw up a social accounting matrix and other empirical studies on the effects of the agricultural and commercial reforms on the production, income and migration of households and the rural sector.

In addition to the above objective, in the first round the survey gathered information on the following features of Mexico's rural households (Chávez Alvarado, 2007):

a) Sociodemographic characteristics of household members.
b) Characteristics of the infrastructure of the dwelling.
c) The work history and characteristics of household members.
d) The history and characteristics of migration of household members.
e) Quantification of the time spent on the family's work in the different economic activities, identifying the members of the household that carry them out.
f) The income structure of the households according to their source and place of origin.
g) The expenditure structure of the households according to its destination: type of supplier and the place where the spending occurred.
h) The costs of productive activities the household is involved in and the place they are done in. Payment of hired labor, spending on inputs, capital and transportation of products.
i) The household consumption on different economic activities.
j) Crops produced, use and characteristics of the land owned by the households (area, quality, distance from the center of the locality, type of landholding, etc.)

During the second round of the survey it was possible to add the following specific aims:

k) Main characteristics of the financial markets.
l) Extend the section on natural resources incorporating specific aspects such as the use and exploitation of medicinal plants.

COVERAGE AND SURVEY PERIOD

With respect to temporal coverage, the reference periods of the survey according to the type of variable were the following:

a) From January 1 to December 31, 2002 and 2007, for the economic questions (income and expenditure), for the first and second rounds, respectively.
b) The moment of the interview for sociodemographic variables (age, sex, religion, language, civil status, educational level) and housing conditions (construction materials and services available)
c) From 1980 to 2002 for the work histories of household members, in the case of the first ENHRUM; for the second survey the period covered 1990 to 2007.

A year is a very long time, and the results that are obtained in an interview concerning this time can be of very low quality. However, with the experience of other similar surveys and during the pilot runs that were carried out before the fielding of ENHRUM, the organizers realized that as long as the questions were adequately formulated, it was possible to obtain good-quality average information for this period.

It is very common for the head of the family or member of the rural household who directs the economic activities to know, with certain precision, the average expenditure and income involved in these activities, even when he or she makes no written register of them. A good example is agriculture. In the case of the ENHRUM, the corresponding section of the questionnaire was divided into three subsections following to the agricultural cycle: activities carried out (i) before sowing, (ii) after sowing and just prior to the harvest, and (iii) during the harvest. This division was very familiar to those interviewed and contributed to a great extent to their recalling the information at each stage, with the consequent high-quality replies on the topic.

However, the researchers participating in the ENHRUM considered the risks involved in using such a long a period of reference for the survey, for which reason the effort made to gather the best information possible not only reflected

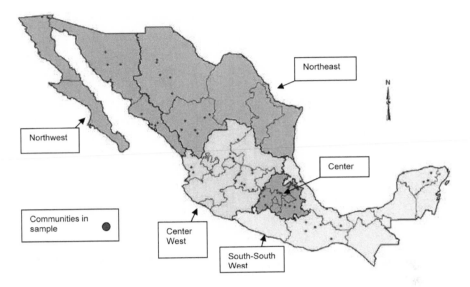

Figure 3.1.

the elaboration of the survey but also, the training of the team. It should be mentioned that in the second round of the survey the informants' memories were tested in the retrospective and job history sections, with the aim of carrying out statistical tests with respect to the quality of the information gathered.

Geographical Coverage

The geographical coverage of the ENHRUM is national in villages of 500 to 2,499 inhabitants. Based on a division of the country into five regions defined by their geographical vicinity in the National Development Plan,[2] the survey was applied in eighty rural communities in fourteen states of the Mexican Republic. Figure 1 shows the distribution of these communities throughout the country. The ENHRUM II was applied in the same localities studied in the first survey.

RESULTS OF THE ENHRUM

Given that the objective of the survey was to gather socioeconomic information on the households from a sociodemographic point of view related to the composition of their income and expenditure, the approach of this composition is based on the hypothesis that rural households diversify their sources of income in order to cover their expenditure; thus each one of them carries out more than one economic activity, among which, of course, one of the main income-generating activities is the migration of individuals from the Mexican rural sector.

Sociodemographic Characteristics of Mexican Rural Households

In this section the rural population is described by means of the presentation and interpretation of the results of a number of sociodemographic variables and basic migratory characteristics.

Table 3.1 shows some sociodemographic characteristics of the sample. The average size of the households is 6.3 individuals, in a range of 1 to 18 members.

Table 3.1.   Descriptive Statistics, ENHRUM, 2002

Variable	*Mean*	Standard *Deviation.*	*Min.*	*Max.*
Household size	5.77	3.02	1	18
Number of children	0.54	0.89	0	8
Age of head of household	48.62	16.11	15	95
No. of years education of head of household	4.47	3.74	0	20
Average number of years education of household members	5.45	2.48	0	16.6
Number of family contacts in internal migration destinations in 1990	0.21	0.56	0	5
Number of family contacts in migration destinations in the United States in 1990	0.11	0.4	0	5
Endowment of land (hectares)	4.8	25.08	0	537.5
Number of heads of cattle in 2001	2.76	13.56	0	252
Tractors property of the household in 2001	0.05	0.22	0	2
Wealth index	0	2.03	−6.28	4.48
Frequency of transport	8.24	5.91	0	24
Lack of access during climatological shocks (Dummy)	0.14	0.34	0	1

Source: ENHRUM, 2002. The sample size is 1765 households.

Table 3.2.   Years of Schooling According to Educational Level

Years of Schooling Completed	Number	Percentage
0	798	10.93%
4–6	2610	35.76%
6–9	1866	25.57%
10–12	573	7.85%
>12	233	3.19%
Total	7,298	100.00%

Source: ENHRUM, 2002.

The average age and number of years' schooling of household heads are 48.6 and 4.47 years, respectively. The average schooling of the rest of the family is 5.46 years. Table 3.2 shows that education, measured in years completed, has a relatively symmetrical distribution, centered in the range of 4 to 6 years of schooling. About 11 percent of household members have studied no school grades at all, while only almost 3 percent have studied twelve or more grades.

LEVEL AND COMPOSITION OF NET RURAL INCOMES

The ENHRUM permits us obtain data on the micro-economic plane of the variety of productive activities of Mexican rural households, which makes it possible to estimate the net incomes from the different activities that the rural households participate in. For example, this study takes into account net incomes from agriculture, livestock raising, and net income from other sources, which include commerce and services. These sources of income were selected since they are ones originating from the main productive activities that generate rural incomes.

There are various methods to obtain net incomes originating from the different productive activities of Mexican rural households. In this research values are not attributed to family income such as work, land, and capital, given that it is not obvious which prices should be used to do this. Thus the net income from productive activities was estimated from the gross production value (using the local prices observed). Income from remittances was obtained in the same way, by adding the amount sent by each member of the household and subtracting the costs involved in the migration of the household members who participated in this activity.

Table 3.3 shows the composition of total net income, which includes the sources used for this study, as well as others sources of income which together make up the total net income. It can be seen that the net income

Table 3.3.   Composition of Net Income According to Source

Variable	Mean	Share
Income from livestock	1,983.38	3.71%
Income from agriculture	6,627.15	12.40%
Government transfers	2,326.39	4.35%
Internal remittances	897.71	1.68%
Remittances from the U.S.	5,888.42	11.01%
Salaries	28,949.05	54.15%
Other income	6,793.2	12.71%
Total	53,465.31	100.00%

Source: ENHRUM, 2002.

from agriculture and livestock income represents more than 16 percent of the total, while remittances account for 11 percent. The most important source of income in Mexican rural households is from wages, which have a share of 54 percent in the total income.

MIGRATION IN RURAL MEXICO

In a similar way to migration on a national level, according to the ENHRUM data base, rural migration rose more than 450 percent from 1980 to 2002—that is to say, it grew 8 percent annually. Over the same period, the number of communities surveyed having international migrants more than doubled. Meanwhile, the proportion of rural Mexican households with international migrants went from 4 percent in 1980 to more than 16 percent in 2002 (see Table 3.4).

Table 3.4.   Migration Statistics in Rural Mexico, by Region*

	Households with Migrants in the USA (%)		Migrants in the USA per Household		Households with Internal Migrants (%)		Internal Migrants per Household	
Region	2002	2007	2002	2007	2002	2007	2002	2007
Southeast	7.53	10.18	0.10	0.17	34.95	43.32	0.89	1.17
Center	14.52	20.40	0.27	0.44	29.32	39.94	0.7	1.02
Center-West	27.75	36.13	0.62	1.01	30.06	34.68	1.02	1.31
Northwest	12.09	15.34	0.23	0.36	22.42	33.92	0.72	0.84
Northeast	19.72	19.82	0.54	0.57	11.67	18.33	0.23	0.46
Total	16.22	20.23	0.35	0.5	25.76	34.05	0.71	0.88

Source: ENHRUM, 2002 y 2007.   * All data for 2007 is preliminary

From the ENHRUM data it can be seen that emigration can be positively correlated with investment (see Table 3.5). At the same time, the descriptive statistics from the data obtained in this survey suggest that migration influences household income and assets. The income and wealth of the households with international migrants are, on average, greater than those of households without migrants. Also, the first group of households has a greater number of productive assets. This might suggest that, on average, the households with migrants have higher standards than households without migrants. (see Table 3.5).

Disparity in income levels also appear to be present when the rural regions of Mexico are compared using ENHRUM data. The households in the two northern regions—specially the northwest—are those which have higher incomes, and are the regions where households have a considerable share of the number of households with international migrants, as well as having a more equal distribution of productive assets.

Table 3.4 contains migratory characteristics according to region. Sixteen percent of households had at least 1 household member living in the United

Table 3.5. Descriptive Statistics for Households with and without Migrants

Variable	Households with International Migrants	Households without International Migrants
Number of migrants in the U.S.	2.16	—
Remittances from the U.S.	29,014.57	—
Income from livestock	3,108.95	1,765.51
Income from agriculture	5,469.34	6,851.27
Government transfers	3,016.27	2,192.85
Income from salaries	19,051.74	30,864.87
Other income	8,743.75	6,415.63
Years schooling of head of household	3.31	4.69
Experience of head of househols	47.86	37.46
Household size	7.91	5.36
Number of children	0.37	0.58
Average number of years education of household	5.46	5.45
Endowment of land (hectares)	7.67	4.25
Heads of livestock owned	6.17	2.10
Tractors	0.11	0.04
Wealth index	0.90	−0.17

Source: ENHRUM, 2002.

States at the beginning of 2002, and 26 percent of households had members living in other parts of Mexico. The average number of migrants going to the United States was 0.35 individuals per household and the figure for migrants within Mexico was 0.71 individuals, which makes a total on average of 1.06 migrants per household.

Table 3.4 also contains preliminary migratory information for the second round of the survey. In this case it is possible to observe that for 2007, 20 percent of households had at least one member living in the United States and 34 percent members living in other parts of Mexico. These figures increased with respect to the number registered in 2002, in both the proportion of households with a migrant member and the average number of individual migrants in each destination.

Table 3.5 includes descriptive statistics of the households with and without international migrants. If we consider the households with migrants in the United States, the average number of migrants is 2.2 individuals, and the annual average sum of remittances is more than $29,000 pesos. The average educational level of each household head is higher in the nonmigrant households than that of the migrants (4.7 and 3.3 years, respectively). There are no significant differences between the schooling of the other family members in the two groups. On average, the migrant households have a larger endowment of productive assets (land, animals, and tractors).

In addition, Figure 3.2 shows us the trend registered with respect to the flow of migrants to national destinations and to the United States. We can observe

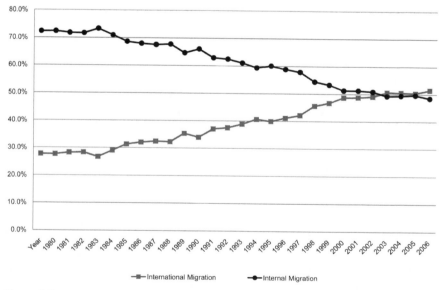

Figure 3.2.

that in 1980, among the total proportion of migrants, the number going to national destinations was considerably greater than to international ones, a trend which remained steady until 2004, when the proportion of migrants going to the United States overtook those going to national destinations. It would be useful to have data for after 2007 in order to be able to know whether this trend holds up despite the immense financial crisis which hit the U.S. labor market during 2008 and 2009.

CONCLUSION

Carrying out a large-scale survey, as in the case of one that is nationally representative, is no easy task. To do this, a large-scale deployment of resources of all kinds is needed: human, economic, infrastructure, logistics, and technical. This document constitutes, in part, the description of those resources for the Mexican National Rural Household Survey. It also presents the results of the survey on the characterization of the population studied from the demographic and economic points of view, putting special emphasis on the phenomenon of migration.

All the stages and components of the survey are transcendental and are related to each other. If one does not fulfill its purpose in time and form, this fact will be reflected in the quality of the information. Thus the efficient and timely planning of every detail will be felt in the successful fulfillment of the objectives.

Concerning the results obtained after the collection and processing of the survey information, it should be noted that in this piece of work only a number of important variables which provide a brief but clear overview of the population studied were presented. This survey is farther-reaching, and the presentation of all the results, in itself, requires another piece of research.

The results permits us to see that from the economic point of view, the rural households are, in fact, characterized by being family units which diversify their sources of income, by means of a varied range of economic activities, and that they produce for both their own consumption and for sale. However, "they are still relatively isolated from the markets" (Yúnez et al., 2000), a situation which can be seen in the small proportion of the products of agriculture and the exploitation of natural resources which are sold. In consequence, the households need to resort to other sources of income. We should also note the shift of the rural population towards work unrelated to the countryside. Although the proportion of people who work there is greater than that of those individuals who work outside, the importance of the latter in terms of income is greater than the former. This is a sign of the low salaries earned in agricultural work. The same behavior is observed in migration to the United States and other parts of Mexico. Although the number and proportion of individuals who migrate

internally is greater than that of those who go to the United States, the income
from remittances of the latter is higher. From these results, it can be understood
that the increasingly evident trend among inhabitants of the rural sector to
exchange typically rural activities for other more profitable ones.

These conclusions lead us to call the attention of policymakers and their
corresponding institutions to give more interest to the rural sector, including
by assigning sufficient resources to research, including censuses and surveys
that generate information reliable and high-quality enough to sustain studies.

In this sense, a necessary project was the fielding of the second round of
the ENHRUM, with the aim of obtaining panel data and permitting us to
follow up on the behavior and changes amongst the rural population. Having
completed this second round, we hope we will be able to carry out more
precise study, among other things, of the dynamics of the phenomenon of
migration which characterizes Mexico's rural population.

APPENDIX 3

Sections of the ENHRUM I and ENHRUM II questionnaire

This appendix contains the sections that make up the ENHRUM I and
ENHRUM II questionnaires fielded in 2003 and 2008, respectively. It is

Table 3.6. Sections Included in the ENHRUM by Wave

ENHRUM I (2002)		ENHRUM II (2007)	
Section No.	Section Name	Section Number	Section Name
1	Housing	1	Recontact sheet
2	Household members	2	Household members
3	Pieces of land	3	Characteristics of pieces of land
4	Crops	4	Annual crop prduction
5	Livestock	5	Permanent crop production
6	Goods and services	6	Accounts for annual and permanent crops
7	Natural resources	7	Livestock
8	Other income and expenses	8	Goods and services
9	Assets	9	Natural resources
10	Inheritance and credit	10	Assets
		11	Housing
		12	Credit
		13	Savings and financial investments
		14	Other income and investments
		15	Exogenous events

important to point out that in some cases, although the names of the sections are the same, they do not have the same numbering in both questionnaires.

The sections added to the 2007 questionnaires are: Recontact Sheet, Exogenous Events, Credit, Savings, and Financial Investments (in these two last sections, although the 2002 questionnaire contains some questions, the 2007 version goes into more detail on both topics; see Table 3.6 for details).

NOTES

1. Instituto Nacional de Estadística, Geografía e Informática (2000).

2. According to p. 10 of the President's 2001–2006 National Development Plan, the regions "are configured in a practical manner in order to coordinate large-scale projects with effects that will transcend the borders of two or more states."

Chapter 4

Beyond Income Differentials

Explaining Migrants' Destinations
in Mexico

M. Estela Rivero-Fuentes

Internal migration is a phenomenon of great demographic and social importance in developing countries. The rapid urbanization of many countries throughout the world during the 1960s and 1970s can be mainly explained by an intense migration from rural to urban areas (Bilsborrow, 1998; Brockerhof, 1999). During the 1980s and the 1990s new patterns of migration emerged in many countries, as migrants started moving from urban centers to other urban centers, and from rural areas to other rural areas. Today internal migration is still the most important factor in determining the distribution of the population in many Latin American, Asian and African countries (United Nations Population Division, 2008). As a result, policy makers need to rely on accurate forecasts of internal migration and on an understanding of the forces driving internal migration when assessing and planning for the future housing, education, and health needs of the different regions in a country.

Despite its importance, our understanding of internal migration is still limited. Past empirical studies attempting to explain why migrants go to some states in a country and not to others have very large residual errors and commonly fail to predict the states that are more likely to receive migrants (see for example, Davies, Greenwood and Li, 2001; Lin and Xie, 1998, Grusky, 1998). In addition, there are very few studies that try to explain the emergence of new patterns of migration in many developing countries during the 1980s, 1990s, and 2000s. Most of the studies that do so give ad-hoc explanations and do not contrast their hypotheses or findings with other alternative explanations (see, for example, for the case of Mexico, Chávez, 1999; Escobar, Bean and Weintraub, 1999; and Liang and White, 1996 for the case of China).[1]

One of the reasons for the poor results of empirical studies of internal migration in predicting migrants' destinations is that most studies are based

51

exclusively on the neoclassical hypothesis of migration, and ignore other factors based on an economic sociology perspective of migration. Such factors, which include past migration trends and trade and infrastructure ties between sending and receiving states, may be instrumental in explaining the distribution of migrants across different destinations, but their relevance has not been empirically tested yet.

This paper attempts to contribute to the literature of internal migration in developing countries in several ways. Taking the case of interstate migration in Mexico in three different periods (1975–1980, 1985–1990, and 1995–2000), I test whether or not the level of past migration, past and recent trade, and administrative and infrastructure ties between states help to explain why migrants from different states of origin go to different destinations. To my knowledge, this is the first study of internal migration in any country that tests the power of variables based on economic sociology explanations to understand migrants' destinations. Furthermore, by comparing the determinants of the distribution of interstate migrants in 1975–1980, 1985–1990, and 1995–2000, this paper moves from ad-hoc explanations to the recent changes in migration patterns in the country.

Background

Most studies that try to explain the distribution of internal migrants in a country rely on the neoclassical theory of migration (see, for example, De Jong, 1999; and Greenwood and Hunt, 2003). Originally formulated by Harris and Todaro in 1970, this theory proposes that individuals migrate because they seek to maximize their expected long-term earnings. In this search, individuals compare their expected earnings in the place of their current residence with the earnings they would expect to make in alternative destinations, given the costs of the migration. If expected earnings somewhere else are greater than expected earnings in their current place of residence, individuals decide to migrate and go to the place where their expected earnings are greatest. The expected long-term earnings in each possible destination are approximated through the average income times the probability of finding a job minus the cost of moving (Harris and Todaro, 1970).

At the aggregate level, the neoclassical theory predicts that the probability of out-migration is positively correlated with the unemployment rate and negatively correlated with the income level of the community or state of origin. Among those individuals who migrate, the probability of moving to any particular destination is positively correlated with the income level and negatively correlated with the unemployment level in the destination and with the distance separating origin and destination (Greenwood, 1985).

Despite its popularity, neoclassical theory does not explain completely why individuals migrating within their country move to the places they do. Studies of internal migration that try to explain the choice of migrants' destinations based on income levels, unemployment, and distance alone generally have very large residual errors and provide a bad fit to the data (Lucas, 1997). Furthermore, in many cases variables measuring economic opportunity in the destination (e.g., unemployment and income levels) are not statistically associated with the probability of migration, or are associated in a direction opposite to what the neoclassical theory would predict (Greenwood, 1985). For example, in a review of the literature on internal migration in developing and developed countries, Greenwood (1985) finds that in many empirical studies the unemployment rate of the place of destination is not significantly associated with, or has a negative effect on, the immigration rate.

One of the possible causes for the failure of the neoclassical theory of migration to explain accurately migrants' destinations is that it assumes that individuals have complete information about all the alternative destinations they can migrate to. In other words, the neoclassical theory assumes that prospective migrants know the distance that separates them from all their potential destinations, and the wages and unemployment rate in each place. Only if they know what to expect in every destination can migrants choose to migrate to the place that maximizes their long-term earnings.

However, individuals might not be equally informed about the conditions in all the potential destinations in a country, or they may consider only some of the states in a country as potential destinations. If when making their migration decisions individuals compare only those places that they have some information about and do not consider places that they are unaware of, even if those places offer higher wages and lower unemployment rates, the predictions of the neoclassical model of migration will be inaccurate.

Contact with individuals who have migrated before, geographical proximity, easy access by transportation, trade, recruitment, and past political, cultural, social, or economic ties between the place of origin and the destination are several of the factors that contribute to individuals' having more information about some destinations than about others. The literature on international migration has already demonstrated that these factors play an important role in determining the direction of international flows. And the explanations articulated in several studies of international migration suggest that these mechanisms might also operate in the case of internal migration. In addition, in the case of Mexico, past migration and relative deprivation have been proved important in explaining the level of migration (Partida Bush, 2006).

According to the theory of social capital of migration, past migrants inform friends and family in their home town about job opportunities in the places they migrated to, and make them aware that they can be better off if they migrate to that destination than if they remain in their place of origin. In addition, individuals who have migrated before help others migrate by helping them find a job or assist them during the migration and settlement process (Choldin, 1973; Massey and Garcia-España, 1987; Massey, 1990). As the number of migrants increases, communities develop a "culture of migration." Migration becomes a rite of passage for young people, even for those who do not have a family or friendship tie with a past migrant (Kandel and Massey, 2002).

The effect of the number of past migrants in the choice of destination has been demonstrated, among other cases, for migrants from the United States (Brastberg and Del Terrel, 1996), Portugal (Borges, 2002), and Italy (Moretti, 1999). Bratsberg and Del Terrel (1996) study the factors that explain the migration of U.S. citizens to sixty-five countries in 1993. These authors find that the probability of U.S. migrants going to a country increases with the number of U.S. citizens already living there, even after controlling for distance, language, and the economic and political conditions of the country of destination.

In the case of Mexican migration, the importance of cumulative causation has been demonstrated for internal and international migration from rural communities (Davis, Stecklov and Winters, 2002; Fussell and Massey, 2004) but not for international migration out of urban areas (Fussell and Massey, 2004). Davis, Stecklov, and Winters (2002) show that in rural communities the number of past migrants who have moved to an urban area increases the probability of new migrants' moving to a city instead than to another rural area. Similarly, the number of migrants who have moved to a rural area increases the probability of new migrants' going to a rural area rather than to an urban area.

Past political and cultural ties between countries are other factor that studies of international migration have found to be associated with migrants' choice of destination. Colonization promotes migration because the population in the colony identifies the colonizing country with some economic conditions that they cannot attain at home. In addition, easier transportation, a shared language, some common cultural traits, and special legal conditions facilitate migration between the two countries (Cohen, 1987; Petras, 1981; Portes, 1978).

In the case of internal migration, it is not political but administrative and commercial ties that might promote migration to some parts of the country. In many developing countries, governmental and commercial activity concentrates in two or three of the largest cities in the country. These cities serve as the administrative centers for the population in the surrounding states, and in many cases they also have a strong influence upon the local mass media (Hardoy, 1983; Portes, Itzingsohn, and Dore-Cabral, 1997). In addition, because of better roads and more options for public transportation, communication with these cities is usually easier than communication with other parts of the country, despite the distance.[2] In consequence, individuals are more likely to identify the city that serves as the administrative center of the region they live in as a place with better opportunities than to identify other places in the country.

Trade and foreign investment are also associated with international migration (Cohen, 1987; Petras, 1981; Portes, 1978; Massey et al., 1998). On the one hand, publicity and the media help to promote lifestyles that are not easily achievable in the communities of origin (Sassen, 1988). On the other, imported merchandise promotes the idea that the place of origin of the goods is a developed and modern place. In addition, individuals working in export processing plants identify the place where their products are destined to as more modern and rich destinations where they can fulfill their new consumer expectations (Fernández-Kelly, 1983). When choosing to migrate in search of better economic opportunities, individuals move to the countries they are already familiar with.

A similar mechanism can operate in internal migration. The history of internal markets and transportation contributes to the generation of independent economic regions of states that trade among themselves and have less contact with other regions in the country (Coatsworth, 1979). When deciding to migrate, people might be more likely to know the conditions in those states that have trade with their state of origin than with those states that do not. Also, they might be more likely to identify these states with better living conditions and more resources than the states they are disconnected from.

Some studies have explored the effect of past migration on the choice of internal migrants' destinations (see for example Davis, Stecklov and Winters, 2002; Zhu, 1998). However, no study has yet explored systematically whether transportation, trade, and past ties between origin and destination contribute to explain internal migration. This study fills that gap in the literature.

INTERNAL MIGRATION IN MEXICO

Mexico is an interesting case study because in many senses the experience of internal migration in Mexico is typical of the experience in many developing countries. Mexico has a high rate of interstate migration, but this rate has decreased slightly with time. According to the population censuses[3], 6.5 percent of the country's population had changed their place of residence between 1975 and 1980,[4] 5.2 percent of the population in 1990 had changed their state of residence in the past five years, and 4.6 percent of the population in 2000 had changed their state of residence in the past five years.

As in many other developing countries, the three largest cities in the country, Mexico City, Guadalajara, and Monterrey, were among the most frequent destinations of migration during the 1960s and 1970s. However, after 1980, migration to these cities diminished, and migrants started moving to other destinations, including medium-populated and border states such as Veracruz, Baja California Norte, and Tamaulipas. The result of these changes in migration is most notable in the percentage of migrants that the Federal District was receiving in 1970. Along with this increase in the destinations of migration after 1980 came a diversification in the destinations. Most migrants in Mexico concentrate in a few destinations, and individuals who migrated between 1975 and 1980 were concentrated in fewer places than individuals who migrated between 1985 and 1990, and between 1995 and 2000. Mexico is divided in thirty-two states. If migrants from all the states in the country distributed randomly across destinations, each state would receive approximately 3 percent of all the migrants in the country. Only eight states in the country received more than 3 percent of the migrants from 1975 to1980. The five states that received most migrants, in order of importance, were: the state of Mexico and the Federal District, where Mexico City is; Jalisco, which houses Guadalajara; Veracruz; and Nuevo León, which houses Monterrey. In 1985 to 1990, the number of states receiving more than 3 percent of interstate migrants in the country had increased to nine, and Nuevo León had stopped being one of the top five destinations. In 1995 to 2000, migrants' destinations had diversified so much that ten states received more than 3 percent of interstate migrants, and Jalisco was not among the top five destinations.

Not all states in the country send migrants to the same destinations. However, migrants from all states diversified their destinations after 1980. Figures 4.1 to 4.3 exemplify this point by showing the distribution of migrants from Hidalgo[5] (which had the tenth largest rate of out-migration in 1975–1980) in the periods 1975–1980, 1985–1990, and 1995–2000.

Individuals who migrated from Hidalgo between 1975 and 1980 moved mostly to four states in the country, and the state of Mexico and the Federal District received each more than 20 percent of these migrants. Veracruz and Puebla also received more migrants that would have been expected if migrants from Hidalgo distributed randomly across destinations, as each of these two states received between 3 percent and 10 percent of migrants from Hidalgo. Migration to the remaining twenty-seven states was very small, and no other state received more than 3 percent of the migrants from this origin.

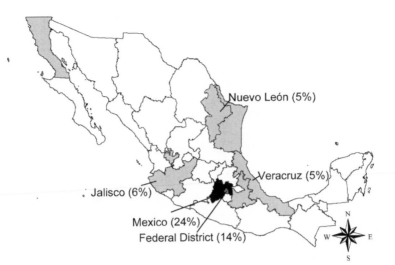

Nuevo León (5%)

Veracruz (5%)

Jalisco (6%)

Mexico (24%)

Federal District (14%)

Percentage of migrants received

- 0-3%
- 3-10%
- 10-20%
- 20% and more

Figure 4.1.

Querétaro
Hidalgo
Puebla
Veracruz

Mexico

Federal District

Percentage of migrants received

- 0-3%
- 3-10%
- 10-20%
- Sending state

Figure 4.2.

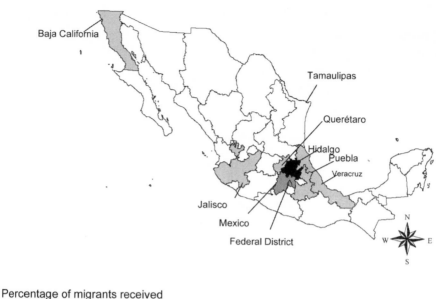

Percentage of migrants received

☐ 0-3%
▨ 3-10%
▨ 10-20%
■ Sending state

Figure 4.3.

However, beginning in 1985, migrants from Hidalgo started moving to other destinations. In 1985–1990, Queretaro received between 3 percent and 10 percent of the migrants from Hidalgo, and in 1995–2000 Tamaulipas, Jalisco, and Baja California also received more than 3 percent of the migrants from Hidalgo.

Mexico is also similar to other developing countries in its urbanization and industrialization pattern. Until the mid-1980s, economic development in Mexico was based on a program of import substitution. This model favored industries that were placed in or near the largest cities of the country, so they could take advantage of economies of scale and abundant labor supply. Consequently, during this period Mexico City, Guadalajara, and Monterrey were not only the largest cities in the country, but also the places where industrialization and economic growth concentrated (Haber, 1989; Escobar, Bean and Weintraub, 1999; Hanson, 1997). During this phase, internal markets in Mexico were structured in clear-cut economic regions that resembled the economic regions during the nineteenth and early twentieth centuries (Unikel, 1975; Moreno Toscano, 1972, 1998; Tamayo-

Flores, 2001). Each region was organized around a city that served as the commercial and administrative center, and most of the states in the region were connected to this city via a modern road or railroad. Also, with the exception of the state containing these core cities, transportation between states of the same region was easier than transportation to other states in the country (Coatsworth, 1979). Consequently, there was an intense exchange of merchandise among states belonging to the same region, but trade with states in other regions occurred mainly through their commercial centers (Bassols Batalla, 1979).

Beginning in the mid-1980s Mexico progressively opened its economy to foreign investment and changed its industrialization policy from import substitution to export production. Contrary to the period of import substitution, the new model of industrialization favored places with low tariffs, low wages, and accessibility to international transportation. As a result, new manufacturing centers, export processing zones, and agro-industries were located mostly in small and medium cities that were not industrial centers before (Escobar, Bean and Weintraub, 1999; Garza, 2000).

In addition, the focus on export processing and the decentralization of industrial production led to a growing trade between states over time. After 1985, trade between states in different regions has increased. This occurred because of the emergence of new productive zones, and because industries fragmented their production in different locations (Hanson, 1997; Herrigel and Zeitlin 2010; van Dooren, 2006). For example, Parnreiter (2002) shows that after 1985, many big companies moved their production facilities from Mexico City to other states in the center or north of the country. Also, the number of companies that have productive plants in several states of the country increased.

The changes in the industrialization policy of Mexico led to many transformations that can have influenced migration patterns. In the late 1980s and early 1990s, a greater number of states experienced economic growth, and wage and unemployment differentials between states may have diminished according to some estimates (Hanson, 1997). The neoclassical economy theory of migration predicts that this alone could have led to a decrease in the intensity of migration and to a diversification in migrants' destinations. Similarly, increased trade between states and the diminishing importance of traditional economic regions might have had an important role in the decreased concentration of migrants' in a few destinations. In the following section I present some hypotheses about the relative importance of each of these factors on the changes in the directionality of migration after 1980.

HYPOTHESES

Historical administrative, commercial and infrastructure ties between states, past migratory trends, and recent trade patterns might help to better explain why migrants move to the states they do, and why their destinations of migration changed after 1980.

The following hypotheses derive from the review of the literature on the directionality of internal and international migration, and from the economic changes Mexico experienced during the last three decades.

Hypothesis 1: Neoclassical hypothesis. The probability that migrants choose one state as its destination is positively correlated with the wages, negatively correlated with the unemployment rate in that state, and negatively correlated with the distance that separates both states. This hypothesis derives directly from the neoclassical theory of internal migration.

Hypothesis 2: Importance of past migration. The probability that migrants choose one state as its destination is positively correlated with the number of individuals from the place of origin that already live in the said destination. This hypothesis derives from the theory of cumulative causation and from past evidence that the destination of new internal migrants in Mexico is associated to the destination of past migrants (Davis, Stecklov and Winters, 2002).

Hypothesis 3: Importance of historical, administrative, infrastructure and trade ties. The probability that migrants choose a state as its destination is positively correlated with historical administrative, trade, and infrastructure ties between the place of origin and destination and with recent trade ties between both places. This hypothesis derives from the literature on international migration that shows that migration between countries is correlated with trade and political exchanges (Cohen 1987, Portes 1978, Fernandez-Kelly 1983), and from the historical economic literature in Mexico that shows that trade between states is determined by its economic regions (Moreno-Toscano 1998, Bassols Batalla 1979).

Data and Variables

This paper uses data from Mexican Population Censuses,[6] from studies of origin–destination of cargo traffic (Secretaría de Comunicaciones y Transportes, 2002), from Mexican road atlases, from Mexican archived historical maps (Ortíz Hernán, 1994; Florescano et al., 1983; Coatsworth,

Table 4.1. Variables and Data Sources, by Period of Analysis

	Period of Analysis and Data Source		
Variable	*1975–1980*	*1985–1980*	*1995–2000*
State-to-state migration rates	1980 Census	1990 Census	2000 Census
Unemployment rate	1970 Census	1980 Census	1990 Census
Unpaid family workers	1970 Census	1980 Census	1990 Census
Labor force earning more than 2 minimum wages	1970 Census	1980 Census	1990 Census
Distance	Road Atlas 1975	Road Atlas 1985	Road Atlas 1995
Historical, infrastructure and administrative ties	Archived historical maps and historical and political economy literature	Archived historical maps and historical and political economy literature	Archived historical maps and historical and political economy literature
Recent trade	Surveys of Origin-Destination 1965 to 1968	Surveys of Origin-Destination 1965 to 1985	Surveys of Origin-Destination 1965 to 1994
Past migrants from *i* to *j*	1970 Census	1980 Census	1990 Census
Past migrants from *j* to *i*	1970 Census	1980 Census	1990 Census
Population size	1970 Census	1980 Census	1990 Census

1984), and from a review of the historical and political economy literature in Mexico (Coello-Salazar, 1965; Duhau, 1988). Table 4.1 shows the variables obtained from each of these sources. I explain next how these indicators where calculated.

MEASURING MIGRATION FLOWS BETWEEN STATES

In this analysis I measure state-to-state migration rates in three different periods. For each time period, I calculate the proportion of those 20 and older who migrated from one state to another (state i to state j), based on the census question about where a person lived five years earlier.[7] I only consider the migration of individuals 20 and older because the model I present is a model of migration for economic reasons. The legal working age in Mexico is 16 years old, but many of those 16 to 19 years old who migrate within Mexico move to attend college. Restricting the population of study to individuals

20 and older selects those who migrated to work. The measure of migration collected by the census is the standard measure used in most censuses around the world. This measure might underestimate migration because it ignores temporal migrants (i.e., those who migrated during the five-year period but returned to their state of origin before the census date), and is thus a conservative estimate. Another caveat of estimates of interstate migration based on population censuses is that they do not consider international migrants (see Rivero-Fuentes, 2005). Still, given that migration is a rare event in some states, population censuses are the best alternative for obtaining estimates of migration rates that are comparable across states. Figure 4.4 presents state-to-state migration rates (per 1,000 inhabitants) in the periods 1975–1980, 1985–1990, and 1995–2000.

Figure 4.4 shows that the intensity of migrant flows varies between states, and that the overall intensity of migration decreased between 1975 and 2000. In 1975–1980, the state-to-state migration rate was greater than 1 per thousand in 50 percent of the cases, there was a greater percentage of states that experienced a migration rate of 5.0 per thousand or more than in 1985–1990 and 1995–2000, and the average migrant flow between any two states was 3.2 per thousand (not shown). In 1985–1990 and 1995–2000 around 70 percent of the state-to-state migration rates were below 1 per thousand, and only 30 percent of the state-to-state pairs had a migration flow greater than 1 per thousand. As a consequence, the average migrant flow between any two states was 1.4 and 1.2 per thousand, respectively (not shown).

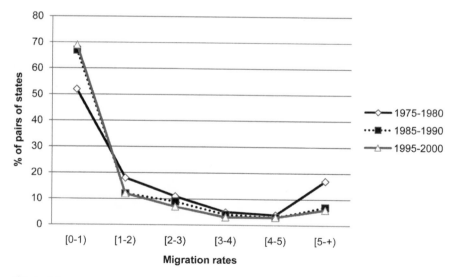

Figure 4.4.

MEASURING THE FACTORS THAT AFFECT
MIGRATION FLOWS BETWEEN STATES

In order to test the predictive power of the neoclassical hypothesis of migration, I calculate the unemployment rate in each state, the proportion of the labor force who are unpaid family workers, the proportion of the labor force earning more than twice the minimum wage at the beginning of the decade preceding the observed migration rate, and the distance between capital cities of any two states.

I calculate the unemployment rate in each state based on the census questions on economic activity (see Table 4.1, above). To measure unemployment, I take the number of people actively looking for a job during the week previous to the census and divide it by the number of people in the labor force. The estimate of the labor force includes the unemployed and all those working in the formal and informal sectors, including self-employed and non-paid family workers. This is the standard measure of open unemployment.

The open unemployment rate underestimates unemployment, especially in places where underemployment and unpaid family work is high (Martin, 2001). This underestimation is the result of those who are considered employed but work part-time or work without pay but are also looking for a job. To control for this underestimation, I use the population census to calculate the proportion of the labor force in each state who are nonpaid family workers.

The third variable used to test the neoclassical hypothesis of migration is the proportion of the labor force in each state who earn more than twice the minimum wage at the beginning of the decade preceding the observed migration rate. This variable intends to measure the earnings level in each state. It is taken from population censuses and includes all earnings from wages, self-employment, sales, rents, and other income-earning activities. I use the proportion of the labor force earning more than twice the minimum wage rather than the average earnings of the labor force because this last information is not available for 1970 and 1980. Data from old population censuses are available only in printed tabulations, and these group earnings in categories.

The neoclassical hypothesis of migration argues that individuals make their migration decisions based on how much better are the employment conditions in the receiving state (j) than in the sending state (i). To capture this effect, unemployment, family workers, and wages enter my statistical models as parity indexes. The unemployment parity index is the ratio of the unemployment rate in the receiving state to the unemployment rate in the sending state. When unemployment in the receiving state is equal to unemployment in the sending state, the unemployment parity index is 1;

when unemployment in the receiving state is larger to unemployment in the sending state, the unemployment parity index is greater than 1; and when unemployment in the receiving state is lower than unemployment in the sending state, the unemployment parity index is less than 1. Similarly, the unpaid family workers parity index is the ratio of the receiving state's to the sending state's proportion of the labor force who are unpaid family workers and the wage parity index is the ratio of the receiving state's to the sending state's proportion of the labor force earning more than twice the minimum wage.

Distance between states is measured through the distance between their capital cities. Using road atlases published in 1975, 1985, and 1995, I calculate the shortest distance in miles through a modern, paved road between the capital cities of each state.

To measure the effect of prior migration networks upon current migrant flows between two states, I use information in the census about place of birth. I calculate a lifetime measure of migration between two states by counting the number of people born in the sending state who now live in the receiving state. This number is then divided by the number of people living in the sending state to create the ratio of past migrants to non-migrants at the beginning of the decade preceding any observed migration rate.

The effect of the ratio of past migrants to nonmigrants on the probability of new migration may not be linear. When migration from the sending state to the receiving state is not very common, any past migrant has a large, positive effect on the probability of others' migrating because he or she offers new information and resources about the receiving state that were not available in the sending state. When migration is more common, the experience of an additional migrant is less important. The population in the sending state is already informed about the conditions in the receiving state, and it is likely that they know some other past migrant who can help them move. To capture this nonlinearity, I also include in the statistical models the squared-term of the ratio of natives from the sending state living in the receiving state to the population in the sending state at the beginning of the decade preceding any observed migration rate.

The effect of past migrants can run both ways. People from the receiving state living in the sending state can also have an effect on migration because they help to diffuse information about their state of origin. I measure this effect by including in my models the number of people born in state the state of destination who lived in the state of origin divided by the total population of state the state of origin at the beginning of the decade preceding any observed migration rate. To capture nonlinearities, I also include the squared-term of this variable.

To measure historical administrative, trade, and infrastructure ties between two states, I observe whether or not the two states were connected by a main road or railroad anytime before 1910; or if they belonged to the same economic and productive region during the nineteenth and early twentieth centuries. I use Moreno Toscano's definition of economic and productive regions during the nineteenth century (Moreno-Toscano, 1998) and Duhau and Coello-Salazar's definition of economic and productive regions during the early twentieth century (Coello-Salazar, 1965; Duhau, 1988). This indicator takes the value of 1 if any two states were connected by a main road or railroad or if they belonged to the same economic and productive region, and the value of 0 otherwise.

To measure recent trade between two states, I observe the cargo traffic between them. I use the Studies of Origin–Destination of Cargo Traffic of the Mexican Ministry of Transport (Secretaría de Comunicaciones y Transportes, 2002) to count the number of cargo vehicles that went from the state of origin to the state of destination and *vice versa* from 1962 (the date when the studies began) until the year prior to the observed migration rate. I then divide this number by the total number of cargo vehicles that started or ended their trip in the state of origin. Based on this information, I construct a categorical indicator that takes the value 1 if the number of cargo vehicles that traveled between two states represents more than 4 percent of all the cargo vehicles that departed or arrived to the state of origin. If the state of origin traded equally with all the other states in the country, one could expect the same number of cargo vehicles to travel between the state of origin and any other state. In that case, each state would be involved in 3.2 percent of all the cargo flows originating in (or going to) that state. States that are involved in 4 percent or more of the cargo traffic exchanges of the state of origin have stronger trade with this state than the average state in the country.

Finally, population size in each of destination is included as a control in the models because more populated states are more likely to have large cities that attract immigration. In addition, information about more populated states might be more readily available than information about less populated states because they are more likely to dominate the national mass media. Table 4.2 shows the mean and standard errors of these covariates.

In Table 4.2 one can see that the unemployment rate has remained constant, on average, in the period of study, but the percentage of the labor force that is self-employed has increased more than 50 percent—from 47 percent to 77 percent. Nevertheless, these numbers show important variation across states, and this variation was greater in 1975 than in 1985 and 1995.

Table 4.2.   **Mean and Standard Deviation (in Parenthesis) of Covariates**

	Period of Observation		
	1975–1980	*1985–1990*	*1995–2000*
Unemployment rate	3.23	3.23	3.23
	(6.38)	(6.07)	(6.16)
% of labor force earning more than twice the minimum wage	3.91	3.06	2.70
	(1.24)	(0.66)	(0.65)
% of labor force self-employed	47.27	53.10	77.48
	(18.77)	(14.97)	(9.75)
% of labor force who is a family worker	19.49	22.93	23.44
	(6.58)	(9.83)	(7.86)
GDP growth rate	7.22	5.23	3.93
	(2.45)	(1.39)	(1.18)
Distance between *i* and *j* in kms	1366.12	1365.89	1278.82
	(1096.41)	(1096.60)	(1039.98)
% population born in *i* living in *j*	0.14	0.14	0.14
	(0.34)	(0.34)	(0.34)
Historical tie between *i* and *j*	0.54	0.54	0.52
	(1.41)	(1.41)	(1.34)
Recent trade between *i* and *j*	0.15	0.26	0.26
	(0.36)	(0.44)	(0.44)
Population size (millions)	0.94	1.58	1.67
	(0.93)	(1.41)	(1.51)
Number of states	32	32	32

Physical and commercial distance between states shortened during the periods of observation. Highway distance between capital cities decreased after 1985 because of the construction of new highways during the late 1980s and early 1990s. At the same time, trade between states has increased. In 1975, any state had, on average, a trade tie with 15 percent of the other states in the country, while on 1995 it had a trade tie with 26 percent of the states in the country.

The presence of migrants, both in the state of origin and in the state of destination changed slightly between these periods. On average, 0.14 percent of the individuals born in one state where living in any given state in the three periods of analyses, but these numbers hide important differences between states and between periods. In 1975–1980, the percentage of migrants from any state living in another state was 6 percent or more in only 15 percent of the cases. In 1995–2000, the percentage of migrants from any state living in another state was 6 percent in 20 percent of the pairs of states *i–j*.

Methods for measuring the effect of the explanatory variables on the distribution of migrants across destinations

I use conditional logit models to evaluate hypotheses 1 to 3. Similar to multinomial models, conditional logit models are used to model discrete choice behavior when individuals can decide between more than two options. Still, conditional logit models differ from multinomial models because the choice is modeled as a function of the characteristics of the options available and not as a function of the characteristics of the individuals deciding.[8] In this case, the probability that migrants go from state i to state j (M_{ij}) is, conditional on the origin, a function of the characteristics of the state of destination (such as population size), of the relationship between state of origin and state of destination (e.g., distance), and of how the conditions in the state of destination compare to the conditions in the state of origin (e.g., unemployment parity index). Conditional logit models have been used to model social behaviors that imply a choice between destinations, such as the choice of destination in U.S. interstate migration (Davies, Greenwood and Li, 2001), tourists' destination choices (Eymann and Ronning, 1997), and the locational choice of foreign direct investors (Coughlin, Terza and Arromdee, 1991).

The conditional models in this paper focus solely on the distribution of migrants across destinations. The models presented below can be understood in terms of either a nested or a hierarchical model of migration wherein individuals decide whether to migrate or not based on the characteristics of their state of origin and the conditions in all other states in the country. Once they have decided to migrate, individuals decide where to move based on the characteristics of all their potential destinations. Rivero-Fuentes (2005) showed that when explaining both the probability of out-migration and the distribution of migrants across destinations, nested logit models and hierarchical logit models of migration that modeled the probability of out-migrating and the distribution of migrants across destinations in two different equations yielded better results than conditional logit models that modeled the probability of out-migration and the distribution of migrants in the same equation. Furthermore, Rivero-Fuentes (2005) also showed that the equation for modeling the distribution of migrants across destinations was the same in nested logit models and in hierarchical logit models.

I fit four different models for each of the three periods of observation. The first model, represented by equation 1, in figure 4.5, is meant to test the neoclassical hypothesis of migration (hypothesis 1).

The neoclassical hypothesis of migration predicts that the probability that migrants from state i go to state j (Mij) is positively correlated with the wage parity index of the two states (W_{ij}) and negatively correlated with the

$$M_{ij} = \frac{\exp(P_j * \beta_1 + FW_{ij} * \beta_2 + U_{ij} * \beta_3 + W_{ij} * \beta_4 + D_{ij} *}{\sum_{\substack{k=1 \\ k \neq i}}^{J} \exp(P_k * \beta_1 + FW_{ik} * \beta_2 + U_{ik} * \beta_3 + W_{ik} * \beta_4 +}$$

$$\frac{* \beta_5)}{D_{ik} * \beta_5)}$$

Figure 4.5.

unemployment parity index (U_{ij}) and with the distance between i and j (D_{ij}). To control for the fact that an underestimation of unemployment due to unpaid work, I include in this model the unpaid family workers parity index (FW_{ij}). To account for the attraction of large cities, I also control for state j's population size (P_j) in all the models. In accordance with hypothesis 1, expect to find that $\beta_3<0$, $\beta_4>0$, and $\beta_5>0$.

The second model (Equation 2, represented in figure 4.6) tests the importance of past migration between states i and j (hypothesis 2).

$$M_{ij} = \frac{\exp\left(P_j * \beta_1 + PM_{ij} * \beta_6 + PM_{ij} * \beta_7 + B_{ij} * \beta_8^2 +}{\sum_{\substack{k=1 \\ k \neq j}}^{J} \exp\left(P_j * \beta_1 + PM_{ik} * \beta_6 + PM_{ik} * \beta_7 + B_{ik} * \beta_8^2}$$

$$\frac{B_{ij} * \beta_9^2)}{+ B_{ik} * \beta_9)}$$

Figure 4.6.

The theory of cumulative causation predicts that the probability that migrants from i go to j is positively associated with the ratio of the natives from i living in j to the population living in i (PM_{ij}). Hence, I expect to find that $\beta_6>0$. Because the natives from j living in i can also help people migrate from i to j, I include in this model the proportion of the population living in i who was born in j (B_{ij}). I expect to find that the effect of this variable on the probability that migrants from i go to j is positive ($\beta_8>0$). The effect of past migration may diminish as migration becomes more common. Hence, I expect to find that $\beta_7<0$ and $\beta_9<0$.

The third model (Equation 3, depicted in figure 4.7) attempts to prove that the probability that migrants from i go to j is positively associated with the presence of historical, infrastructure, and administrative ties between i and j (H_{ij}) and with recent trade between i and j (T_{ij}).

$$M_{ij} = \frac{\exp(P_j * \beta_1 + H_{ij} * \beta_{10} + T_{ij} * \beta_{11})}{\displaystyle\sum_{\substack{k=1 \\ k \neq i}}^{J} \exp(P_k * \beta_1 + H_{ik} * \beta_{10} + T_{ik} * \beta_{11})}$$

Figure 4.7.

According to hypothesis 3, I expect to find that $\beta_{10} > 0$ and $\beta_{11} > 0$.

Finally, the fourth model (equation 4, in figure 4.8) controls for the correlation between all the explanatory variables. I expect to find that hypotheses 1, 2, and 3 hold even after controlling for the association between explanatory variables.

$$M_{ij} = \frac{\exp\big(P_j * \beta_1 + FW_{ij} * \beta_2 + U_{ij} * \beta_3 + W_{ij} * \beta_4 + D_{ij} *}{\sum_{\substack{k=1 \\ k \neq i}}^{J} \exp\big(P_k * \beta_1 + FW_{ik} * \beta_2 + U_{ik} * \beta_3 + W_{ik} * \beta_4 + D_{ik}}$$

$$\frac{\beta_5 + PM_{ij} * \beta_6 + PM_{ij}^2 * \beta_7 + B_{ij} * \beta_8 + B_{ij}^2 * \beta_9 + H_{ij}}{* \beta_5 + PM_{ik} * \beta_6 + PM_{ik}^2 * \beta_7 + B_{ik} * \beta_8 + B_{ik}^2 * \beta_9 +}$$

$$\frac{* \beta_{10} + T_{ij} * \beta_{11}\big)}{H_{ik} * \beta_{10} + T_{ik} * \beta_{11}\big)}$$

Figure 4.8.

In the conditional logit models above, the effect of the explanatory variables on the probability that migrants from i go to j is nonlinear and difficult to interpret because the β coefficient appears both in the nominator and in the denominator. The β coefficients, however, can be easily interpreted in terms of the odds that migrants from state i go to state j instead of to state g (M_{ij}/M_{ig}). Take equation 1 as an example. If two states j and g do not differ on anything but on their unemployment rates and U_{ij} is one unit larger than U_{ig}, the odds that migrants from state i go to state j instead of to state g are given by $exp(\beta_3)$. This is the interpretation I favor in the discussion of results that follows.

Discussion of Results

Table 4.3 presents the estimates of exp(β) for the four models fitted in the three periods of observation.

All the coefficients in Table 4.3 are significant with a $p<0.001$, and support the three hypotheses of this paper. However, the explanatory power of these hypotheses is not the same in the three periods of observation.

Table 4.3. Conditional Logit Model Estimates Predicting Migrants' Destination Choice.*

Variable	Period	Parameter	Model 1	Model 2	Model 3	Model 4
Population Size (millions)	1975–1980	$exp(\beta_1)$	1.214	1.078	1.186	0.993
Unpaid Family Workers Parity Index	1975–1980	$exp(\beta_2)$	0.706			0.937
Unemployment Parity Index	1975–1980	$exp(\beta_3)$	0.730			0.751
Wage Parity Index	1975–1980	$exp(\beta_4)$	1.913			1.202
Distance (100 miles)	1975–1980	$exp(\beta_5)$	0.774			0.942
Past Migration from i to j	1975–1980	$exp(\beta_6)$		1.082		1.057
Squared Past Migration from i to j	1975–1980	$exp(\beta_7)$		0.999		0.999
Past Migration from j to i	1975–1980	$exp(\beta_8)$		1.022		1.005
Squared Past Migration from j to i	1975–1980	$exp(\beta_9)$		0.999		0.999
Historical, Infrastructure and Admin. Ties	1975–1980	$exp(\beta_{10})$			3.749	1.975
Recent Trade Ties	1975–1980	$exp(\beta_{11})$			3.354	1.800
% Deviance Explained	1975–1980		60.576	74.978	66.610	83.308
Population Size (millions)	1985–1990	$exp(\beta_1)$	1.107	0.967	1.156	0.888
Unpaid Family Workers Parity Index	1985–1990	$exp(\beta_2)$	1.856			1.968
Unemployment Parity Index	1985–1990	$exp(\beta_3)$	1.206			0.939
Wage Parity Index	1985–1990	$exp(\beta_4)$	8.691			2.216

Variable	Period	Parameter	Model 1	Model 2	Model 3	Model 4
Distance (100 miles)	1985-1990	$exp(\beta_5)$	0.820			0.982
Past Migration from i to j	1985–1990	$exp(\beta_6)$		1.066		1.042
Squared Past Migration from i to j	1985–1990	$exp(\beta_7)$		0.999		0.999
Past Migration from j to i	1985–1990	$exp(\beta_8)$		1.036		1.015
Squared Past Migration from j to i	1985–1990	$exp(\beta_9)$		0.999		0.999
Historical, Infrastructure and Admin. Ties	1985–1990	$exp(\beta_{10})$			2.885	1.782
Recent Trade Ties	1985–1990	$exp(\beta_{11})$			2.549	1.644
% Deviance Explained	1985–1990		54.857	80.784	56.288	85.047
Population Size (millions)	1995–2000	$exp(\beta_1)$	1.240	0.999	1.206	0.971
Unpaid Family Workers Parity Index	1995–2000	$exp(\beta_2)$	0.670			1.061
Unemployment Parity Index	1995–2000	$exp(\beta_3)$	0.455			0.743
Wage Parity Index	1995–2000	$exp(\beta_4)$	11.225			3.005
Distance (100 miles)	1995–2000	$exp(\beta_5)$	0.848			0.993
Past Migration from i to j	1995–2000	$exp(\beta_6)$		1.055		1.041
Squared Past Migration from i to j	1995–2000	$exp(\beta_7)$		0.999		0.999
Past Migration from j to i	1995–2000	$exp(\beta_8)$		1.032		1.023
Squared Past Migration from j to i	1995–2000	$exp(\beta_9)$		0.999		0.999
Historical, Infrastructure and Admin. Ties	1995–2000	$exp(\beta_{10})$			2.048	1.881
Recent Trade Ties	1995–2000	$exp(\beta_{11})$			2.203	1.232
% Deviance Explained	1995–2000		51.182	79.868	49.212	82.887

* All the coefficients are significant with a p<0.001

In the three periods of observation, the parameter $exp(\beta_1)$ is significantly larger than 1 in models 1 and 3, implying that even after controlling for the economic conditions in the state of origin and destination, distance, and historical, administrative, and trade ties, migrants were more likely to go to more populated states than to states with smaller population size. Nonetheless, in 1985–1990 and 1995–2000, the effect of population size changes signs when one introduces past migration patterns in the models (models 2 and 4). This result shows the change in the directionality of migration after 1985. When choosing between destinations that had the same presence of past migrants, movers started turning toward less populated states rather than toward more populated states.

As predicted by the neoclassical hypothesis of migration, migrants tended to go to states that are closer in distance and that have higher wages and lower unemployment than their state of origin. The coefficients of unemployment parity index, wage parity index, and distance have the predicted sign in model 1, and this association holds even after one controls for past migration patterns and historical, infrastructure, administrative, and trade ties (model 4).

The effect of wages on the directionality of migration $(exp(\beta_4))$ increased substantially after 1980. According to the results of model 4, in 1975–1980, migrants were 20 percent more likely to go to a state where the proportion of the labor force earning high wages was double the proportion of the labor force earning high wages in their state of origin than to a state where the proportion of the labor force earning high wages was equal to the proportion of the labor force earning high wages in their state of origin. In 1995–2000, migrants were thrice as likely to go to a state where the proportion of the labor force earning high wages was double the proportion of the labor force earning high wages in their state of origin than to a state where the proportion of the labor force earning high wages was equal to the proportion of the labor force earning high wages in their state of origin.

This increased effect of wages can be the result of the homogenization of wages between states, particularly after 1990. As states tended to exhibit fewer differences in wages, any small difference had a large impact on migrants' destination choice.

In the three periods of analysis, unemployment was a disincentive for migration to a state. In 1975–1980 and in 1995–2000, migrants were almost 25 percent less likely to migrate to a state whose unemployment rate was double the unemployment rate of their state of origin than to a state with the same unemployment rate than their state of origin $(exp(\beta_3)=0.75$ in model 4). In 1985–1990 this effect is lower, but still significantly lower than 1 $(exp(\beta_3)=0.94$ in model 4).

The negative effect of distance on the probability of migrants going to a particular destination is captured on the coefficient of road distance between capital cities $(exp(\beta_5))$. Comparing two destinations that do not differ on anything but on their distance from the origin, migrants in 1975–1980 were 6 percent more likely to go to the closest of these two destinations. In 1985–1980 and 1995–2000 the effect of distance was smaller, but still negative. In 1985–1990, migrants were 2 percent more likely to go to the closest destination, and in 1995–2000 migrants were 1 percent more likely to go to the closest destination.

The coefficients of the ratio of past migrants from the state of origin in the state of destination to the population living in the state of origin $(exp(\beta_6))$ and of the proportion of the population living in the state of origin who were born in the state of destination $(exp(\beta_8))$ demonstrate the significance of the hypothesis of cumulative causation for domestic migration in Mexico. In the three periods of observation, the odds that new migrants move to a particular destination rather than to any other state in the country increases with the number of people from their state of origin that have migrated there $(exp(\beta_6)>0$ in models 2 and 4). These odds also increase with the presence of natives from this destination who have migrated in the opposite direction $(exp(\beta_8)>0)$.

At the same time, the parameter estimates $exp(\beta_7)$ and $exp(\beta_9)$ show that the importance of these variables in the new destinations of migration is not linear, and that it diminishes as the number of people who have migrated to a given destination increases $(exp(\beta_7)<1$ and $exp(\beta_9)<1$ in the three periods of observation).

Model 3 is meant to show that the level of migration between two states is positively correlated with the presence of historical, administrative, and infrastructure ties and with recent trade between origin and destination. Controlling for population size, in 1975–1980 migrants were 2.7 times more likely $(1-exp(\beta_{10}))$ to move to a state that belonged to the same economic region or that was historically connected to its state of origin than to a state without these ties. Similarly, migrants were 2.4 times more likely $(1-exp(\beta_{11}))$ to move to a state that had strong trade with their state of origin than to a state with no trade connection with their state of origin.

Historical, administrative, and trade ties are correlated with distance and with past migration trends. Consequently, the effect of historical, administrative and trade ties on the destination of migration diminishes after one includes all the other explanatory variables in the model (model 4). However, even after these controls, $exp(\beta_{10})$ and $exp(\beta_{11})$ are significantly larger than 1. The effect of historical and administrative ties is larger than the effect of recent trade ties in the three periods of observation.

The positive and significant effects of past migration, recent trade, and historical, administrative, and infrastructure linkages of model 4 demonstrate that migrants are more likely to go to states they have more information about. On the other hand, the coefficients of unemployment parity index, wage parity index, and distance show that when choosing between states they have comparable information about, migrants are more likely to go to destinations that have lower unemployment rates and higher wages and that are closer in distance.

These results show that the destinations of interstate migration in Mexico are explained by a combination of the neoclassical hypothesis of migration, of cumulative causation and past migration trends, and of the importance of historical, administrative, infrastructure, and trade ties between states. Indeed, the percentage of deviance explained by models 1, 2, and 3 indicates that none of these hypotheses alone can completely explain migrants' destinations in Mexico. The percentage of deviance explained by model 4, which includes all the explanatory variables together, is always larger than the percentage of deviance explained by any of the other three models.

If one looks at the models that test each of these hypothesis independently (models 1, 2, and 3), the model for the cumulative causation and past migration patterns (model 2) has the largest explanatory power in the three periods of observation. But the explanatory power of this hypothesis increased notably after 1975–1980, the period of largest interstate migration in Mexico. The variables that capture the effect of past migrants and population size explain 75 percent of the variation in migrants' destinations in 1975–1980, and 80 percent of the variation in migrants' destinations both in 1985–1990 and 1995–2000.

On the contrary, the explanatory power of the models for the neoclassical hypothesis and for historical, infrastructure, administrative, and trade ties (models 1 and 3, respectively) decreased over time. The explanatory power of historical, infrastructure, and administrative ties decreased more than the explanatory power of the neoclassical hypothesis. Controlling for population size, the four variables of the neoclassical hypothesis explained 61 percent of the variation in migrants' destinations in 1975–1980, 55 percent in 1985–1990, and 51 percent in 1995–2000. The two variables of historical, infrastructure, and administrative ties, and recent trade ties explained 67 percent of the variation in migrants' destinations in 1975–1980, 56 percent in 1985–1990, and 49 percent in 1995–2000.

These changes indicate that states' economic conditions and historical, infrastructure, administrative, and trade ties between states were determinant in establishing the destinations of interstate migration during 1975–1990, when the largest flows of migration were just starting. As interstate migration increased and the number of past migrants grew, migrants' destinations became more determined by past migration patterns than by historical and trade links between states or than by the economic conditions in the state of destination.

CONCLUSION

This paper contributes to the literature on internal migration in developing countries by showing that migrants' destinations are affected by some factors that have been proved important in explaining the directionality of international migration, but that had been disregarded in past studies of internal migration. I show that in the case of interstate migration in Mexico, migrants' destinations cannot be predicted solely, as the neoclassical model of migration states, by distance and wage and unemployment differentials. Migrants in Mexico are more likely to go to states they have more information about. Past migrants, trade between states, and historical, infrastructure, and administrative ties between states help to diffuse information about different destinations, and thus are positively correlated with the probability that migrants move to a certain state.

There have been important changes in interstate migration in Mexico after 1985. The overall level of interstate migration decreased after 1985, and the destinations of migration diversified. Before 1980, migrants concentrated in a number of states. In more recent periods, migrants are less concentrated in a few states and have started migrating to new states. Historical, infrastructure, and administrative ties were of particular importance in determining migrants' destinations before 1985. However, after 1985, migrants' destinations are more determined by wage and unemployment differentials (or the lack thereof) between states and by past migrants' destinations than by historical, infrastructure, and administrative ties between states.

The allocation of migrants across destinations has important consequences for the distribution of the population in a country. It is important to understand what drives individuals to concentrate in some states and not in others, and how changes in the economic policy of a country affect migrants' destinations.

Studies from an urbanization perspective have noted that in some instances the shift from import-substitution to export-oriented development leads to a redistribution of the population away from the largest cities in the country. This happens when the new manufacturing centers are located away from the largest cities and have the capability to generate abundant employment because migrants start moving to new, farther-removed destinations. However, when the new industrial centers are close to the largest cities the result is a more acute concentration of the population. New industrial centers merge with the old metropolitan centers, resulting in a megalopolization (Portes, Itzingsohn and Dore-Cabral, 1997).

The changes in migrants' destinations in Mexico coincide with the process of economic liberalization that Mexico went through after 1985. The establishment of new agro-industries and manufacturing zones across the country lead to lower wage and employment differentials between states (Hanson, 1997). In consequence, the incentives for migrating to the traditional industrial centers (like Mexico City or Jalisco) diminished, while the incentives for migrating to new development poles (like the central states or to the Gulf of Mexico) increased. The diversification in trade between states seems to be one of the factors that allows potential migrants to realize the changes in the structure of job opportunities in different regions of the country.

The results of this research bring a new dimension to the conclusions of Portes and colleagues. They suggest that the long-term impact on the distribution of the population of a change from import-substitution to export-oriented development does not depend solely on the location of the new manufacturing centers, but also on the way trade between states is reorganized, and on the changes in regional wage and unemployment inequalities.

A similar explanation might be behind the changes in migrants' destinations in other countries, like China (Liang and White, 1997; Poston and Mao, 1998), that have experienced a transformation in their economic policy recently. All the studies that try to explain the directionality of internal migration in China rely exclusively on economic variables such as wages, unemployment and investment in the state of destination. If the results presented in this paper apply to other contexts, future concentrations of migration might be better predicted by also taking into account the structure of historical, administrative, infrastructure, and trade ties between states, as well as past migration patterns.

One of the arguments raised in this paper is that past migration, infrastructure, administrative ties, and trade between states contribute to the explanation of migrants' destinations because these factors are related to migrants' awareness about different potential destinations. There may be other variables that are also associated to the knowledge that potential migrants have about the different states in a country, but more research is needed to identify them.

NOTES

1. One exception, for the case of Mexico, is the work of Partida Bush (2006), who attempts to explain intermunicipal flows in Mexico testing for hypothesis derived from different theories that were initially developed to understand international migration.

2. In the case of Mexico, for example, there are few direct bus routes between medium-sized cities.

3. In this study I use the estimates of internal migration of the 1980 population census revised by Virgilio Partida, who kindly shared his work with me.

4. This percentage refers to individuals that in 1980 lived in a state different to the state they lived in 1975. The calculation excludes migrants to the United States and those that in 1975 were alive, but died before 1980.

5. This state was chosen as an example because it is one of the states that send most of their migrants to Mexico City and because it has a medium rate of out-migration. However, the diversification in migrants' destinations shown here for Hidalgo is also observed in all the other states in Mexico.

6. I am thankful to Virgilio Partida for facilitating his estimates of internal migration for the period of 1975–1980 based on the 1980 population census.

7. The question in 1980 was about the last state of residence and the year of the migration. In this case, I take the migration during the last five years, and assume that those who migrated moved only once during the period 1975–1980. This assumption has been commonly used in the literature of internal migration in Mexico (see Partida (2006) and Chávez (1999), among others), and is supported by the results of surveys like ENADID, MMP, and EDER, which show that those individuals who migrate within Mexico move an average of only 1.2 times in their lifetime.

8. For more information on conditional logit models, see Hunt (2000) and McFadden (1978).

Chapter 5

Internal Migration and Human Development

The Case of Mexico

Gabriel Lara-Ibarra and Isidro Soloaga

Several studies have documented how internal migration is related to demographic and economic characteristics such as education, wage levels, and family structure. We here extend this literature by estimating the likely impact of migration flows on the computation of the Human Development Index (HDI), which is calculated by the United Nations Development Programme and is used as a summary measure for a region's health, education, and income levels. Furthermore, the HDI is used to compare and contrast the standard of living across populations at different levels of disaggregation. Therefore, it is of interest to estimate how domestic migration affects this well-being indicator: Does the indicator improve because of domestic migration? Is the impact symmetric in origin and destination areas? Is the overall impact beneficial? Moreover, this paper provides evidence to assess whether a given change in the HDI is due to public policy or to migration.

To estimate these impacts for the case of Mexico, we use information from the 2000 population census, and estimate a counterfactual state-level HDI had no internal migration occurred. We find that the overall impact on the HDI is small in magnitude. However, the small overall effect is the result of opposing effects of migration on the components of the index.

MIGRATION AND HDI

The Human Development Index (HDI) has three components: education, health, and income. The education component uses adult literacy rates and school attendance rates. The health component is based on the life expectancy at birth. The income component uses GDP per capita (UNDP [2004]). In light of the importance and magnitude of migration flows in Mexico, we could expect that an index based on these components will be affected by the population composition. The aim of this study is to estimate at the state level the importance of internal migration flows on the HDI components. Specifically, we compare the estimate of the states' HDI with a counterfactual HDI had no internal migration occurred.

The basis of our analysis is the fact that migration impacts (whether positively or negatively) the indicators used to calculate the HDI both in the destination and origin regions. Regarding the education component, when a person emigrates, whether she attends school or knows how to read and write affects—ceteris paribus—the school attendance rates and the literacy rates of the destination and origin regions. This is because her migration modifies the percentages upon which the education index is calculated. Regarding the income index, we could argue that when an emigrant's salary leaving State i to live in State j is higher than the average salary in State i, this implies— ceteris paribus—a drop in the HDI of State i. In the same way, there will be an impact on the destination region j depending on the part of the salary distribution where the immigrant is placed. Recalculating the health index is not possible because, as is not the case with education and income, which are personal attributes, life expectancy is an attribute of a given population and thus cannot be considered a personal trait of a particular migrant. The IDH re-estimation presented here is based only on changes arising from the education and income components.

An implication of the process described above is that the identification of the factors of HDI changes in time is complex. Assume, for example, that the HDI in State j in 1995 is higher than in State i due to a better level of demographic and economic variables. These factors may constitute a *pull factor* for migrants leaving State i. For a large enough number of emigrants—especially emigrants from State i to State j with lower levels of education and income per capita than the average person in i and j—the HDI in j will be lower in the year 2000. Thus, migration could constitute a confusing factor in the estimation of the impact of demographic and economic variables on changes in the HDI. The destination state could yield a decrease in the State's HDI even if some demographic and economic indicators have improved. This impact is of the same nature as the "Todaro effect" in which, despite aggressive policies to contain the unemployment rate, this does not decrease due to the continuous inflows of migrants who are attracted precisely by the policies implemented.[1]

Table 5.1. Migrant Population, as % of Local Population in the State. Year 2000

State	Immigrants, as % of the Population	Emigrants, as % of the Population*
Aguascalientes	4.49	2.09
Baja California	9.23	2.61
Baja California Sur	9.51	3.75
Campeche	4.89	4.13
Coahuila de Zaragoza	3.18	2.98
Colima	5.67	3.84
Chiapas	1.15	2.28
Chihuahua	4.54	1.63
Distrito Federal	4.38	9.07
Durango	2.65	4.49
Guanajuato	2.02	1.61
Guerrero	1.71	4.53
Hidalgo	3.89	3.51
Jalisco	2.46	2.26
México	5.25	3.35
Michoacán de Ocampo	2.36	2.69
Morelos	5.38	3.15
Nayarit	4.00	4.46
Nuevo León	3.36	1.75
Oaxaca	2.23	4.06
Puebla	2.58	2.96
Querétaro de Arteaga	5.60	2.31
Quintana Roo	14.12	4.10
San Luis Potosí	2.21	3.21
Sinaloa	3.82	4.82
Sonora	3.48	2.50
Tabasco	2.32	3.89
Tamaulipas	5.98	2.51
Tlaxcala	4.08	2.76
Veracruz Llave	2.24	5.42
Yucatán	2.69	2.63
Zacatecas	2.45	3.38

Source: Own estimations, based on XII Censo de Población. INEGI.
* Refers to the total number of migrants originated in the State of the first column that were living in other States in 2000

THE CASE OF MEXICO

In Mexico, more than 3.5 million people changed their place of residence between 1995 and 2000.[2] This important flow of people should make us expect some impact on the indexes measured in the HDI. Furthermore, the impact will not be uniform across states (see Table 5.1). In states such as Quintana Roo, Baja California, and Baja California Sur—where the immigrant population represented over 10 percent of the resident population in 2000—it is possible to find changes of higher magnitude than in states like Chiapas or Guerrero, where immigrants represent just above 2 percent of the population. In terms of the impact in the origin region, emigrants represent between 1 percent and 4.5 percent of the population on their states of origin. The only exceptions are Distrito Federal (9 percent) and Veracruz (5.4 percent).

Methodology

The methodology used to estimate the impact of migration is different for each HDI component. However, in both cases we recalculate the state level HDI in 2000 had no internal migration flows occurred between 1995 and 2000. The information on migration flows is obtained from the twelfth population census (INEGI [2000]). A brief description of the methodologies employed for each component follows.

EDUCATION

The education index is calculated as a weighted average of the adult literacy rate and the school attendance rate.[3] First, we calculate the education index for each state using individual information from the 2000 census.[4] Next, we calculate the education index netting out migration flows by creating "virtual states" composed of all the people that lived in the state in 1995.[5] By comparing the actual education index with the education index of the virtual state, we get an estimate of the effect of migration. We argue that migrants' characteristics affect the estimated education index. It is obvious that literacy is an asset that a person carries wherever he or she goes. For the case of school attendance, we must assume though that if a person is studying and attending school in 2000 in the destination region, he or she would be studying should he or she have continued to live in his or her state of origin.

Income

In the case of income we use information on monthly income collected in the 2000 Employment National Survey (ENE in Spanish). We take several

$$Y_{kij} = \gamma_0 + \sum_i \gamma_{1i} Z_{ki} + \sum_i \gamma_{2i} Z_{ki} M_{ki} + \sum_{i=2} \delta_{1i} State_i$$

$$+ \sum_i \sum_j \delta_{2ij} State_{i, i \neq j} \cdot State_j + e_k$$

Figure 5.1.

individual characteristics and run a wage equation including controls for the individuals' migration status. We estimate then the following equation:

where Y_{kij} denotes the wage of individual k who lives in state i in 2000 and who lived in State j in 1995. Z_k is a vector that includes individual characteristics such as educational attainment, labor experience, family structure, and other labor characteristics. M_k is a dummy variable equal to 1 if the individual changed his or her state of residence between 1995 and 2000. The equation in Figure 5.1 includes state fixed effects. Finally, we also include interaction terms for each possible combination of state of destination and origin.[6]

Equation (1) is estimated using ordinary least squares. The estimated coefficients are used to calculate a counterfactual state income per capita in the absence of migration. In other words, what would be the income per capita in State i if all emigrants stayed and no immigrants from other States arrived to State i? We do this in two steps. First, the coefficients obtained from the estimation of equation (1) are used to calculate the salary that each individual would receive in his or her state of origin. Second, by aggregating the estimated salaries at the state level, we obtain an estimate of the income per capita of a "virtual state" in the absence of migration. We present now four examples of how this procedure is applied:

- An individual who lives in Quintana Roo in 2000 and who in 1995 also used to live in Quintana Roo.
- An individual who lives in Quintana Roo in 2000 and who in 1995 used to live in Puebla.

- An individual who lives in Puebla in 2000 and who in 1995 also used to live in Puebla.
- An individual who lives in Puebla in 2000 and who in 1995 used to live in Quintana Roo.

The estimated wages for the status quo and the counterfactual are based on the equations shown in tables 5.2 to 5.5 :

Following the presentation in UNDP (2004), we transform the estimated wages to the PPP in 2002 USD. The transformed wages constitute the basis for the income index.[7] It is important to note the following points: First, using the estimated coefficients from equation (1) allows us to purge out any possible wage "premiums" that immigrant workers sometimes have in the destination regions.[8] Second, foreigners are treated as if they were natives from their state of residence in 2000. This allows us to capture the

Table 5.2.   Estimated Wages Based on Migration Status and Residence Status in 2000

State of Residence

1995	2000	Wage on	
Q Roo	Q Roo	Status Quo	$\hat{y}_{kij} = \hat{\gamma}_0 + \hat{\gamma}_{1base}Z_{kbase} + \hat{\gamma}_{1qroo}Z_{kqroo} + \hat{\delta}_{1qroo}Qroo$
Q Roo	Q Roo	Conterfactual	$\hat{y}_{kij} = \hat{\gamma}_0 + \hat{\gamma}_{1base}Z_{kbase} + \hat{\gamma}_{1qroo}Z_{kqroo} + \hat{\delta}_{1qroo}Qroo$

Table 5.3.   Estimated Wages Based on Migration Status and Residence Status in 2000

State of Residence

1995	2000	Wage on	
Puebla	Q Roo	Status Quo	$\hat{y}_{kij} = \hat{\gamma}_0 + \hat{\gamma}_{1base}Z_{kbase} + \hat{\gamma}_{1qroo}Z_{kqroo} + \hat{\gamma}_{2base}Z_{kbase}$ $M_{ik} + \hat{\gamma}_{2qroo}Z_{kqroo}M_{ik} + \hat{\delta}_{1qroo}Qroo +$ $\hat{\delta}_{2qroopue}Qroo^*Pue$
Puebla	Q Roo	Conterfactual	$\hat{y}_{kij} = \hat{\gamma}_0 + \hat{\gamma}_{1base}Z_{kbase} + \hat{\gamma}_{1pue}Z_{kpue} + \hat{\delta}_{1pue}Pue$

Table 5.4.   Estimated Income Based on Migration Status and Residence Status in 2000

State of Residence

1995	2000	Wage on	
Puebla	Puebla	Status Quo	$\hat{y}_{kij} = \hat{\gamma}_0 + \hat{\gamma}_{1base}Z_{kbase} + \hat{\gamma}_{1pue}Z_{kpue} + \hat{\delta}_{1pue}Pue$
Puebla	Puebla	Conterfactual	$\hat{y}_{kij} = \hat{\gamma}_0 + \hat{\gamma}_{1base}Z_{kbase} + \hat{\gamma}_{1pue}Z_{kpue} + \hat{\delta}_{1pue}Pue$

Table 5.5. Estimated Income Based on Migration Status and Residence Status in 2000

State of Residence			
1995	2000	Wages on	
Q Roo	Puebla	Status Quo	$\hat{y}_{kij} = \hat{\gamma}_0 + \hat{\gamma}_{1base}Z_{kbase} + \hat{\gamma}_{1pue}Z_{kpue} + \hat{\gamma}_{2base}$ $Z_{kbase}M_{ik} + \hat{\gamma}_{2pue}Z_{kpue}M_{ik} + \hat{\delta}_{1pue}Pue$ $+ \hat{\delta}_{2pueqroo}Pue^{*}Qroo$
	Puebla	Conterfactual	$\hat{y}_{kij} = \hat{\gamma}_0 + \hat{\gamma}_{1base}Z_{kbase} + \hat{\gamma}_{1qroo}Z_{kqroo} + \hat{\delta}_{1qroo}$ $Qroo$

effect of *internal migration* on the income indexes.[9] Finally, we are aware that this exercise only takes into the account the direct effects on migration on income, and that we do not model the indirect effects that the immigrant inflow (outflow) would have on the labor market of the destination (origin) region. Nonetheless, previous studies have found that immigration does not have significant effects on local labor markets (Card [2005]), or that the effect is economically small (Longhi et al. [2005]).[10] We calculate the indexes following the methodology in UNDP.[11]

RESULTS

Education

Table 5.6 presents the results for the recalculation of the education index. The counterfactual indexes present slight changes for all states, with Quintana Roo having the largest change (1.66 percent). This result is in line with our expectations in light of the large share of immigrants in the Quintana Roo population in 2000. It is notable that Quintana Roo is negatively affected by migration. The estimated education index for this state is 0.8153. However, the index is estimated to be 0.8289 in the absence of migration. This implies that the state was a recipient of immigrants with educational characteristics[12] that were below the average of the native population in 1995. Two other states present a similar result. Baja California and Baja California Sur's education index is higher (roughly by the same magnitude as Quintana Roo's difference) when the migration effect is purged. Another way to compare whether a state was positively or negatively affected by migration is to analyze the state's relative ranking in the absence of migration.[13] Quintana Roo's educational ranking is 4, Baja California Sur's 3, and Baja California's 2 places higher once we purge migration effects.

Table 5.6. Education Index

State	Indicators 2000				Indicators 2000, Net of Migration				
	Alphabetization rate	Assistance rate	Education index	National ranking	Alphabetization rate	Assistance rate	Education index	National ranking	Change in %
Aguascalientes	95.17	63.27	0.8454	7	95.06	63.24	0.8445	7	-0.10
B. California	96.50	62.05	0.8502	4	96.56	65.65	0.8626	2	1.46
B. California S.	95.70	62.92	0.8477	6	95.91	65.87	0.8590	3	1.33
Campeche	88.10	64.69	0.8030	23	88.14	64.93	0.8040	21	0.13
Coahuila de Zaragoza	96.11	62.63	0.8495	5	96.10	62.88	0.8503	6	0.09
Colima	92.78	63.30	0.8296	12	92.83	63.37	0.8301	13	0.07
Chiapas	76.95	56.97	0.7029	32	77.17	56.52	0.7028	32	0.00
Chihuahua	95.16	61.08	0.8380	9	95.04	62.67	0.8425	9	0.53
Distrito Federal	97.09	69.93	0.8804	1	97.15	71.00	0.8843	1	0.45
Durango	94.54	62.05	0.8371	11	94.51	61.25	0.8342	12	-0.34
Guanajuato	87.91	58.50	0.7811	26	87.81	58.46	0.7802	25	-0.11
Guerrero	78.20	63.29	0.7323	31	78.04	62.04	0.7271	31	-0.71
Hidalgo	85.00	64.77	0.7826	25	84.94	63.87	0.7791	26	-0.44
Jalisco	93.52	61.56	0.8287	13	93.48	61.66	0.8288	15	0.01
México	93.55	64.30	0.8380	10	93.50	64.60	0.8387	10	0.08
Michoacán	85.97	58.89	0.7694	29	85.89	58.57	0.7678	29	-0.21
Morelos	90.69	63.30	0.8156	17	90.71	63.58	0.8167	18	0.14
Nayarit	91.02	64.49	0.8218	16	91.12	63.78	0.8201	17	-0.21

Nuevo León	96.65	62.11	0.8514	3	96.65	62.63	0.8531	5	0.20
Oaxaca	78.30	63.30	0.7330	30	78.39	61.92	0.7290	30	-0.54
Puebla	85.27	60.62	0.7705	28	85.22	60.02	0.7682	28	-0.30
Querétaro	90.15	61.80	0.8070	21	89.74	61.55	0.8034	22	-0.45
Quintana Roo	92.45	59.68	0.8153	18	91.98	64.71	0.8289	14	1.67
S. L. Potosí	88.58	64.12	0.8042	22	88.61	63.13	0.8012	23	-0.38
Sinaloa	91.99	64.18	0.8272	14	92.87	64.57	0.8344	11	0.87
Sonora	95.63	65.56	0.8560	2	95.69	66.16	0.8584	4	0.28
Tabasco	90.21	63.57	0.8133	19	90.35	62.74	0.8114	19	-0.23
Tamaulipas	94.81	62.21	0.8394	8	94.75	63.82	0.8444	8	0.59
Tlaxcala	92.12	62.74	0.8233	15	92.08	62.50	0.8222	16	-0.13
Veracruz Llave	84.99	63.34	0.7777	27	85.37	61.62	0.7745	27	-0.41
Yucatán	87.59	63.90	0.7969	24	87.52	63.10	0.7938	24	-0.40
Zacatecas	91.85	60.01	0.8124	20	91.80	59.37	0.8099	20	-0.30

Notes: The maximun level (100) and the minimun level (0) are those used by UNDP
Source: Own estimations, based on XII Censo de Población. INEGI.

Among the most benefited states from the migration phenomenon we find Jalisco, Nuevo León, and Sonora. Each of the states falls two places in the educational ranking based on the counterfactual education index.

These results provide evidence of the relevance of analyzing both the magnitude of the migration phenomenon and the composition of immigrants when recalculating educational indexes. The states with the highest changes after controlling for migration include states with both high and low concentrations of immigrants/emigrants.

Income

The index income yield higher changes than those found for the education index. Table 5.7 presents the results for the income index recalculation.[14] The income indexes changed between –3 percent and 4.4 percent. It is important to mention that only nine states showed a negative change in the index—that is, migration had a positive impact in terms of income per capita. This number is twice as large in the education index recalculation. The states that benefited the most from migration (i.e., those with the largest drops in the purged income index) are those with the largest concentrations of immigrants: Quintana Roo, Querétaro, Baja California Sur, and Baja California. Among the states that were negatively affected by migration, half yield changes above 1 percent. In this group—states where people with salaries higher than the average are emigrating, and at the same time people with salaries below the mean are immigrating—the states with the largest changes are Oaxaca (4.43 percent), Chiapas (3.9 percent), Veracruz (3.83 percent), Puebla (2.96 percent), and Guerrero (2.69 percent).

With respect to the relative ranking, in half of the cases the states did not change their relative position. The state with the largest change was Quintana Roo, which in the absence of migration would have a rank four places higher. Tlaxcala and Michoacán would climb two places in the absence of migration, whereas Puebla, Sonora, and Veracruz would fall two places.

Human Development Index

Using the new indexes—by each component and net of migration effects—we can re-estimate the HDI and evaluate the total impact of migration on the calculation of the index. Table 5.8 presents the results of this exercise. The changes in the states' HDI are above 0.5 percent in only four cases (Chiapas, Oaxaca, Sinaloa, and Veracruz). An important result

Table 5.7. Income Index

State	Indicators 2000			Indicators 2000, Net of Migration			
	GDP per capita* Income Index		National Rank	GDP per capita* Incomer Index		National Rank	Change in %
Aguascalientes	1,724	0.4752	12	1,701	0.4729	12	-0.49
Baja California	2,555	0.5409	2	2,505	0.5376	3	-0.61
B. California S.	2,211	0.5168	4	2,147	0.5118	4	-0.96
Campeche	1,190	0.4134	20	1,183	0.4123	21	-0.26
Coahuila	1,904	0.4918	7	1,914	0.4926	6	0.17
Colima	1,549	0.4573	13	1,554	0.4579	13	0.14
Chiapas	607	0.3011	32	652	0.3129	32	3.90
Chihuahua	1,998	0.4998	5	1,969	0.4974	5	-0.48
Distrito Federal	2,726	0.5517	1	2,739	0.5525	1	0.14
Durango	1,211	0.4163	19	1,242	0.4205	19	1.03
Guanajuato	1,243	0.4206	17	1,248	0.4212	18	0.15
Guerrero	751	0.3366	30	793	0.3456	30	2.70
Hidalgo	901	0.3670	28	940	0.3741	28	1.92
Jalisco	1,780	0.4805	10	1,785	0.4810	9	0.11
México	1,502	0.4522	14	1,496	0.4516	14	-0.15
Michoacán	988	0.3822	25	1,004	0.3850	27	0.73
Morelos	1,308	0.4291	16	1,316	0.4301	16	0.23
Nayarit	1,177	0.4115	21	1,217	0.4171	20	1.37

(Continued)

Table 5.7. Income Index (Continued)

State	Indicators 2000			Indicators 2000, Net of Migration			
	GDP per capita*	Income Index	National Rank	GDP per capita*	Incomer Index	National Rank	Change in %
Nuevo León	2,518	0.5384	3	2,518	0.5385	2	0.01
Oaxaca	640	0.3098	31	695	0.3236	31	4.44
Puebla	968	0.3789	26	1,036	0.3902	24	2.96
Querétaro	1,763	0.4789	11	1,709	0.4737	11	-1.09
Quintana Roo	1,927	0.4938	6	1,763	0.4790	10	-3.01
San Luis Potosí	1,095	0.3995	23	1,126	0.4041	22	1.15
Sinaloa	1,373	0.4373	15	1,423	0.4432	15	1.35
Sonora	1,805	0.4829	9	1,883	0.4899	7	1.45
Tabasco	1,106	0.4012	22	1,107	0.4013	23	0.04
Tamaulipas	1,810	0.4833	8	1,796	0.4820	8	-0.27
Tlaxcala	1,025	0.3885	24	1,033	0.3897	26	0.33
Veracruz Llave	949	0.3756	27	1,035	0.3900	25	3.83
Yucatán	1,234	0.4194	18	1,262	0.4232	17	0.90
Zacatecas	841	0.3555	29	877	0.3623	29	1.92

* PPP 2000 US dollars

Notes: The maximun income level (40000) and the minimun income level (100) follow used by UNDP.

Source: Own estimations, based on XII Censo de Población. INEGI.

Table 5.8.   Human Development Index

State	HDI 2000	National Rank	HDI 2000, net of migration	National Rank	Change, in %
Aguascalientes	0.7166	8	0.7156	9	−0.15
Baja California	0.7435	2	0.7465	2	0.41
Baja California Sur	0.7307	4	0.7328	4	0.29
Campeche	0.6746	21	0.6745	21	0.00
Coahuila de Zaragoza	0.7242	5	0.7247	6	0.07
Colima	0.7040	13	0.7044	13	0.06
Chiapas	0.5974	32	0.6013	32	0.65
Chihuahua	0.7235	6	0.7241	7	0.10
Distrito Federal	0.7569	1	0.7585	1	0.21
Durango	0.6897	16	0.6902	16	0.07
Guanajuato	0.6722	23	0.6722	23	−0.01
Guerrero	0.6204	30	0.6217	30	0.21
Hidalgo	0.6509	29	0.6521	29	0.19
Jalisco	0.7119	10	0.7122	10	0.03
México	0.7053	12	0.7053	12	0.00
Michoacán de Ocampo	0.6542	26	0.6546	28	0.06
Morelos	0.6888	17	0.6895	17	0.10
Nayarit	0.6831	18	0.6844	18	0.19
Nuevo León	0.7412	3	0.7417	3	0.08
Oaxaca	0.6116	31	0.6148	31	0.53
Puebla	0.6525	27	0.6555	26	0.45
Querétaro de Arteaga	0.7012	14	0.6982	15	−0.42
Quintana Roo	0.7105	11	0.7100	11	−0.06
San Luis Potosí	0.6707	24	0.6712	24	0.08
Sinaloa	0.6943	15	0.6987	14	0.63
Sonora	0.7225	7	0.7256	5	0.44
Tabasco	0.6739	22	0.6734	22	−0.08
Tamaulipas	0.7158	9	0.7170	8	0.17
Tlaxcala	0.6768	19	0.6768	19	0.01
Veracruz Llave	0.6516	28	0.6553	27	0.57
Yucatán	0.6748	20	0.6750	20	0.03
Zacatecas	0.6592	25	0.6607	25	0.22

Source: Own estimations, based on XII Censo de Población. INEGI.

Table 5.9.   Percent Changes in the Components of the HDI

State	Education Index	Health Index	Income index	HDI
Aguascalientes	−0.10	—	−0.49	−0.15
Baja California	1.46	—	−0.61	0.41
Baja California Sur	1.33	—	−0.96	0.29
Campeche	0.13	—	−0.26	0.00
Coahuila de Zaragoza	0.09	—	0.17	0.07
Colima	0.07	—	0.14	0.06
Chiapas	0.00	—	3.90	0.65
Chihuahua	0.53	—	−0.48	0.10
Distrito Federal	0.45	—	0.14	0.21
Durango	−0.34	—	1.03	0.07
Guanajuato	−0.11	—	0.15	−0.01
Guerrero	−0.71	—	2.70	0.21
Hidalgo	−0.44	—	1.92	0.19
Jalisco	0.01	—	0.11	0.03
México	0.08	—	−0.15	0.00
Michoacán de Ocampo	−0.21	—	0.73	0.06
Morelos	0.14	—	0.23	0.10
Nayarit	−0.21	—	1.37	0.19
Nuevo León	0.20	—	0.01	0.08
Oaxaca	−0.54	—	4.44	0.53
Puebla	−0.30	—	2.96	0.45
Querétaro de Arteaga	−0.45	—	−1.09	−0.42
Quintana Roo	1.67	—	−3.01	−0.06
San Luis Potosí	−0.38	—	1.15	0.08
Sinaloa	0.87	—	1.35	0.63
Sonora	0.28	—	1.45	0.44
Tabasco	−0.23	—	0.04	−0.08
Tamaulipas	0.59	—	−0.27	0.17
Tlaxcala	−0.13	—	0.33	0.01
Veracruz Llave	−0.41	—	3.83	0.57
Yucatán	−0.40	—	0.90	0.03
Zacatecas	−0.30	—	1.92	0.22

Source: Own estimations, based on XII Censo de Población. INEGI.

is that for most States the change in the index is positive.[15] That is, for most
states in the country, the migration phenomenon had a negative effect in
the HDI. Six states are benefited by migration, or more specifically, by the
composition of the immigrants arriving to them. The states in this group
are Aguascalientes, Campeche, Guanajuato, Querétaro, Quintana Roo, and
Tabasco.

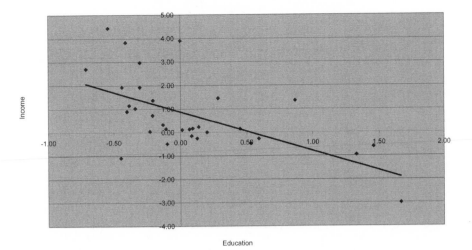

Figure 5.2.

The importance of evaluating the changes in both the overall HDI and in its components should be noted. Table 5.9 presents a summary of the estimated impacts of migration in percentage terms. This is due to the information it provides about the composition of immigrants/emigrants in each state. For two-thirds, the composition of immigrants/emigrants led to changes in the HDI components in opposite directions (see Figure 5.2). We explain now, as an example of the use of this research, the case of Quintana Roo. Migration negatively affected the education index. On the other hand, migration also affected positively the income index. Thus, we can infer that migration in Quintana Roo can be explained by any of the following phenomena: (a) the State is receiving people with low education and/or that do not attend school; (b) the state is expelling literate people and/or who are attending school in 2000; (c) the state is receiving people with a higher than average income; (d) the state's emigrants belonged to the left tail of the income distribution.

CONCLUSION

When we evaluate the impact of migration in the calculation of the HDI, we find that in overall terms, it is negative for most of the states in Mexico. That is, in the absence of migration, ceteris paribus, twenty-six states would have recorded a higher HDI. The impact of the migration phenomenon is different if we look at the two components of the HDI, and in fact the impact is in opposing directions. In this study the estimated changes in the HDI are driven by changes in the income index. On the other hand, we find evidence that the most important factor in the impact of migration is the composition and characteristics of the immigrant population, and not their magnitude with respect to the native population.

NOTES

1. Todaro (1969).

2. Approximately 3.6 percent of the population in 2000 (INEGI).

3. Literacy rate refers to the percentage of people who can read and write, and who are less than 15 years old. School attendance rate relates to the percentage of people who are between 6 and 24 years old and who are attending school (PNUD [2004]).

4. PNUD (2004) used INEA (2004) data to calculate the education index. The indexes we present here use information from the census and are substantially similar to the ones reported in the HDI report 2004. Our exercise relies on estimating the change in the HDI component once migration effects are purged out. Thus, the differences in levels should not be of great concern.

5. For instance, the virtual State of Puebla is comprised of all the people who reside in the state in 1995, regardless of their current state of residence.

6. The results of the estimation are available from the authors.

7. We are aware that total income may be underestimated in the ENE. However, in this analysis it is not necessary to replicate the income index presented in the Human Development Reports. The main objective is to assess the importance of changes due to migration on its calculation. Additionally, wages are the main source of total income.

8. Our estimates show that immigrants have, on average, a salary "premium" of around 20 percent when working in a different state from the state of their birth.

9. Additionally, we implicitly assume that the impact of children who are less than 5 years old on the recalculation of the income index is not significant.

10. The authors found that a 1 percentage point increase of immigrants on the labor force raises wages by 0.119 percent.

11. We use the minimum and maximum values in the Human Development Report UNDP 2004.

12. Specifically literacy and school attendance rates.

13. The relative ranking is also used in HDI Reports. In this ranking, the state with the highest index is ranked first.

14. It is important to mention that the indexes found here should not be evaluated in absolute terms. Due to the methodology employed, the estimated indexes are much lower than the ones presented in HDI Reports. It is necessary to focus on the relative changes of the indexes.

15. It is worth emphasizing that this is a short-term analysis (5 years).

Chapter 6

Gender Differentials in Emigration by Level of Education

Mexican-Born Adult Migrants in the United States

B. Lindsay Lowell and Carla Pederzini

The volume of international mobility has increased sharply in the past half-century and the character of the migration has changed in several ways. The population of international migrants more than doubled between 1960 and 2000 from 76 million to 159 million (Özden et al., 2011). This increase came in part from increases in the rate of emigration and, to a greater degree, from the significant growth of the migrants' source country populations (Lowell, 2007). At the same time, many observers have discerned an increasing feminization of international migration as measured in the increasing percentage of females in the total flow of migrants (Martin, 2007). The most significant increase took place in Europe, where the percentage of migrants who are female rose from 47.7 percent in 1975 to 53.4 percent in 2005. Asia and North America are the two exceptions to this trend, showing a decreasing female participation (Fry, 2006). As of 2005, about 49.6 percent of the world's international migrants were women, up from 46.8 percent in 1960 (UN Population Division, 2005).

Women's role in the evolution of global mobility patterns has been linked to the study of the causes and consequences of the migration of the highly skilled. Does the feminization of migration appear among the highly skilled, and what effect does that have on development? Of course, highly skilled mobility raises the specter of an adverse brain drain, but it also raises the possibility of a favorable brain gain as skilled migration links developing countries to the globalizing phenomenon (Lowell and Findlay, 2002). And many developed nations are seeking to compete with each other to attract highly skilled migrants in order to boost their own economic fortunes. Women's part in these processes has been mostly unknown. Indeed, the skill composition

95

of international mobility has been a source of much speculation until the creation of new data sets in the middle part of the last decade. In turn, with a short lag, these data were extended to include the female contribution to international migrant stocks (Dumont, Martin and Spielvogel, 2007; Docquier, Lowell and Marfouk, 2009).

We now know that women play a significant part in the mobility of the college-educated, and that the world's highest rates of emigration are of tertiary-educated women. Estimates for the year 2000 show that the female rate of emigration varies by major region of birth (Docquier et al., 2009). There is some relationship to the source country's level of economic development, insofar as tertiary-educated African women have a high rate of emigration. The highest rates of tertiary educated female emigration are found from "other" Oceania and the Caribbean—e.g., small and poor island nations. Interestingly, relatively high rates of emigration are also found for secondary educated females from Central America and the Caribbean, perhaps reflecting a unique regional migration process. Whereas rates of tertiary emigration are greatest for almost all other countries in the world, Mexico and Central America demonstrate the highest rates, as measured by available data sets, from among adults who have completed secondary education. The reasons for this difference are unknown, and raise the question of whether the pattern of skilled emigration for Mexico and Central America systematically varies from the typical.

One limitation of most all existing national data estimates of emigration is that they tend to classify skill as completed adult education and identify only three levels of education: primary, secondary, and tertiary. The international and national definitions of these levels of education vary, creating some error in the measures, but, more important, the tertiary level of education lumps together different levels of education. In the first place, the international definition of tertiary education tends to start with at least one year or more of post-secondary education (some college). A casual examination of the data often surprises experts who expect to see figures more in line with traditional "college-educated" statistics of bachelors and above or four years and more. What is more, some college, bachelor's, master's, doctorate, and professional degrees reflect increasing years of education and training in specialized skills. While there has been a spate of new research using the new data on gender migration by skill, there remains little research that has addressed the issue of female migration in its many dimensions (Docquier et al., 2008).

In particular, this chapter contributes to a better understanding of the nuances of how international mobility varies within the tertiary-educated population—it does so with a case study of migration from Mexico to the United States. Latin America and the Caribbean was the region of the world which showed the greatest growth rate in highly qualified outmigration between 1990 and 2007 (Lozano and Gandini, 2010). Just as there is little study of the differences in mobility within the tertiary-educated population, there has been little study in particular of skilled mobility in the Mexico–U.S. context. Notable exceptions include Cruz-Piñeiro and Ruiz-Ochoa (2010), who explore the scope of preferential visas, mainly H-1B and NAFTA visas, granted to highly qualified Mexicans, and their impact on the documented migrant flow.

The perception of Mexican migration, the preponderance of which is to the United States, is that of a mass emigration of low-skilled males of whom many are legally unauthorized to work. But in terms of the numbers, Mexico as of the year 2000 was the third largest nation having a tertiary-educated population living abroad. Only the United Kingdom, the Philippines, and India have larger numbers, although still of roughly the same magnitude, while China and Germany have smaller numbers (Docquier et al., 2008). It is also the case that highly educated female Mexicans are more likely to migrate than are males, albeit we shall see that "highly educated" needs to be qualified in terms of those who complete specific tertiary degrees.

While we focus here on the demographics and possible causes of the mobility of highly skilled women, we note that women's education has been demonstrated to have substantial positive effects. Besides generating private returns for individual women from labor market participation, women's education has strong impacts on numerous other outcomes, such as children's health and mortality, as well as women's own fertility and reproductive health. A large literature exists which has demonstrated that the social returns to investing in women's education outweigh the social returns to investing in men's education (Schultz, 1993; King and Hill, 1993). Other studies have shown that it is important not just to improve overall education levels of men and women, but to reduce gender gaps between men and women as well. There is some evidence that gender inequality in education is associated with reductions in GDP per capita as well as other indicators of development such as life expectancy and infant mortality (King and Hill, 1993). If equality in educational attainment between the sexes is not achieved, improvements in social indicators can only be achieved at much higher levels of economic growth.

The implication of this is that the benefits of increasing the numbers of educated women are more than just an increase in income or in productivity. Women's involvement in the globalization of mobility has real and, as yet, not fully explored consequences. Women tend to have more significant impacts than men on children's health and mortality. Econometric tests of the impacts of highly educated women's emigration finds adverse impacts on source countries' infant mortality, under-five mortality and secondary school enrollment rate by gender (Dumont, Martin and Spielvogel, 2007). These effects are greater both for women than men and for skilled women than for less skilled women. The importance of these consequences of the migration of the highly skilled makes it important to better document gender differentials in migration and to better understand its causes. Many observers believe that the roots of the feminization of highly skilled emigration can be found in gender differentials in educational opportunity in the migrant-source country.

Fortunately, within Latin America gender differences in education are generally lower than in other developing countries, although the growth rate in overall education levels has been less than in other regions (Knodel and Jones, 1996; Grant and Behrman, 2010). Furthermore, substantial progress has been made in the last decades at eliminating gender differences in education. Since 1960, there has been a large expansion in education within the region and sharp falls in gender differences between men and women. Primary school enrollment and completion statistics show no differences by gender in most countries, and to a large extent these trends carry over to secondary education (Duryea et al., 2007). In Mexico, women have historically had less access to education than men, reflected in today's higher male literacy rates, but that is changing (Gandini and Castro, 2007). In the past two decades, the educational gender gap has closed to a point at which girls at the primary school level show higher school participation than boys. Increases in female labor force participation have been associated with the narrower gender gap in education (Creighton and Park, 2010). The average years of education achieved by Mexican women over the age of 15, however, is still a year-and-a-half less than that of men. Nevertheless, the expansion of education by the Mexican state has resulted in a fundamental shift in gender opportunities (Creighton and Park, 2010). A major (conditional) cash transfer program (Progresa-Oportunidades) benefits around one-fifth of all Mexican households. The program grants scholarships to boys and girls attending school and has created incentives for female school attendance in marginal communities where girls receive larger scholarships than boys. The lower opportunity cost of school attendance for girls is also mentioned as a possible cause for greater female attendance (Mier y Teran and Pederzini, 2010).

This chapter uses Mexican and U.S. data sources to examine gender differentials in emigration for the year 2010, as well as to explore some simple first-order explanations for the forces that drive these differentials. The first section starts with the basics, namely a description of gender differentials in Mexico–to–United States migration by age group to establish that emigration is greatest in the prime ages of 25 to 54, and that Mexican males are more likely to emigrate than females. We then describe the data and definitions that we use to explore gender differentials by education and migrant generation in more detail. We use both Mexican and U.S. data sources, define comparable and detailed levels of completed education, and distinguish between child and adult migrants to the United States. Next we turn to the core of the chapter and discuss gender differentials by detailed levels of completed education for adult U.S. migrants, finding that female emigration exceeds male only among doctorate degree holders. Yet we also find alternate patterns of male–female emigration propensities that vary by specific levels of education across three age cohorts of Mexican migrants. The chapter ends with sections that examine gender differentials in labor force outcomes in Mexico and the United States. We find that highly educated Mexican female migrants do not close the labor force participation gap with males and, surprisingly, do relatively less well in the United States than women in Mexico. We reach no definitive conclusions, but it appears that highly educated Mexican women migrate primarily for family and not economic reasons; and we speculate that assortative mating and Mexican marriage markets may explain some of the otherwise inexplicable gender differentials in emigration and labor markets that we find.

HAS MEXICAN MIGRATION BECOME FEMINIZED?

Mexico remains a country in which males make up the greatest percent of the annual flow of migrants to, and the stock of residents abroad in, the United States. There appears to be, nevertheless, some feminization of the emigrant flow. There is some evidence that greater numbers of young and often unmarried women leave Mexico than in the past (Cerrutti and Massey, 2004; Marcelli and Cornelius, 2001). And the available data show that, at least from 1990 to 2000, there has been a greater rate of out-migration of tertiary-educated females than of males. We return to this observation below, but first examine the more fundamental gender differentials in emigration by age group.

One way to see the marked male domination of the *total* migrant stream is to compare the percentage of all Mexican emigrants who reside in the United States. Figure 6.1 shows that the percentage of Mexican males who reside in the United States reaches a high of nearly 20 percent in the 35–44 year age group when a lesser 15 percent of females emigrate. The emigration rate (see definition below) of males and females is more similar at both the younger and older ages. It is hard to escape the fact that males dominate Mexican migration. As of 2010, our estimates show a male–female sex ratio of the population in Mexico of 0.94, while the sex ratio of the Mexican born in the

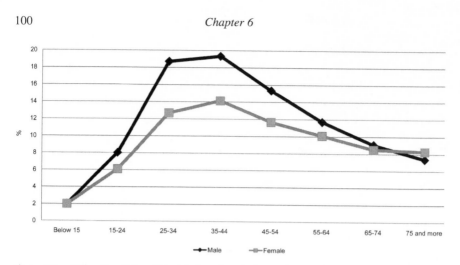

Figure 6.1. **Emigration Rates of the Mexican Population to the U.S. by Age Group, 2009–2010**

United States is 1.26 and is substantially higher. It has long been known that a good part of Mexico's relatively low male–female sex ratio can be mainly explained by the high rates of emigration among Mexican males (Bean, King and Passel, 1983).

There may be unique ways in which Mexican migration is becoming feminized, one of which may be a policy related boost to the traditional higher U.S. stay rates of women. First, the legalization of 2.3 million formerly undocumented Mexicans in 1986–1988 helped stabilize women migrating to, and resident in, families in the United States. Then, starting in the 1990s, the United States increased its enforcement of border crossings, which appears to have contributed to a slowing of the historical pattern of circular Mexico–to–United States migration. In an earlier investigation of the feminization of Mexican migration we concluded that based on a comparison of U.S. and Mexican data sources,

> While females have been relatively less likely to migrate from Mexico, females who do migrate to the United States have a greater tendency to remain. This pattern is at least consistent with the findings discussed above that, as the Mexican data indicate, circular or return migration has increased since 1997. (Lowell, Pederzini and Passel 2008)

In short, the percentage of males among Mexican migrants is greater than females, but that has been changing somewhat. Moreover, the causes of the general trend toward the feminization of the migrant share may be associated to some degree with the legalization provisions of two decades ago and subsequent enhancement of border enforcement. Greater deterrence at the border has made it riskier to cross the border, and there is a consensus that this has led to greater crossing costs, smuggler fees, and so forth, and a reduction in the pace of circulation of migrants between the United States and Mexico. Women are especially affected by these changes, and, the top-side data suggests, more than many males who shuttle back and forth, tend to stay in the United States once they enter.

We have also identified another clear pattern of the feminization of Mexican emigration. Using 2000 Mexican and U.S. census data, we have estimated the rate of outmigration by gender and the completed education of adults (Lowell, Pederzini and Passel, 2008). Those estimates demonstrated that male emigration rates are greater than female among migrants with secondary education or less, the single greatest source of the differential in emigration across age groups discussed above. At the same time, female rates of emigration are greater than male from high school though college and doctorate degrees. Mexican migration of the highly educated has been feminized since 1990, just as has been the case for most migrant streams globally. What our earlier estimates have shown, and which we reinforce below, is a unique pattern of emigration of the tertiary-educated in the case of Mexico. In the current chapter we update the estimates of emigration by education to 2010, once again using Mexican and U.S. Census data.

MEASURING MEXICAN EMIGRATION

The data analyzed in this chapter draw on Mexican and U.S. sources. For Mexico we use the 2010 National Survey of Employment and Occupation (ENOE), a nationally representative sample. The ENOE public microdata are one of several Mexican samples that have been introduced in the last decade and they provide reliable, quarterly information on the Mexican population. At the time of this writing the 2010 Mexican census microdata were not available. For the United States we tabulate the public microdata from the 2009 American Community Survey (ACS), since the 2010 national microdata are not yet available. The ACS is the only large sample of the resident population that includes a large number of detailed questions in its survey.[1] The survey takes place each month throughout the year and is combined into an annual total for tabulation. In some cases, especially for estimates by age groups, we tabulate a combined sample of the 2007, 2008, and 2009 ACS to achieve larger and more reliable sample sizes.

We measure the emigration "rate," actually the percentage of all Mexican-born persons (stock) living in the United States, following the literature as *Emigration rate* $= E_{USA}/(E_{USA} + P_{Mexico})$, where the emigration rate includes in the denominator both the Mexican-born emigrant population residing in the United States (E_{USA}) and the population resident in Mexico (P_{Mexico}). We also follow others in restricting the population of interest to adults—persons ages 25 and older—to limit the population to persons old enough to have, for the most part, completed their highest level of education. We further restrict the adult population to persons no older than 54 years of age, because we are interested in the population in the prime working and family years, and we have seen the greatest rates of Mexican emigration occur from 25 to 54 years of age.

All emigrants and the population resident in Mexico are differentiated by their highest completed education. The literature prefers completed education for many reasons, as contrasted with years of education, which is useful as a rough measure of schooling but which does not capture the value added of a completed degree. Mexico and the United States have a roughly similar system of education, but there are notable differences that keep the comparison from being a perfect fit. That, of course, can be said about most cross-country comparisons of educational systems. We use the standard self-report of years of education and completed degrees in the ENOE and the ACS. The comparison is made as follows: less than primary education includes all adults who have not completed at least six years of education, while primary completers report having completed six years of education (primaria). Middle school is the first level of secondary education (secundaria) and includes adults who report up to twelve years of education but not having completed high school (preparatoria); and we include here non-tertiary type technical degrees granted in Mexico. A high school or secondary completion includes a "GED" in the United States and is similar in Mexico. A post–high school level of completion includes all adults reporting at least one year of post-secondary education, including technical degrees. A bachelor's degree includes adults reporting having completed that degree, as does a master's degree and the doctorate or professional degree.

A final distinction is made in the measurement of Mexican-born migrants by "decimal generation," or what is commonly referred to as the 1.0 and 1.5 generations. All foreign-born persons reporting Mexico as their country of birth comprise the sample for the United States; this is the "first generation." The first generation can be further distinguished by their age at migration, where adults are likely to be independent or members of their family of procreation, while child-to-teen arrivals are likely to be dependents or members of their family of orientation. Of equal importance for our purposes here, child arrivals are likely to have completed their primary, secondary, and particularly any tertiary education in the United States. Thus, their behaviors are governed by a different set of selective forces than those conditioning adult migrants who, in turn, are more likely to have either completed their education in Mexico or moved to the United States to complete their tertiary education. We distinguish the decimal first generations with self-reports of year of arrival in the United States and, in turn, we estimate age at arrival assigning those coming at age 18 or younger to the 1.5 generation, and older arrivals to the 1.0 migrant generation.[2]

COMPLETED EDUCATION AND MALE–FEMALE RATIOS

Table 6.1 shows the estimated adult population 25–54 years of age by level of completed education in Mexico and in the United States by first decimal-generations. The number of adults with higher education is substantially less than that of adults with lesser education. Indeed, only about one-seventh of Mexican-born males in the United States have completed a tertiary education, which is roughly equivalent to the completion rates achieved by Mexican-born females. There are a *total* of 1.14 million tertiary-educated Mexican-born, and 414,000 thousand with a bachelor's degree or better, out of an adult population of 7.5 million adult residents in the United States. The 1.0 generation makes up the lion's share of the U.S. resident population of Mexican born, while there only about 500,000 in the population of the 1.5 generation Mexican-born with a tertiary education of any type. The numbers of the 1.5 generation are small, because most migration occurs in the adult ages, and relatively few adults bring Mexican-born children with them.[3]

Otherwise, there are notable differences in tertiary completion rates by place of residence and generation. It is striking, and little recognized, that a bachelor's degree is more common among adults resident in Mexico (12.8 percent) than among the Mexican-born resident in the United States (4.1 percent).[4] Yet, there is little difference in the percentage of Mexican residents or Mexican-born U.S. residents who go on to complete a master's or doctorate degree. The other notable fact is that 1.5 generation Mexican-born women in the United States are more likely to have completed a tertiary education than are 1.5 generation males (21 percent vs. 14 percent), as well as, either the male or female 1.0 generation (ca. 14 percent).[5] The tendency for the 1.5 generation of Mexican-born women to perform most favorably in tertiary education parallels that of native-born women in the United States.

There are two ways in which these patterns of college completion play themselves out in terms of migrant selectivity. The one in which we are primarily interested is the propensity to emigrate by level of education, but the literature

Table 6.1.   Number and Percentage of Males and Females Ages 25–54 by Educational Level in Mexico and in the United States

	Male			Female		
	In Mexico	*In the U.S.*		*In Mexico*	*In the U.S.*	
Level of Education		*Gen 1.0*	*Gen 1.5*		*Gen 1.0*	*Gen 1.5*
Below Primary	2803478	364569	184874	3720110	294227	99706
Primary	4219423	490983	245880	5208819	422542	143253
Middle School	6350447	745556	522334	7720035	594229	352301
High School	2263135	623219	432440	2146233	471570	318943
Post High	907712	195986	185048	812491	168950	175650
Bachelor's	2748753	103060	59526	2630369	98451	47860
Master's	239696	24083	9849	201483	16032	16328
Ph.D.	28590	14855	4751	15261	15775	3890
Total	19561234	2562311	1644702	22454801	2081776	1157931
Percentage within Group						
Below Primary	14.3	14.2	11.2	16.6	14.1	8.6
Primary	21.6	19.2	14.9	23.2	20.3	12.4
Middle School	32.5	29.1	31.8	34.4	28.5	30.4
High School	11.6	24.3	26.3	9.6	22.7	27.5
Post High	4.6	7.6	11.3	3.6	8.1	15.2
Bachelor's	14.1	4.0	3.6	11.7	4.7	4.1
Master's	1.2	0.9	0.6	0.9	0.8	1.4
Ph.D.	0.1	0.6	0.3	0.1	0.8	0.3
Total	100.0	100.0	100.0	100.0	100.0	100.0

Source: United States: American Community Survey, 2009; Mexico: National Survey of Employment and Occupation, 2010

also commonly refers to selectivity in terms of the male–female sex ratio of the migrant population within classes of education. Table 6.2 first shows emigration rates (percent of all Mexican born in the United States) by level of education, as well as the male–female ratio of those separate emigration rates (relative propensity to emigrate). Next, it shows the traditional male–female sex ratio (male over female population) by level of completed education. These are two ways in which the literature gauges male–female differences in migrant selectivity.

In terms of the more typically studied male–female sex ratios, for the population with less than a high school education the sex ratios are low in Mexico and high in the United States. Somewhat surprisingly, there are many more males (1.87) relative to women with a doctorate degree in Mexico, as well as somewhat more males relative to females in other tertiary levels of education.

Table 6.2. Ratio of Male-Female Emigration Rates and the Male-Female Sex Ratio in Mexico and the United States by First-Generation

| Level of Education | *Emigration Rate 1.0 Generation* | | | *Sex Ratio in Mexico and the United States* | | |
	Male	*Female*	*Ratio Male/ Female*	*U.S. emigrants (1.0 Gen)*	*U. S. emigrants (1.5 Gen)*	*Residents in Mexico*
Below Primary	0.11	0.07	1.52	1.24	1.85	0.75
Primary	0.10	0.07	1.35	1.16	1.72	0.81
Middle School	0.10	0.07	1.43	1.25	1.48	0.82
High School	0.19	0.16	1.17	1.32	1.36	1.05
Post High	0.15	0.15	1.04	1.16	1.05	1.12
Bachelor's	0.04	0.04	1.00	1.05	1.24	1.05
Master's	0.09	0.07	1.28	1.50	0.60	1.19
Ph.D.	0.31	0.45	0.68	0.94	1.22	1.87
Total	0.11	0.08	1.33	1.23	1.42	0.87

Source: United States: American Community Survey, 2007–2009; Mexico: National Survey of Employment and Occupation, 2010

In the United States, however, there is an alternating pattern by level of education that differs for the 1.0 and 1.5 generations. For the 1.0 generation migrants, males are somewhat under- or equally represented among both bachelors and doctorate degree holders, but overrepresented among master's degree holders; the sex ratio is 1.50. For the 1.5 generation, males are under or equally represented among the master's or post–high school educated, but strongly overrepresented among the bachelor's (1.24) and doctorate degree holders (1.22). What this shows is that there is no simple pattern of selectivity that varies linearly by level of education; rather, the pattern varies by level of education, place of residence, and generation in the United States.

In terms of the rate of emigration, table 6.2 restricts its measure to the first (1.0) generation of adult arrivals. The reason is as follows. Even though our measures are for prime-age adults, or persons ages 25–54, many Mexican migrants come to the United States as youth. Persons who enter the United States before attaining adulthood are different from adult migrants in at least two ways. First, most but not all youth migrants (1.5 generation) accompany family members or relatives, and thus are not making the decision to migrate.[6] Second, youth migrants are more likely than residents in Mexico to complete their primary and secondary education, because the U.S. system produces higher rates of completion than Mexico's. Finally, the literature on these issues also makes the distinction between youth and adult migrants and focuses on adult migrants.[7] The rate of Mexican emigration (1.0 and 1.5 generations) is reduced with the removal of the youth generation (1.5) for males from 17.7 percent to 10.8 percent, and for females from 12.6 percent to 8.1 percent: a 36.1 percent and 35.7 percent reduction in the measured rate respectively. In other words, rates of emigration are reduced by just over one-third with the exclusion of the 1.5 generation from the estimates.

Table 6.2 demonstrates that high school and doctorate degree holders have the highest rates of emigration. Indeed, if the four tertiary levels of educational completion were averaged, which is how the major cross-national data sets are constructed, then rates of Mexican emigration would be highest in high school, or at the secondary level. Unlike nearly all other nations, Mexico's highest rate of emigration is at the secondary level of education. When the tertiary level of education is examined closely, however, those with some college or with bachelor's degrees have fairly low rates of emigration. At the next higher level of education, migrants with a master's degree, males especially, have yet higher rates of emigration. Migrants with a doctorate degree, females especially, have the highest rates of Mexican emigration of all the educational groups: 31 percent for males and 45 percent for females.

At first blush it appears as if highly educated women are more likely to emigrate than are males, but that holds primarily only for adults with a doctorate degree.[8] Otherwise, for all adult (1.0) migrants the male propensity to emigrate is higher than females for those with a master's degree; it is also higher than women for all emigrants with a high school degree or less. Once again, there is no linear pattern of increasing feminization with higher degrees, but rather an alternating pattern in the male–female propensity to emigrate by level of education. On average, males with less than tertiary education are more likely to emigrate than are females; however, the pattern varies for each of the four levels of tertiary education. Among the tertiary-educated, males are less or no more likely to emigrate than females with a doctorate or bachelor's degree, but males are more likely to emigrate than are females with a master's degree. We do not know what forces are generating these patterns which are unique to given levels of education.[9]

ADULT EMIGRATION (1.0 GENERATION) BY EDUCATION AND AGE COHORT

We are interested in the pattern of emigration rates by age which may indirectly capture period-of-emigration patterns. On the one hand, increasing economic ties between Mexico and the United States might be associated with an increasing propensity of the highly skilled to emigrate. For example, it was thought that the 1994 North American Free Trade Agreement (NAFTA) would boost skilled mobility and it included a special "TN" class of admission for highly skilled workers. Then, too, Mexico's 1994–1995 peso crisis is thought to have disproportionately impacted its middle class and, perhaps, emigration of the better-educated. If this were the case, then today's U.S. resident Mexican born in the 45–54 age group might benchmark a period of emigration of the highly skilled. More prosaically, the dynamics of Mexican demography might be associated with a steadily increasing propensity to emigrate by level of completed education, a pattern that has been observed over time and that is linked to improved educational completion in Mexico (Lowell and Suro, 2002). These effects of economic integration and the improving levels of education might be associated with increasing rates of emigration of the highly skilled from the earliest to the most recent age cohorts.

Figures 6.2, 6.3, and 6.4 show emigration rates for first (1.0) generation adult migrants by level of education for three age cohorts, the eldest being those 45–54 and the youngest, contemporary cohort being 25–34 years of age. There is an increasing rate of emigration over the three age cohorts, as can be seen by contrasting the rates of emigration from the oldest to the youngest cohort. From the oldest to the youngest cohort the average tertiary, post-secondary rate of emigration increases for males from 11.4 percent to 14.4 percent and for females from 13.3 percent to 16.1 percent. At the same time, from the oldest to youngest cohorts, the rate of emigration for the high school educated decreases for males from 24.0 percent to 21.0 percent, and for females from 24.9 percent to 15.6 percent. Thus, while the rates of emigration are greatest among adults with a secondary education, those rates appear to have been declining while rates of emigration among the tertiary educated have been increasing. Over these three age cohorts, the average emigration rate for adults with less than a secondary education has been fairly

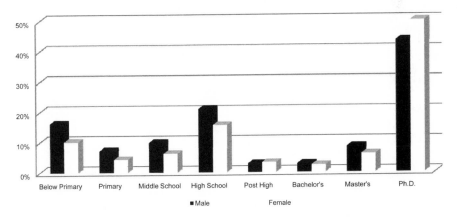

Figures 6.2.   Emigration Rates by Level of Completed Education, 2009–2010 (Mexican Born Adult Population 25–34)

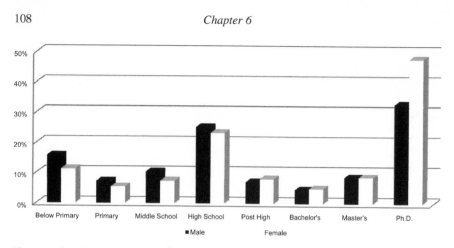

Figures 6.3. Emigration Rates by Level of Completed Education, 2009–2010 (Mexican Born Adult Population 35–44)

unchanged at 11.1 percent of males and roughly 7.0 percent of females. On balance, therefore, the trend has been a tempering of Mexico's uniquely high rate of emigration for adults with secondary education, and an increasing rate of emigration of the most highly tertiary-educated.

Within broad educational groupings, the pattern across cohorts is the same—i.e., there is no marked difference for any given age cohort by detailed level of education from that seen for the average for all age cohorts. The most distinctive or greatest rates of emigration are for adults with doctorate degrees. At the high school level, more males emigrate than females. Then the next highest rate of emigration is for doctorate degree holders, where females

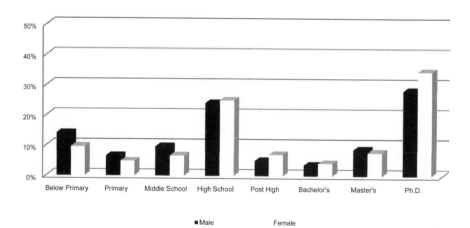

Figures 6.4. Emigration Rates by Level of Completed Education, 2009–2010. (Mexican Born Adult Population 45–54)

emigrate at higher rates than males with a doctorate degree. These reversed gender differentials in the propensity to emigrate among masters as opposed to doctorate degree holders remain mostly unchanged over the three age cohorts.

LABOR FORCE OUTCOMES IN MEXICO AND THE UNITED STATES

It is possible that highly educated women are migrating to the United States to seek better job opportunities than they can achieve in Mexico. If women's motive to migrate to the United States is largely motivated by a desire to improve their working conditions, then that should show up in improved female outcomes in the United States compared to Mexico. We explore that possibility by comparing Mexican-born women's participation in the labor market, and their work earnings, *relative* to men in Mexico and in the United States. This is an exploratory analysis, and we examine relative outcomes for prime-age workers.

Table 6.3 shows the labor force participation rates of men and women resident in Mexico and participation rates for the Mexican born in the United States. Mexican-born women's labor force participation rates are lower than most native-born women in the United States, which conforms to the casual observation that Mexican culture emphasizes women's role as homemakers. Otherwise, the tendency in either country is for women's labor force participation to increase as their completed education increases, even though there is

Table 6.3. Labor Force Participation of Mexican-Born Adults (25–54) by Gender and Education Level (Percent)

	Male			Female		
		In the United States			In the United States	
Completed Education	In Mexico	Gen 1.0	Gen 1.5	In Mexico	Gen 1.0	Gen 1.5
Below Primary	89.0	91.6	89.8	38.8	50.6	52.9
Primary	93.8	94.1	93.7	44.4	53.0	54.3
Middle School	95.5	93.4	90.7	53.7	53.1	58.3
High School	96.2	94.4	92.3	58.7	56.6	67.6
Post High	88.0	94.2	92.4	67.4	63.5	79.5
Bachelor's	96.3	94.4	96.2	78.2	60.4	84.1
Master's	97.7	91.9	98.3	87.3	72.1	90.2
Ph.D.	98.4	92.2	93.8	96.5	59.5	84.2
Total	94.1	93.4	91.7	53.2	54.8	64.5

Source: United States: American Community Survey, 2007–2009; Mexico: National Survey of Employment and Occupation, 2010

little change for male participation by their level of education. Yet, there are some markedly different patterns for women in Mexico compared with the United States. For women with a high school education or less, the rate of labor force participation in Mexico is less than in the United States (48.9 percent versus 56.3 percent). But for women with tertiary education, on average, the rate of labor force participation is greater in Mexico than in the United States (82.4 percent versus 73.1 percent). This shows that highly educated women are, in fact, less likely to work in the United States than they are Mexico.

We also want to know women's rate of labor force participation relative to men in order to explore whether or not education leads to different patterns of female participation. Figure 6.5 shows female labor force participation rates as a percent of males in Mexico and in the United States (the ratio of female-to-male participation rates). Two distinctive patterns stand out. The 1.5 generation of women in the United States show a participation rate relative to men that increases in a more or less linear fashion with increasing education. The 1.5 generation has rates of participation that are much lower than men's through high school, but which improve markedly with increasing levels of post–high school education. Women close the participation gap with men as they gain more education.

The relative participation rates of the first (1.0) generation women, however, show a distinctive pattern in Mexico that is mirrored in the United States. Women's labor force participation increases relative to men's participation for adults with primary, secondary, and some post-secondary education. But then women's participation declines relative to men's participation for adults with a bachelor education, only to increase sharply relative to men

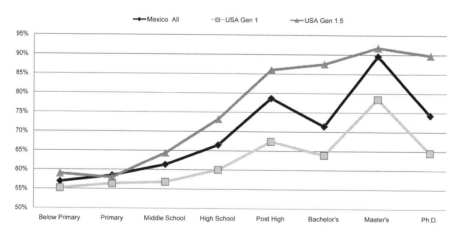

Figures 6.5. Female Labor Force Participation Rate as Percent of Male (25–54) by Education Level

for adults with a master's degree and then decrease for adults with a doctorate degree. This pattern holds, inexplicably, for women in Mexico and for the 1.0 generation Mexican-born women resident in the United States. What is more, generation 1.0 women in the United States actually have lower levels of labor force participation relative to men than do women residing in Mexico.

Next, Figure 6.6 shows women's average hourly earnings relative to men's for full-time, prime-age workers. Women who work full-time earn less than men in both nations. In Mexico, women average 86.5 percent of men's hourly wage. In the United States, first 1.0 generation women earn 80.2 percent of 1.0 generation men's hourly wage, and first 1.5 generation women earn 86.5 percent of that paid to Mexican-born 1.5 generation men. Otherwise, there is little wage premium for women relative to men in Mexico or among the 1.0 generation in the United States. The 1.5 generation females, on the other hand, earn more relative to men at higher levels of education. Perhaps the most remarkable pattern in Mexico is the sharp decline in Mexican women's earnings relative to men among doctorate degree holders. Mexican women with doctorates earn about 83.0 percent of male earnings in the United States, but in Mexico women with doctorates earn just 59.2 percent of male earnings.

On the one hand, these outcomes suggest one possible reason that female emigration rates for doctorate degree holders are much higher for women than for men. Even though women with doctorates experience little increase in relative labor force participation by moving to the United States, the women who do work experience markedly improved earnings relative to

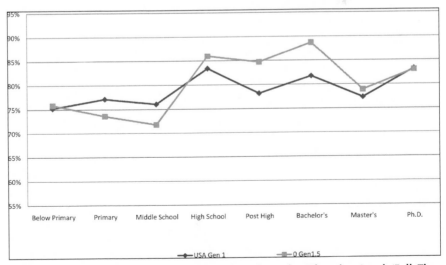

Figures 6.6. Female/Male Hourly Wage of Mexicans by Education Level (Full Time Workers 25–54)

men. On the other hand, there are few other sharp female–male differences in relative earnings by level of education and the overall patterns of labor force participation raise questions for which we have no clear answers. Why do highly educated women in Mexico have higher relative labor force participation rates than Mexican-born 1.0 generation women in the United States? Why do female-to-male labor force participation rates demonstrate an alternating pattern: low among bachelor degree holders, highest among master degree holders, and then declining again among doctorates? Why is this pattern replicated in Mexico and the United States, what factors diffuse these female–male patterns that are distinctively related to level of education?

WHERE AND WHY MEXICANS COMPLETE COLLEGE DEGREES

The foregoing suggests that there are differences between the genders in the reasons they migrate to the United States, but that economic factors may play a strong role in female migration only among the doctorate degree holders. Table 6.4 tabulates a random sample known as the National Survey of College Graduates (NSCG), fielded in 2003, which includes only U.S. residents with a bachelor's degree or better. The table divides the Mexican-born population between those who complete their high school education abroad (1.0 generation) and those who complete high school in the United States (1.5 generation). It further divides the population into the place where they complete their college education. The table omits the trivial percentage of the (1.5) generation who, having already been in the United States as youth, go abroad to complete a college education. The table also shows survey responses to the question about the primary reasons given for migrating to the United States.

The first panel of table 6.4 shows that among the Mexican born who complete high school in the United States and go on to complete a U.S. college degree, the greatest share completes a bachelor degree, 64.9 percent of women, 74.7 percent of men. Women with a U.S. high school degree are more likely to continue on to complete a graduate degree than are the males. This is consistent with the observation that women in the United States achieve somewhat higher degree completion on average than men.

Of Mexicans who complete their high school in Mexico, most also complete their college in Mexico and not in the United States. Some 77.7 percent of Mexican women and 79.7 percent of men with a Mexican high school degree go on to complete their college degrees in Mexico. Among these men

Table 6.4. Place of College Education by Highest Completed Degree and Place of High School Education, Percent by Gender.

	College Mexico		College USA		
	Bachelors	*Graduate*	*Bachelors*	*Graduate*	*Total*
High School Mexico					
Women	62.2	15.5	9.4	12.9	100.0
Men	52.0	27.7	5.6	14.6	10.0
High School, USA					
Women	8.7		64.9	26.4	100.0
Men	1.9		74.4	23.7	100.0

Note: Just 44.1 percent of this sample of Mexican born are U.S. high school graduates. The NSCG sample includes only bachelor degree holders or better; it is a subset of the 1.5 generation. Almost all Mexican-born with a U.S. high school degree go to college in the United States and the sample size is insufficient to estimate their college completion abroad separately.
Source: Authors' tabulations of the 2003 National Survey of College Graduates (NSCG).

as compared with women, however, about twice the percentage complete a graduate degree in Mexico abroad before migrating to the United States (27.7 percent 15.5 percent). This suggests that Mexican male migrants with graduate degrees may be more able than women to use their advanced degree in the United States.[10] Unfortunately, the sample size of the NSCG does not permit us to fully explore whether the graduate degree most favored by males is a master's degree, as implied by the analysis above, or a doctorate degree. At the same time, a small percent of either gender who complete their high school in Mexico report migrating to the United States to complete their college degree (just 13.8 percent, on average). Both genders are somewhat more likely to have migrated and completed a graduate degree, but there is little difference between these men and women in their rate of bachelor versus graduate degree completion.

Table 6.5 shows the primary reason reported for migration in the NSCG by all Mexican-born residents in the United States. For both genders, those who complete their high school in the United States (1.5 generation) report family reasons as the primary motivator of their migration. This makes a good deal of sense, as these 1.5 generation youth migrants mostly come to the United States with their immediate families or to reunify with them. Even male 1.5 generation Mexicans are most likely to report family as their major reason for being in the United States. But for U.S. high school completers (1.0 generation) there is a tendency for men more than women to report education or economics as their primary reason for migrating, especially among those who complete a graduate degree.

Table 6.5.   Primary Reason for Migrating to the United States by Highest Completed Degree and Place of High School Education, Percent by Gender

| | High School Mexico | | | | High School, USA | |
| | College, Mexico | | College, Mexico | | College, USA | |
Reason by Gender	Bachelors	Graduate	Bachelors	Graduate	Bachelors	Graduate
Women						
Family	67.2	47.4	37.5	33.3	77.1	72.3
Education	14.8	15.8	37.5	44.4	12.9	12.8
Economics	8.2	21.1	12.5	7.4	4.3	14.9
Professional	1.6	5.3	0.0	14.8	0.0	0.0
Other	8.2	10.5	12.5	0.0	5.7	0.0
Total	100.0	100.0	100.0	100.0	100.0	100.0
Men						
Family	29.1	9.1	28.6	20.4	61.3	51.5
Education	13.9	22.7	42.9	59.2	16.3	21.2
Economics	48.1	40.9	28.6	12.2	17.5	24.2
Professional	2.5	20.5	0.0	8.2	0.0	0.0
Other	6.3	6.8	0.0	0.0	5.0	3.0
Total	100.0	100.0	100.0	100.0	100.0	100.0

Note: Professional reasons include better scientific opportunities.
Source: Authors' tabulations of the 2003 National Survey of College Graduates.

There are sharper gender differences for Mexican migrants who complete their high school in Mexico, with differences between those with a bachelor's compared with a graduate degree. A relatively small percentage of either gender reports education as their primary motivation to migrate. Women are more motivated by family reasons than are men, while men tend to report economic motivations for their migration. Women migrants who complete a bachelor degree in Mexico are more than twice as likely as men to report family reasons for migrating (67.2 percent versus 29.1 percent). These women are one-fifth as likely as men to report economics as their primary motivator. A yet greater difference occurs among Mexicans who complete their graduate degree in Mexico. Women with graduate degrees from a Mexican institution are more than five times as likely as men to report family reasons for migrating (47.4 percent versus 9.1 percent), while women with graduate degrees are half as likely as men to report economic motivations. In other words, at the highest level of degree completion, the distinction between family and economic motivations are greatest. Women with graduate degrees appear to be migrating primarily for family reasons, and to a far lesser degree for educational or economic reasons than are men.

CONCLUSION

This chapter documents a particular pattern of the feminization of international migration for Mexico-to-U.S. migration, a pattern worth examining in its own right. Little has been known about gender differences in international mobility until fairly recently, and there have been only a handful of efforts that focus on Mexican migration. A growing and fairly new research literature has generated initial international measures of female and male emigration by level of education. However, those data, for pragmatic reasons, divide education into primary, secondary, and tertiary levels, obscuring possible differences by more detailed levels of schooling. Our research uses nationally representative Mexican and U.S. data to make those detailed comparisons. We also contribute to the small literature that includes a focus on the little recognized phenomenon of skilled Mexican migration (Cruz-Piñeiro and Ruiz-Ochoa, 2010; Lozano and Gandini, 2010).

We affirm the fact that Mexico-to-U.S. migration is mostly dominated by men, but that a pattern of feminization occurs among the highly educated. We revisit out earlier research in this chapter with new information and updated data (Lowell, Pederzini and Passel, 2008). We confirm some of our 2000 findings for 2010: namely, that a greater share of males with a secondary education or less is engaged in Mexico-to-U.S. migration than are women. Indeed, the rate of male emigration is so substantial that the sex ratio of males to females residing in Mexico is well below 1. Male emigration has substantially depleted the number of young males particularly among the lesser-educated Mexican population. Mexico's high school–educated population shows the highest rate of emigration among Mexicans, in contrast to migration from most all other nations. Over the past three decades, and for three cohorts of Mexican migrants, however, we find a tempering of Mexico's uniquely high rate of emigration for adults with secondary education and an increasing rate of emigration at the highest levels of tertiary education.

Of the various patterns within the tertiary level, three stand out. First, women have higher emigration rates than men on average among the tertiary-educated, but this is primarily due to the substantially higher emigration rate of female doctorate holders. Second, whereas our earlier research found that *all* (1.0 and 1.5 generation) Mexican-born women had higher rates of emigration at the differing tertiary levels, we find that after subtracting the 1.5 generation only female doctorates are more likely to emigrate than males. By subtracting the 1.5 generation, we reduce the emigration rates for *all* Mexican emigrants by a little more than one-third. Third, there is no linear increase of the 1.0 generation woman's propensity to emigrate compared with a man's as their education increases, but rather there are male–female differences that are specific and alternating between successive degrees. Mexican-born 1.0 female adult migrants compared with men are less likely to emigrate for individuals with "some college," equally likely for individuals with a bachelor's degree, much less likely for individuals with a master's degree, and much more likely to emigrate for individuals with a doctorate degree. We do not know what forces are generating these alternating patterns at successive levels of tertiary education.

Next we examine some possible motivators for female migration by looking at gender differentials in Mexican versus U.S. labor market outcomes to see if there are systematic advantages for highly educated women to emigrate. We find that there is not a simple storyline. One might expect that with increasing education women would be more likely to participate in the labor market and to close the wage gap with males. This simple observation holds only for 1.5 youth migrants who are educated and socialized in the United States; there is a linear improvement of female labor market outcomes with education. But for Mexican-born 1.0 generation there is no simple linear story of improved labor market outcomes with increasing education. The 1.0 generation female emigrants in the United States not only have lower participation rates than the 1.5 generation, but also than women in Mexico. Within the tertiary level there is a pattern that is specific and alternating between successive degrees. Compared with men, 1.0 generation women have low participation rates at the bachelor's level, high participation rates relative to men with masters, and lower participation rates relative to men with doctorates. Surprisingly, this alternating pattern is the mirror of the same female–male pattern of labor force participation observed in Mexico.

There are many Mexican-American "paradoxes," but perhaps most relevant is that Mexican-American women have higher fertility than women resident in Mexico (Frank and Heuveline, 2005). While the fertility paradox has not been fully solved, there appears to be a parallel in the labor force behavior of Mexican emigrants. Most of the 1.0 generation adult emigrants, nearly 80 percent, completed their tertiary education in Mexico. They are socialized in Mexican society and its educational system and, apparently, they carry those values and household strategies with them into the United States. Thus, their household's improved earning power enables them to retain fundamental Mexican values—female emigrants are more likely than Mexicans in Mexico to be homemakers than workers. At least this explanation appears consonant for the female participation ratios relative to men for bachelor and doctorate degree holder. For adults with a master's degree the situation appears different, women close the participation gap with men with master's degrees. It may be that master's degrees, being more professionally and technically oriented, help explain why women who achieve a master's degree work at relatively high rates.

The very high female versus male rate of emigration among women with doctorate degrees may have something to do with the substantial gain in relative earnings they experience by moving from Mexico to the United States. Whereas women doctorates in Mexico earn just 59 percent of the earnings of men, in the United States the 1.0 generation women earn 83 percent as much as their Mexican-American male doctorate counterparts. The female earnings gap in Mexico is actually greatest among doctorates as compared to all other educational groups. So while in the United States the 1.0 generation female migrants are rather unlikely to work relative to males, there is a significant earnings incentive for the migration of female doctorates who do work. We interpret these findings to suggest that the Mexican earnings gap for Ph.D. women partly explains the high rate of women's Ph.D. emigration, but only partly.

In order to get a better understanding of the reasons why Mexican women migrate, we examined data for 2003 from a U.S. sample of adults with a bachelor's degree or better. The survey asked migrants their reason for moving to the United States. Those data show that women are several times more likely than men to report that family was the primary reason they chose to migrate. Men, on the other hand, were substantially more likely than women to report economic motivations. Women migrants with a graduate degree were less likely than women with a bachelor's degree to report family as a migrant motivator; and more likely to report economic reasons for their migration. While these findings are consistent with the notion that women invest in higher education with some interest in pursuing better job opportunities, their migration remains primarily motivated by family reasons. At the same time, these findings are consistent with the likelihood that assortative mating is contributing to the gender differentials that we observe in migration, as well as research findings that education shapes the marriage markets and choices of highly educated Mexican women (Chiswick and Houseworth, 2010; Kelly and Dalmia, 2010; Attanasio and Kaufmanny, 2010; Lafortune, 2010). We are unable to substantiate these possibilities in this research, but these findings may provide some impetus to better understand how marriage markets interact with migration decisions to shape the unique pattern of male–female migration differentials among highly educated Mexicans that we observe.

NOTES

1. The decennial U.S. census prior to 2010 included an enumeration of all households that were asked a few basic questions ("short form") followed by a large random sample with a detailed survey released as public microdata form (the "long form"). However, during the last decade the annual American Community Survey has replaced the former decennial census samples.

2. While it may be correct to note that self-reports of year of arrival may be biased, typically assumed to underreport the earliest or initial age of arrival, the results appear to be robust in terms of the systematic differences in the 1.0 and 1.5 generation as estimated for our purposes here.

3. Migrants tend to have their children once in the United States. This generalization holds regardless of legal status and, in part, is the context for one of the Mexican "paradoxes" in which Mexican-born women have higher fertility rates in the United States than those who remain in Mexico.

4. Mexico has a high share of its population with a bachelor's degree, but a comparatively small share with any graduate degree. Yet Mexico's bachelor population appears to do fairly well by remaining in Mexico as compared with its graduate population, which finds better opportunities in the United States. This may be due in part to the fact that the type of knowledge and skills taught in B.A. and B.S. programs in Mexico, generally much more specific than in the United States, are not valued in the U.S. labor market. Extremely well educated migrants face the prospect of reapplying for professional certification if they wish to practice their profession in a high GDP country. Comparing tertiary educated migrants in the United States, Lozano and Gandini (2010) find that those with a bachelor's degree find themselves in a disadvantaged position—i.e., the proportion of those who get a job below their educational level is larger than in higher educational levels. What is more, bachelor graduates can earn higher relative salaries in Mexico than in the United States which also reduces their incentive to emigrate. Interestingly enough, Gallup Polls conducted in Latin America in 2005 and 2006 also suggest a curvilinear pattern in the relationship between education and the desire to migrate: relative to people with a primary education or less, Latin Americans with a high school education are more likely to express a desire to migrate. Those who possess a college degree or higher are less likely to report a desire to migrate compared with high school graduates, and roughly as likely as those with very little education to report a desire to migrate (Torres and Pelham, 2008).

5. Young males are more likely to migrate for working reasons while young women who migrate with their families are more likely to be enrolled in school.

6. Simply put, the behavior of youth migrants cannot be attributed to the range of factors in which we are interested. The one caveat which is, perhaps, somewhat unique to Mexico is the migration of Mexican youth for employment, which occurs particularly among lesser-educated males.

7. In terms of Mexican investment in the education of migrants, the "waste" is higher for adult migrants who have completed their education in Mexico.

8. There is an apparent higher rate of emigration among *all* females among master degree holders, but the removal of the youth (1.5) migrants from that calculation reveals that adult-emigrant males with master's degrees are slightly more likely than females to emigrate. This occurs because 1.5 generation women in the United States are more likely than males to complete a master's degree.

9. Again, there is no "linear" pattern by level of education. However, simple correlations show a strong inverse association between male–female sex ratios in Mexico and male rates of emigration by level of education: high rates of male emigration are associated with lowered Mexican sex ratios. Conversely, simple correlations show a strong positive association between male–female sex ratios in the United States and male rates of emigration: high rates of male emigration are associated with higher U.S. sex ratios.

10. To some extent, women's high relative rate of emigration to the United States would also decrease the share of women with graduate degrees in Mexico.

Chapter 7

Mexicans in and out of the United States

Facts on Job Search and International Migration

Alfredo Cuecuecha and Silvio Rendon

In this chapter we contend that migration patterns between Mexico and the United States are not explained merely by wage differentials between the two countries, but also by job turnover, in particular, job-to-job transitions. To document this we provide detailed descriptive evidence coming from census data, employment surveys, and panel data for the two countries. We show that job-to-job transitions match the patterns of migration, both in stocks and flows, from Mexico to the United States. We also show that the U.S.–Mexico wage differential does not match these patterns equally well, even when the U.S.–Mexico wage differential is adjusted by differences in employment probabilities. We interpret this result as indicating that a more dynamic labor market in Mexico could potentially reduce migration rates from Mexico to the United States.[1]

International migration, particularly between neighboring countries such as Mexico and the United States, goes both ways. The flows going in and out of the United States reveal a very intensive and dynamic relation between the two countries. In 2000, around 10 percent of the Mexican labor force was in the United States, with migration rates of 11.68 percent, according to Chiquiar and Hanson (2005), and return migration rates of 42.6 percent (Jasso and Rosenzweig, 1982) and 66 percent (Reyes, 1997). These flows reveal that Mexican migrants leave Mexico to seek better economic perspectives in the richer neighbor, but they do so with the prospect of returning to their country of origin where they prefer to live.

The explanation for this pattern of migration cannot rely exclusively on the obvious large international wage differentials between the two countries, for these differentials only generate one-directional migration (Sjaastad, 1962). The phenomenon of return migration requires including other mechanisms in the explanation, such as incomplete information, heterogeneity in preferences for origin, and higher returns to capital or human capital in origin countries.[2] However, a common feature of these mechanisms is that migrants emigrate and then return to their origin countries after achieving a goal. These migrants are called "target savers" (Massey et al., 1987) and these mechanisms are called life cycle explanations (Yang, 2006). None of them, however, bases their analyses on the comparison of the origin and destination labor markets.

Comparative studies of Mexico and the United States focus on regulations and labor market flexibility. The Mexican labor market is known to be less flexible than other OECD and industrial countries (Calderón-Madrid, 2000; Heckman and Pages-Sierra, 2000). However, Mexico has a relatively flexible labor market in terms of job turnover, more so than other Latin-American economies (Maloney, 1997; Frenkel and Ross, 2004). Recent studies mostly focus their attention on the social networks formed by migrants (Piore, 1979; Massey et al., 1987; Massey et al., 1993; Faist, 2000; Delechat, 2001; Munshi, 2003; Massey and Aysa, 2005; Garip, 2008).

This chapter focuses on a comparison of job turnover between Mexico and the United States, in particular in exit from unemployment, job loss and job-to-job transitions.[3] We find that patterns of exit from unemployment and job loss are not substantially different between the two countries. Moreover, these two job transitions tend to converge over age between the two countries, and even to be better in Mexico than in the United States. However, job-to-job transitions are substantially higher in the United States than in Mexico, and this difference is persistent, unlike the other job transitions. This important difference between the two labor markets, together with large and persistent wage differentials, may be the main source of migration and return migration. We show that trends in job-to-job transition rates are very similar to trends in migration flows from Mexico to the United States, and to return migration flows, from the United States to Mexico. Mexicans seek in the United States the job mobility that they do not find in their country of origin.

The remainder of the chapter is organized as follows. The next section describes the different datasets used, as well as the criteria chosen to select the sample and the moments used in the estimation. Section 3 presents the descriptive analysis of these data. Section 4 compares our results with other studies. Finally, Section 5 summarizes the paper's main conclusions.

DATA

We are using data from five sources: the Mexican Migration Project (MMP 124) data set, the Mexican and the US Censuses of 2000, the first to fourth quarters waves of the Mexican Urban Employment Survey (ENEU-*Encuesta*

Nacional de Empleo Urbano) for 1999, and the January to December waves of the Current Population Survey (CPS) for 1999. For these data sets, we select subsamples from 15- to 45-year-old males, who are not disabled or incarcerated, for whom there is more than one observation, except in the censuses.[4]

The MMP 124 was developed by Princeton University and Universidad de Guadalajara. It surveys 124 communities in twenty-one Mexican states from 1982 to 2008 and is representative of rural Mexico. We use this source for the migration rates and flows of Mexicans going into the US and returning from the US, as well as for the job-to-job transitions. This is the only available source for job-to-job transitions for Mexicans in Mexico and in the US. Our sample from this source contains 9,225 individuals. We use the average of the migration rates of the 124 communities over time, so that we maximize the number of observations by ages that meet all our selection criteria.

Annual wage incomes in PPP dollars come from a 10 percent sample of the 2000 Mexican Census and from a 5 percent sample of Mexicans in the US Census (IPUMS database). After performing the selection by age, gender, incarceration and disability, we end up with approximately 1.7 million observations from the Mexican Census, and with approximately 134 thousand observations from the US Census.

Mexican and American employment surveys are our sources of information on unemployment rates, exit from unemployment, and job loss. For Mexico we select 113 thousand observations from the first to fourth quarter waves of the ENEU of 1999, which is representative of urban Mexico. It is a quarterly rotating panel which contains information on employment transitions and wages. From the observed quarterly transitions we compute the annual transitions, i.e., we calculate the probability that an individual in a given quarter is observed a year later with a different employment status. January to December waves from the CPS 1999 are our corresponding source of information for the US. From this source, also a rotating panel on employment transitions and wages, representative for the US population, we select individuals born in Mexico, and obtain a sample of around 3 thousand individuals. We annualize the monthly employment transitions in a similar way as we proceeded with the Mexican sample. Further details on the sample selection and the choice of data sources are provided in the Appendix.

WAGE DISTRIBUTIONS, JOB TURNOVER, AND MIGRATION

Wage differentials between the United States and Mexico are persistent over the life cycle. They widen over average wages, but are stable over log-wages; dispersion of log-wages is relatively small. Table 7.1 shows wage variables

Table 7.1.   Wages in US Dollars

Country		Mexico				United States		
	Source	Age			Source	Age		
Variable		16–25	26–35	36–45		16–25	26–35	36–45
Annual Wage	Mx. Census	3073	4997	5779	US. Census	9279	18651	21793
Annual Log wage	Mx. Census	7.69	8.11	8.2	US. Census	9.09	9.74	9.87
Standard Deviation	Mx. Census	0.64	0.79	0.89	US. Census	0.92	0.76	0.82

characterizing the wage distributions by country and age bracket, data coming from the Mexican census and the U.S. census.

Average wages start off at similar levels at early ages, but in the United States they go up much faster, so that the wage gap widens with age. This is captured by a long-lasting difference in log-wages, which show a fairly stable difference over age. The standard deviation of log wages initially decreases and the increases slightly with age in the United States, while it increases monotonically in Mexico. Differences in the standard deviation of log-wages are not substantial: in both countries they are around 0.8. The initial high standard deviation of log-wages in the United States may be explained by the relatively few young Mexican migrants. As the migration process occurs the dispersion of wages ends up exhibiting similar trends in the United States and in Mexico.

Table 7.2 shows unemployment variables by country, age bracket and dataset. Unemployment rates are higher Mexico than in the United States for young cohorts but fall faster in Mexico than in the United States, so that for older cohorts they are higher in the United States than in Mexico. Something similar happens with exit from unemployment and job loss: initially they are

Table 7.2.   Employment Transitions. Rates and Flows in %

Country		Mexico				United States		
	Source	Age			Source	Age		
Variable		16–25	26–35	36–45		16–25	26–35	36–45
Unemployment Rate	ENEU	34.85	4.43	3.72	CPS	26.49	6.69	9.82
Job taking	ENEU	60.17	95.04	94.81	CPS	74.7	92.95	85.89
Job loss	ENEU	29.67	3.73	3.31	CPS	22.08	6.42	8.74
Job-to-Job	MMP	10.51	6.57	4.51	MMP	26.73	18.99	14.78

Table 7.3. Migration. Rates and Flows in %

Country	Mexico			United States			
	Source	*Age*		*Source*	*Age*		
Variable		16–25	26-35	36–45		16–25	26–35	36–45
Migration rate stock					MMP	11.2	16.18	14.73
Migration flow from	MMP	3.6	2.95	1.95	MMP	34.53	14.05	10.88

better in the United States than in Mexico, but over time they improve in Mexico and end up overtaking those in the United States. However, average job-to-job transitions decrease and are always higher in the United States than in Mexico. These transitions will prove to be very important in accounting for the migration patterns observed.

Table 7.3 shows that the migration stock is 11 percent among individuals 16 to 25, 16 percent among individuals 26 to 35, and 15 percent among individuals 36 to 45. It is also shown that both migration and return migration flows are decreasing, but the former are, on average, 2.9 percent, while the latter are, on average, 14 percent.

We can now try to link these variables and inquire at a descriptive level, which features of the labor markets are more closely related to the migration patterns observed.

Figure 7.1 shows the U.S.–Mexico differential in job-to-job transitions by age and the migration rate by age, from age 16 to 65. Both series have a similar pattern: they both show an inverted U pattern. They differ in the speed at which they reach their maximum: in the case of the U.S.–Mexico differential in job-to-job transitions the maximum is reached at age 19, while for the migration rate, the maximum occurs at age 29. This relation is more than a simple correlation, since Rendon and Cuecuecha (2009) show that there is a causal relationship between the two series and that the importance of the U.S.–Mexico differential in job-to-job transitions can actually dominate the importance of the U.S.–Mexico wage differential.

Figure 7.2 helps to clarify why the U.S.–Mexico differential in job-to-job transitions dominates the U.S.–Mexico wage differential. The figure shows the U.S.–Mexico log wage differential in 2000 PPP dollars and the migration rate by age. Both series show an inverted U pattern. The speed at which they reach their maximum differs considerably. The U.S.–Mexico wage differential in PPP dollars reaches its maximum at age 60, while the migration rate reaches its maximum at age 29, as mentioned previously. This implies that from age 29 onward an increasing U.S.–Mexico wage differential coexists

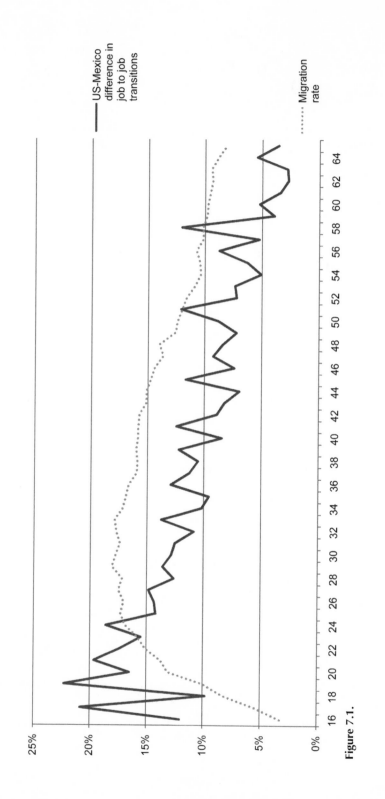

Figure 7.1.

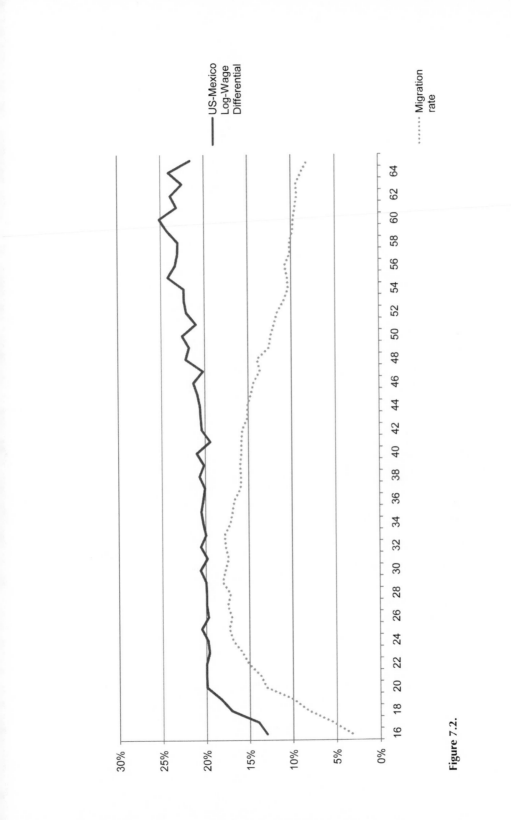

Figure 7.2.

with a decreasing migration rate. This pattern itself would prove that traditional migration theory (Sjaastad, 1962) cannot explain the migration pattern from Mexico to the United States.

Figure 7.3 shows the U.S.–Mexico wage differential adjusted by the employment probabilities. Once we adjust by employment differentials, the expected U.S.–Mexico wage differential follows a pattern that matches better the migration rate pattern. The expected wage differential increases rapidly to reach a maximum at age 19 and reduces up to age 46. The migration rate reaches a maximum by age 29. After age 46, the expected wage differential shows a very volatile pattern. For example, between age 46 and age 65 the expected wage differential reaches its global minimum at age 63 (–30), while it reaches its second highest level of all ages at age 60 (40 percent).

As shown in Figure 7.4, the reason for this dramatic change in the ability of the U.S.–Mexico wage differential to explain the migration rate pattern seems to be the fact that the U.S.–Mexico employment differential is negative for almost all ages, with the notable exception of the ages 18 to 24, when the U.S.–Mexico employment differential is positive.

This dramatic importance of the employment probability led us to explore in more detail how the migration rate is linked to differences between Mexico and the United States in the job search process. We have already shown the importance of the job-to-job transition probability. Figures 7.5 and 7.6 show the relation that exists between the migration rate and two other important job search probabilities, which are the exit from unemployment and job loss. They show that while they have the potential to explain some of the variations observed in the migration rate, they do not seem to match the migration rate as well as the job-to-job transition probability.

Specifically, Figure 7.5 shows the U.S.–Mexico differential in exit from unemployment probabilities, while Figure 7.6 presents the U.S.–Mexico differential in job loss. The U.S.–Mexico differential in exit from unemployment is positive and rises at early ages only to decline consistently from age 22 and up to age 56. From this age on, the U.S.–Mexico differential in exit from unemployment increases. The U.S.–Mexico differential in job loss follows an inverted U shape with a maximum at age 46.

Given that transition probabilities of the job search process measure flows in and out of unemployment and jobs, we decided to show how these transitions in the job search process are related to transitions between Mexico and the United States. Figure 7.7 shows the relation between the U.S.–Mexico job-to-job transition differential and the Mexico–U.S. migration flow. There is a clear relationship between these variables: the differential in U.S.–Mexico job-to-job transitions reaches its maximum at age 18, while the U.S.–Mexico flow reaches its maximum at age 19. Both series experience a decline after that age.

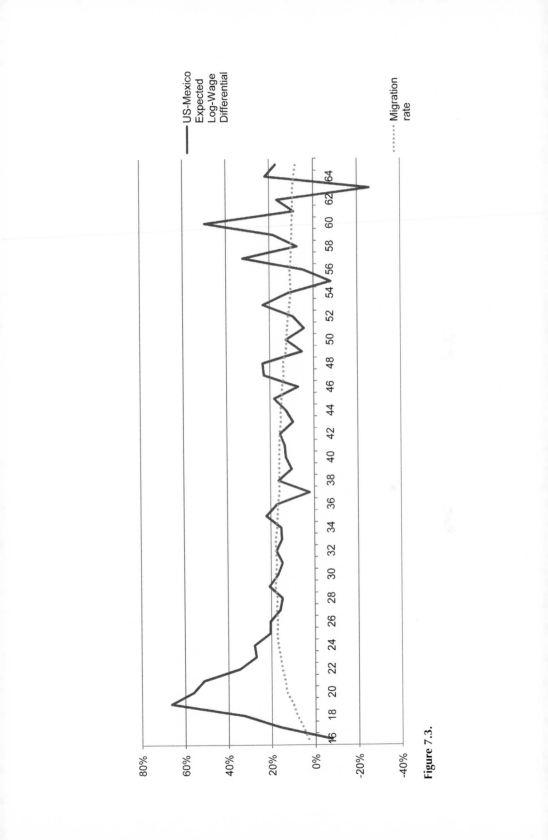

Figure 7.3.

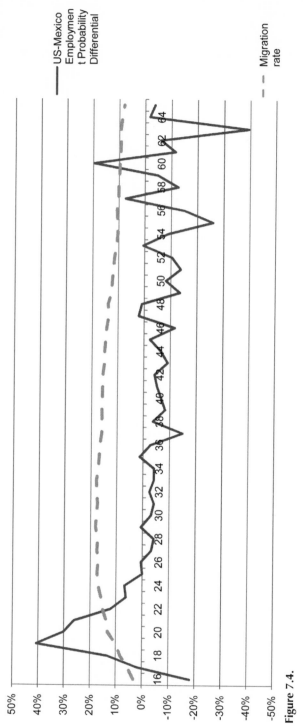

Figure 7.4.

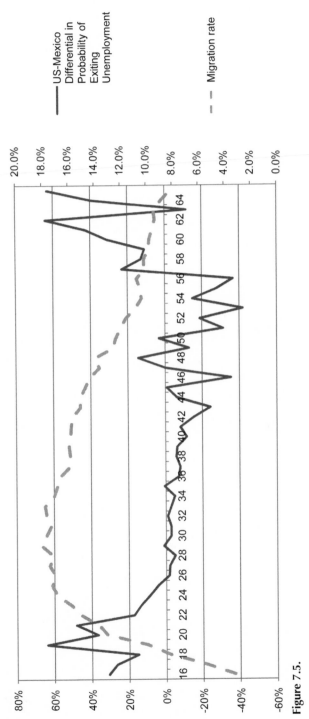

Figure 7.5.

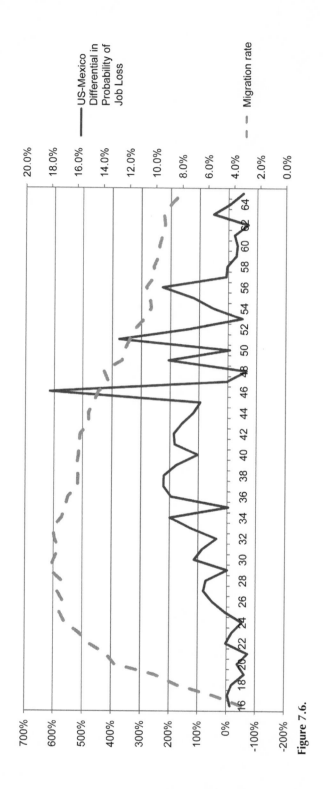

Figure 7.6.

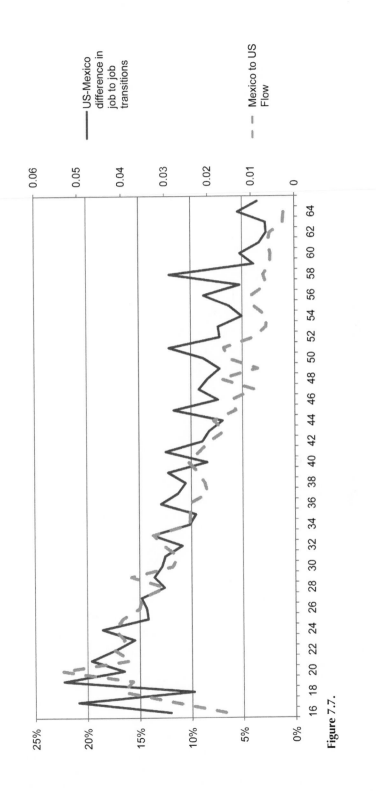

Figure 7.7.

Figure 7.8 shows the relation between the U.S.–Mexico differential in job-to-job transitions and the return flow United States to Mexico. These two flows experience their global maxima at age 19, and the two series show a decline afterward. Consequently, these figures demonstrate that there is a clear relation between the U.S.–Mexico job-to-job transition differential and the migration flow and the return flow, both of which govern the stock of Mexican migrants in the United States.

Figures 7.9 and 7.10 show the relation between the Mexico–U.S. migration flows, the return flow United States to Mexico and the U.S.–Mexico differential in exit from unemployment. The figures show that the U.S.–Mexico differential in exit from unemployment has the variability to explain the U.S.–Mexico migration flow, but that the relationship with this flow is not as clear as the one presented before between the U.S.–Mexico job-to-job transition and the U.S.–Mexico migration flow.

Finally, Figures 7.11 and 7.12 show the relation between the Mexico–U.S. migration flow, the return flow U.S.–Mexico and the U.S.–Mexico differential in job loss. These figures also show that there is variability in the job loss that can potentially explain the U.S.–Mexico return flow. However, it is not such a clear relationship as the one shown between the U.S.–Mexico differential in job-to-job transition and the migration and return flows.

COMPARISON WITH OTHER SOURCES

The numbers from different sources provided in this paper are similar to those for other studies on migration and labor markets in Mexico and the United States. The migration rates reported here are comparable to those of Chiquiar and Hanson (2005:246). These authors show that the migration rate in 2000 for Mexican males 16 to 25 years old was 17.58 percent, above the MMP 124 migration rate of 11 percent. For males 26 to 35 years old, they estimate the migration rate at 15.49, slightly below the MMP 124 migration rate of 16 percent. And for males 36 to 45 years old they estimate a migration rate of 12.21 percent, while the MMP 124 migration rate is 14 percent.

Based on the CPS 1994–2003 March waves, Blau and Kahn (2007) report an unemployment rate for males in the United States of 13 percent, and that 6 percent of Mexican males in the United States are out of the labor force. To simplify our analysis, we include as unemployed individuals those outside the labor force, and calculated a non-employment rate of 19 percent. Taking into account the different definitions, our numbers are similar to those reported in the literature.

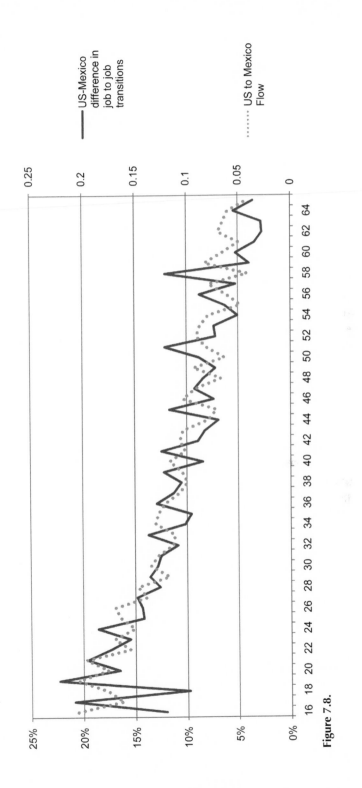

Figure 7.8.

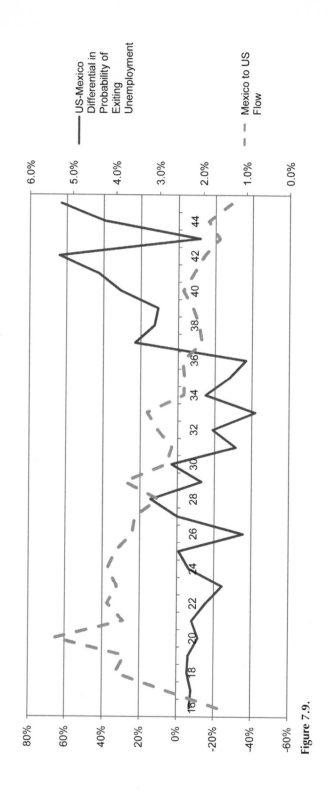

Figure 7.9.

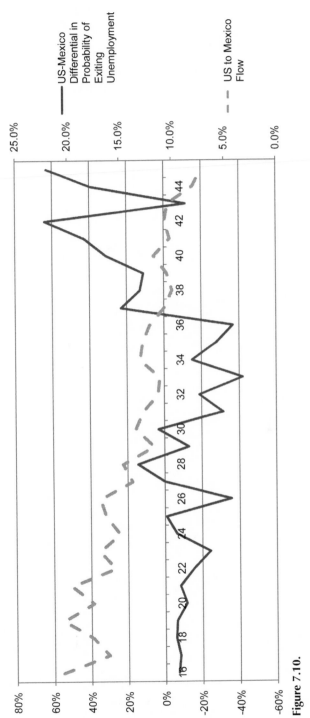

Figure 7.10.

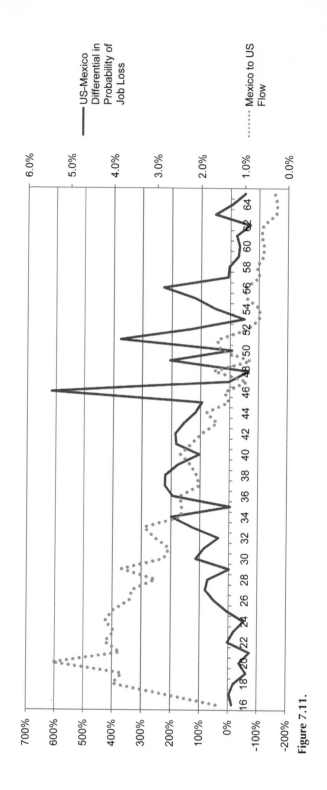

Figure 7.11.

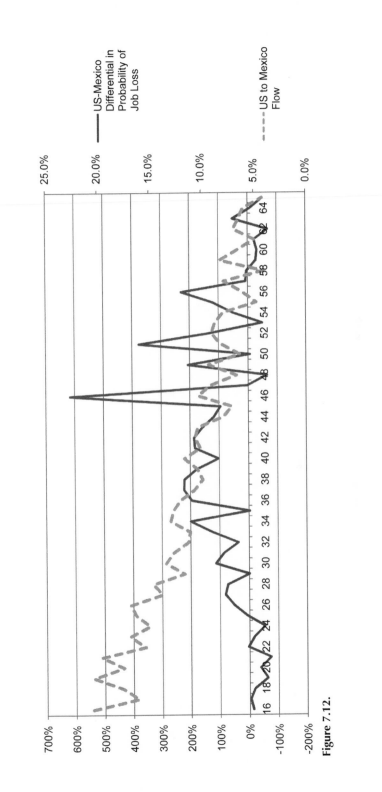

Figure 7.12.

Taking into account differences in sample and frequencies, our estimations of probabilities of exit from unemployment and of job loss are comparable to those shown by Calderón-Madrid (2000). His quarterly rates imply an annual job loss rate of 30.66 percent and an annual exit from unemployment of 34.59 percent. Although our reported job loss is smaller and our exit from unemployment is higher, if we use his sample selection rules, we obtain similar figures.

Our estimated wages are somewhat higher than the numbers of Card and Lewis (2007). We obtain a mean hourly wage for Mexicans in the 2000 U.S. census of $12.89 per hour for males 16 to 45 years old. Card and Lewis report an average annual wage income of $16,816 for that year, perhaps because through including individuals who work less than full time shifts, so that if individuals worked fifty-two weeks and forty hours per week, that annual wage income is equivalent to approximately $8.08 per hour. We leave an in-depth analysis of this aspect for future research.

CONCLUSION

In this paper we provide descriptive evidence of the importance of job-to-job transitions in explaining migration patterns from Mexico to the United States, both stocks and migration flows. We also document that neither stocks nor migration flows could be explained only by the U.S.–Mexico wage differential.

We also show that other moments of the job search process do not have the same importance as job-to-job transitions in explaining the migration of Mexicans to the United States. These results imply that Mexicans migrate to the United States not only because wages are higher in the United States than in Mexico, but also because Mexicans are looking for a job reallocation process that they cannot find in Mexico.

APPENDIX TO CHAPTER 7

Sample Selection and Construction of Variables

We obtain from the Mexican Migration Project 124 the data for the job search history in the United States and Mexico, as well as the data for the migration history of individuals. We use the longitudinal data files, from which we use 9,225 individuals that comply with all our sample selection rules: males between 15 and 45 years old who are not disabled or incarcerated (see Table 7.4 for details). The MMP files are obtained with retrospective questions that

Table 7.4. Sample Selection (Individuals)

	MMP	Mx. Census	US Census	ENEU	CPS
All	17,764	4,938,130	234,159	234,423	7,477
15 to 45	9,245	2,263,840	172,778	164,286	5,603
Excluding disabled	9,225	1,693,627	133,977	157,463	5,570
Individuals with 2+ periods	9,225	-	-	112,649	3,402

provide the individuals' labor and migration history. The individuals included in the survey are obtained through a random sample of individuals in the communities that are included in each wave of the survey. The surveys are conducted during the winter season when many migrants return home for the holy days. Individuals that are not found in the community are then contacted in the United States during the next summer season. This implies that the MMP only loses individuals in cases where the entire household has left the community. The major disadvantage of using the MMP 124 files is that we can face recall bias and that over time changes in the sample come not only from the pass of time but also for the change in communities sampled. Our measurement of job-to-job transition also fails to detect short unemployment spells, since the questionnaire asks about annual changes in job status.

We obtain annual wages from the 2000 Mexican census (the 10 percent sample publicly available) and the 2000 U.S. census (the 5 percent sample from the IPUMS database). In both cases we select only males who are not disabled, who are not incarcerated, and who are between 15 and 45 years old. In the case of the Mexican data, we transform the data in pesos to 2000 PPP dollars. In the case of the U.S. census, we only include individuals who claim to have been born in Mexico. (See Table 7.4 for details on the number of observations.)

The information for the unemployment and the dynamic flows in and out of unemployment comes from the ENEU 1999 (first- quarter to fourth-quarter waves). We use the same sample selection criteria mentioned above.[5] (See Table 7.4 for details.) Individuals are defined as employed if they claim to have done paid work for at least one hour during the week prior to the survey. We considered as employed individuals that claim to be temporarily ill or on vacation. Every other individual is considered unemployed, including those out of the labor force. Unemployment is measured using the average rate of unemployment by age. Exit from unemployment is obtained measuring the number of individuals leaving unemployment quarter to quarter by age. We then obtained the weighted average for the year. We follow the same procedure to obtain the number of individuals that lost their job. Finally we use this information to calculate the annual transition probabilities. The main

Table 7.5. Balance of the Panels (Individuals)

	Data set		
Variable	MMP	ENEU	CPS
Periodicity	Annual	Quarterly	Monthly
N	9225	112,649	3,402
Periods	%	%	%
2	0	25.88	23.07
3	0	26.68	20.43
4	0.02	47.44	54.85
5+	99.98	—	1.65

disadvantage of using this data set is that it is only representative of urban Mexico. We use it, however, because it provides us with quarter to quarter individual information on the employment transitions.

Our final source of information is the CPS 1999 January to December waves. They are representative of the U.S. population. The CPS is a rotating panel that provides the information on unemployment and employment transitions. We apply the same sample selection criteria mentioned for other sources (see Table 7.4 for details). In the case of CPS, individuals are considered employed if they claim to have done paid work in the week prior to the census. We also considered as employed those individuals who claim to be temporarily ill or on vacation. We obtain the average rate of unemployment for the entire sample by age. The exit from unemployment is measured with the number of individuals that left unemployment from one month to another, while the job loss is measured with the number of individuals that lost their jobs from one month to another. With this information we obtained the annual transition rates. The major disadvantage of the CPS is that it potentially underestimates illegal Mexican migrants.

Table 7.5 provides details on the number of individuals that appear on average in the different panels that are used in the paper. ENEU and CPS show the periodicity to be expected in rotating panels, while in the MMP 124 most observations are carried out for more than five years.

CHOICE OF SOURCES

This article could have been written with all information from the MMP 124 data set. However, a comparison between different sources shows that there are important variations between the MMP 124 and other data sets. Table 7.6 illustrates this.

Table 7.6. Descriptive Statistics. Choice of Sources

Country		Mexico				United States		
	Source		Age		Source		Age	
Variable		16–25	26–35	36–45		16–25	26–35	36–45
Annual Log wage (dollars)	Census	7.69	8.11	8.20	Census	9.09	9.74	9.87
Standard Deviation	Census	0.64	0.79	0.89	Census	0.92	0.76	0.82
Annual Log wage (dollars)	ENEU	9.04	9.51	9.55	CPS	9.46	9.86	9.96
Standard Deviation	ENEU	0.75	0.75	0.95	CPS	0.52	0.48	0.47
Annual Log wage (dollars)	MMP	6.63	7.18	7.24	MMP	10.01	9.90	9.91
Standard Deviation	MMP	3.05	2.82	2.76	MMP	0.38	0.38	0.43
Unemployment Rate (%)	ENEU	34.85	4.43	3.72	CPS	26.49	6.69	9.82
Exit from Unemployment (%)	ENEU	60.17	95.04	94.81	CPS	74.70	92.95	85.89
Job Loss (%)	ENEU	29.67	3.73	3.31	CPS	22.08	6.42	8.74
Unemployment Rate (%)	MMP	1.63	0.65	1.11	MMP	1.12	0.36	0.62
Exit from Unemployment (%)	MMP	19.83	18.28	7.58	MMP	27.45	36.06	23.16
Job Loss (%)	MMP	0.20	0.10	0.15	MMP	0.13	0.07	0.20

The MMP 124 wage data shows a pattern with age which is not found either in the Census data or wage data from ENEU or CPS. We select the census data since the ENEU wage data is only representative of urban Mexico.

The MMP 124 unemployment and employment transition data also shows patterns not observed in the ENEU or CPS data. Since both CPS and ENEU are specialized in measuring employment levels and employment transitions, we decided to use them instead of the MMP 124 employment data.

Chapter 7

NOTES

1. In Rendon and Cuecuecha (2009) we propose and estimate a dynamic model of migration and job search that more formally accounts for the observed migration patterns. This model gave us the theoretical guidance to organize the descriptive statistical and the issues analyzed in the present paper.

2. There is a vast literature about these mechanisms. See Cuecuecha (2008) for a detailed description of these mechanisms and extensive explanations of the migration process of Mexicans in the United States.

3. There is a body of literature that has studied the relation between the level of unemployment and migration (Harris and Todaro, 1970, Bencivenga and Smith, 1997). In this paper we focus in the relation between migration and the flows going in and out of unemployment, as well as the flows between different jobs.

4. We report how we construct the final sample and the impact of each of these selection criteria, in the appendix.

5. We also exclude individuals that left the rotating panel because they change address and the survey did not follow them. (i.e., "hogares mudados" in the ENEU database).

Chapter 8

The Vulnerability of Mexican Temporary Workers in the United States with H-2 Visas

Paz Trigueros-Legarreta

The participation of Mexican workers in the H-2 visa program has its origins in the *Immigration Reform and Control Act* of 1986 (IRCA), which widened the scope of these visas created ex-profeso for Caribbean workers in the 1940s and converted into H-2 visas under the so-called *McCarren Act* of 1952, for Caribbean workers.[1]

The law of 1952 also created H-1 visas in order to attract temporary qualified workers during periods of labor shortage. The H-1 program would be oriented toward specialized workers, and the H-2 program toward those who were unqualified. At this time, it was not at all clear what was meant by "specialized," for which reason a very wide range of professions were included under this category of visa.

The IRCA inaugurated the strategy of greater reliance on the importation of temporary workers, with the aim of satisfying the new needs of employers,[2] but avoiding the settling of such workers permanently in the country.[3]

At the beginning of the 1990s there was a turnabout on temporary hiring. The challenges of the scientific and information revolutions and the transformations in production processes imposed the need to increase the local offer of highly qualified workers through the importation of foreigners with extraordinary skills. On the one hand, priorities in migration policy were modified, increasing the number applicants selected for their job skills from 54,000 to 140,000 per year, which would be shared out through a system of preferences based on qualification levels (Alarcón, 2000). And on the other hand, the system of temporary visas was reformed.

It is for this reason, that although at present there are fourteen categories of visas for "non-immigrant workers,"[4] only two (H-2A and H-2B) are assigned to those with few qualifications (see Table 8.1).

Table 8.1. Classes of Admission for Non-Migrant Workers in the United States

H-1A	Temporary program for professional nurses (1990–1995)
H-1B	Temporary workers with "specialty occupation"
H-1C	Registered nurses participating in the Nursing Relief for Disadvantaged Areas Act of 1999
H-2A	Agricultural workers, does not require qualifications
H-2B	Non-agricultural workers, does not require qualifications
H-3	Workers who enter the United States to receive some sort of training.
O-1	For workers with extraordinary ability/achievement in the sciences, arts, education, business, or athletes.
O-2	Workers' assistants O-1
P-1, P-2 and P-3	For internationally recognized athletes, entertainers and artists, under reciprocal exchange programs or unique programs.
Q-1	For participants in international cultural exchange programs.
R-1	Workers in religious occupations
TC and TN	TC visa for professional workers from 1989–1993 as part of the Free Trade Agreement between the US and Canada, and, since then, the "TN" visa as a result of the signing of NAFTA between Canada, the US and Mexico.
Other visas which in practice are used to import temporary workers	
J-1	Exchange visitors
L-1	Intra-company transferees

Source: Grieco, 2006, Appendix A.

In general there are strong objections to temporary work visas on the part of the U.S. population, above all among labor organizations, professional groups, unions, and non-governmental organizations. They argue that these visas lead to the importation of workers who accept inferior conditions to those historically achieved by local workers and cause numerous violations of their labor rights. The criticisms of the H-2 visas are more serious, as it is claimed that the presence of this type of workers impedes the development of technologies capable of substituting unskilled workers. On the other hand, the businesses that require these workers lobby continually not only for these visas to be maintained, but also for the numbers to be substantially increased.

The aim of this article is to analyze the evolution the H-2 visas have undergone, the limitations imposed in the legislation and the effects when they are implemented, specially the vulnerability to which the workers who enter on them are exposed.

H-2 VISAS: EVOLUTION AND WORKING CONDITIONS

Evolution

The turnabout on immigration policies described above had an important effect on ways of hiring foreigners in the United States. If temporary hiring had been prohibited since the Immigration Law of 1885, the new regulations changed this trend. The country was no longer prepared to open its arms to foreigners in general as it had been since the nineteenth century. Now it became much more selective. This is why, to fill the gaps in the demand for workers, it increasingly resorted to temporary workers, which explains why non-immigrant worker visas have increased much more rapidly, despite the new labor priorities.

Before beginning the analysis of the behavior of these visas, I should mention that it is very difficult to know exactly how many of them there are, in light of the complexity of the way they operate. On the one hand, the Department of Labor (DOL) certifies that the demand fulfills the legal requirements and gives the employer permission to apply to the State Department, which issues visas through a consulate. Then, the Citizenship and Immigration Services Office (USCIS) of the DHS[5] registers the number of admissions across the different border crossing points and migration offices. However, as the DOL permits a worker to do two or more certified activities on one visa, the number of certifications is greater than the number of visas. On the other hand, the State Department only issues visas to workers who are outside the country and not to those inside; but some countries' citizens can apply for a visa the moment they cross the border, as is the case with Canada. Last, the Department of Homeland Security registers entries, so if a person enters the country a number of times with the same visa, he or she will be included in the registers as often as he or she crosses the border. Taking these limitations into account, I will use the information from the DHS, as in some cases the numbers recorded by the State Department are far lower than the total, since many of the recipients are already in the United States, as is the case with a large proportion of the immigrant visas (green cards), or those nationalities exempted by law from requiring a visa.

The abovementioned trends imposed by the new migration policy can be seen in Figure 8.1. While the number of working immigrants admitted between 1990 and 2008 only grew threefold from 58,192 to 166,511, the number of temporary worker visas rose almost seven times during the same period (from 144,880 to 943,431). It was from 1993 that this trend began to be visible, reaching its highest point between 1996 and 2001. Although the number fell for some years, it rose again from 2004 onward.

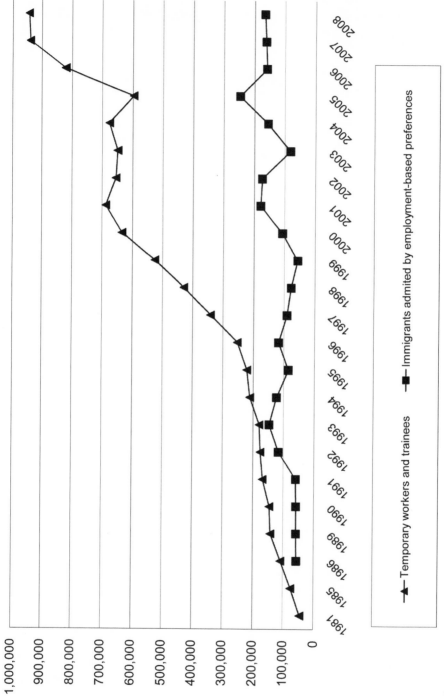

Figure 8.1.

Legend: ◀ Temporary workers and trainees   ■ Immigrants admitted by employment-based preferences

The acceptance of temporary H-2 visas by business owners has evolved slowly. The availability of recently legalized workers on the one hand, and of a numerous group which, despite not having obtained a residence permit, have stayed in the country, constitute an important supply of labor, easily used and got rid of when no longer needed—above all in the case of those who are undocumented.

In 1989 only 3,965 H-2A visas and 9,575 H-2B visas were issued. The latter rose more quickly than those of agricultural workers, being applied for by a growing number of businesses, above all those connected with seasonal tourism, for which they have become indispensable. Figure 8.2 shows a growing trend up to 2007, when admissions reached 155,000, although this seems to change in 2008, which saw a reduction of 45,000.

The growth in the number of H-2A visas has been much slower. Up until 1996 admissions did not reach 20,000, and although in the subsequent years they went up to nearly 30,000 annually, the gap in relation to H-2B non-agricultural activity visas gradually widened from then on, although the latter were limited to 66,000. For this reason it is surprising to see the drastic change that began in 2006, when this number doubled from 22,000 in 2004 to 46,000 in 2006, and to 173,000 in 2008. However, we must take in account that the number of admissions between 2007 and 2008 increased also because of the more complete recording of pedestrian admissions along the Southwest border. On the other hand we should not lose sight of the fact that we are dealing with a much smaller number than the approximately 1.2 million agricultural workers who, according to Martin (2007:3–4), work annually in the United States.

When they were created, the H-2 visas constituted almost all of the temporary visas (90 percent in 1989 and 86 percent in 1990),[6] but when the modifications to the law came into force in 1990, their importance in the total number gradually fell to 18.9 percent in 1995; at present it represents 25.7 percent of the total. The increase in the number of H-1B visas has visibly overtaken them due to the demand which appeared insatiable until 2007. Businesses that used these visas, especially those in computing and systems, have lobbied and applied pressure in various ways in order to exceed the established limit of 65,000 per year, an activity which has paid off, as can be seen in Figure 8.2. However, in this case a downward trend can also be seen which is corroborated by the news of sluggishness in reaching the upper limit established by the State Department in 2009.

As seen in Table 8.2, the mass of workers coming from India and Mexico make up a third of all temporary workers (15.9 percent and 15.5 percent, respectively). They are followed by Japan with 8.7 percent, Canada with 8.5 percent, and the United Kingdom with 8.1 percent. However, while

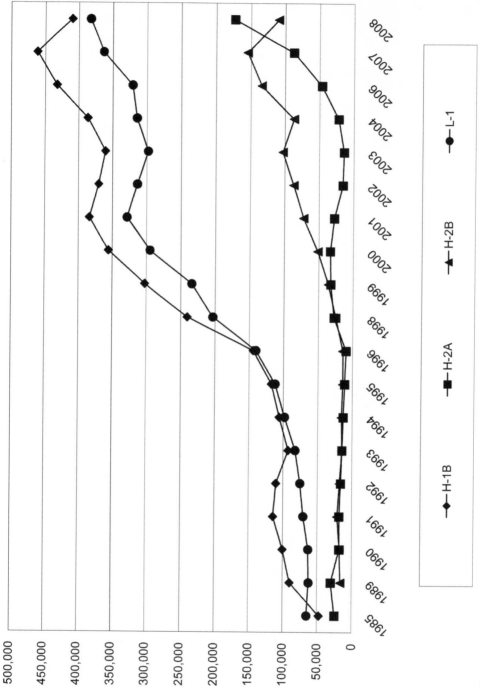

Figure 8.2.

Table 8.2.   Distribution of Admissions According to Visa Type and Main Countries Providing these Types of Workers, 2007 (Percent)

Country of Origin	H-1B	H-2A	H-2B	L-1	Others	Total %	Total Abs.
India	51.4	0.003	0.3	16.8	31.4	100	306,400
Mexico	6.0	26.4	35.0	7.1	25.4	100	300,346
Japan	8.6	D	D	21.5	69.7	100	167,548
Canada	15.9	0.3	1.5	10.9	71.4	100	164,836
United Kingdom	16.2	0.03	1.1	34.3	48.3	100	157,144
Germany	14.7	D	D	27.3	57.8	100	86,256
France	20.9	0.004	0.1	29.8	49.2	100	67,647
South Korea	23.6	D	D	13.9	62.2	100	48,739
Australia	11.8	0.2	3.5	25.2	59.2	100	37,710
China	46.9	D	D	16.9	36.2	100	35,461
Brazil	26.7	0.1	2.5	34.2	36.4	100	35,008
Jamaica	7.9	14.5	55.0	1.9	20.6	100	27,184
Total	23.9	4.5	8.0	18.8	44.7	100	1,932,075

Source: Based on information from the U.S. DHS Statistical Yearbook for 2007, Table 32.D Data withheld to limit disclosure.

61.5 percent of those from Mexico are H-2, only 0.3 percent of those from India and 1.8 percent from Canada enter on this type of visa. In contrast, H-1B visas make up 6 percent of those from Mexico, and 51.4 percent of those from India. It is interesting to note that among workers from Europe, the most common visa is the L-1, which, as has already been mentioned, though it is not strictly speaking for workers, is used by transnational companies to move workers to head-offices and subsidiaries in the United States and, on occasion, to avoid visa applications with stricter requirements.

H-2 visas are also important for other underdeveloped countries, most notably Jamaica as well as Mexico, as 69 percent of its citizens arrive with these visas,[7] and only 7.9 percent with H-1B.

WORKING CONDITIONS OF H-2 WORKERS

The working conditions of these workers depend a lot on the employer, the type of work, and how far the workplaces are from the cities. However, in most cases, they are jobs described as "dirty, dangerous and demanding"

(Waller, 2006:6). In spite of these conditions, many of those who enter on these visas leave a much worse situation in their countries of origin and are not interested in entering without documents.

The aim of *H-2A visas* is the *admission of agricultural workers* to carry out certain activities, which are by nature temporary. Amongst the obligations

Table 8.3. Characteristics and Requirements for H-2 Visas

	Visa type	
	H-2A	*H-2B*
General	Admission of agricultural workers	Non-agricultural workers with or without qualifications, but temporary in character
Duration	1 year which can be extended for 2 more	
Salary	The highest amongst the Adverse Effect Salary, the prevailing and the minimum for the region where the work is to be done	The DOL accepts the prevailing salary rate indicated by the employer
Demands on employers	Housing, food, transportation,[a] work tools and, access to compensation for medical costs; pay for lost time and any permanent injury caused by the work. Documents which specify working conditions. Guarantee at least ¾ of the time mentioned in the contract.	The only worker benefit is payment for the return journey when they become unemployed or are fired.
Rights	Exemption from social security tax Access to free LSC advice	Do not have these rights
Participating government agencies	Department of Labor (certification); Office of Citizenship and Immigration Services (authorizes visas) Department of State (issues visas)	
Activities included	Those related to agriculture (tobacco, fruit and vegetables), irrigation, livestock, cattle and sheep, poultry, horses etc.	A wide range, most notably gardeners, forestry workers, hotel and lodging, construction, stables, sports instructors, seafood processors.
Caps	No caps	66,000 visas per year

Source: From a number of sources included in the bibliography at the end of the text.
[a] This includes both the cost of the place where they live to the work center and payment for the return journey if three-quarters of the days of work in the contract are fulfilled, as well as adequate transport to and from their lodgings to the work place.

imposed on employers that ask for H-2A workers are: (1) pay the same or higher salary than that received by United States residents,[8] (2) provision of a document in which the details of the worker's total income and employment condition are established,[9] (3) transport from the place the worker is to be found initially and to the next workplace when the contract ends, (4) housing with the minimum standards established at federal level, (5) agricultural tools and implements, (6) food or facilities where the workers themselves can prepare it, (7) compensation insurance, and (8) guarantee of at least three-quarters of the total amount of work offered (see Table 8.3) (Wassem and Collver, 2001:3). All these requisites are aimed at making the hiring of foreigners more onerous than hiring local workers.

It should be pointed out that although these workers are exempt from paying social security and can receive advice from the Legal Services Corporation (LSC),[10] they are not covered by the Migrant and Seasonal Agricultural Worker Protection Act, which regulates working standards and conditions in agriculture; nor by the Federal Unemployment Tax Act, which sets out unemployment benefits. Nor are they covered by Social Security (regulated by the Federal Insurance Contributions Act) which authorizes the right to collective bargaining (Wassem and Collver, 2001).

Legal protection for H-2B workers is far less regulated, as the IRCA only sets out as a guideline that they should have no adverse effect on local workers, either on salaries or on working conditions; nor did the DOL establish the necessary regulations to make protection for these workers effective (Southern Poverty Law Center, 2007).

This is why the employer's declaration referring to the "prevailing wage rates"—that is, the average wage paid to similarly employed workers in the same occupation and field of employment—are accepted. Regarding working conditions, transport, etc., it only establishes that if the worker becomes unemployed before his or her visa runs out, the employer must pay for his or her return transport (Brenan Center, 2007).

On the other hand, these workers are precluded from resorting to LSC and, for the same reason, precluded from having access to free legal support to defend themselves against violation of their rights by the employers (Abel and Kaufman, 2003).

Of course, there is also an immense gulf between the hiring conditions of H-1B and H-2 workers as is shown in Table 8.4, even though they are all necessary for U.S. economy. The former are not tied to a single employer (because of the portability of the H-1B status), but instead can choose the job that is most suited to them without losing their visa rights. They can move around freely all over U.S. territory. The visa is valid for three years and can be extended for another three. They can opt for permanent residence at the end of six years and have many facilities for taking their families with them.[11]

Table 8.4. Some Differences Between H-1 and H-2 Visas

H-1B	*H-2*
Portability of H-1B status	No portability status
Lasts for a total of 6 years	Lasts for only 3 years
Can apply for a permanent visa	No possibility of changing status
The employer has no obligation to show that it covers a temporary need	For H-2B demonstration of a temporary need is required
Although there is a cap of 65,000, employers' demands, from 2000 to 2003 the number increased to 195,000. They are exempt from a number of investigation agencies.	H-2B visas have a cap of 66,000, although in 2006 and 2007 it was established that the cap was only for workers hired for the first time.
Freedom of movement	Strict control, above all in the case of agricultural workers and those in non-urban zones.
Facilities to travel with the family	Almost impossible to travel with the family

Source: Based on information from various sources included in the bibliography at the end of the text.

From the legal point of view, the DOL, through the Employment and Training Administration (ETA), provides the hiring certification for H-2A workers, after carrying out investigation to prove that there are no workers resident in the United States interested, qualified, and available at the time and place required to do the job or provide the service mentioned in the application, and also that this job or service does not adversely affect the wages and conditions of the workers similarly employed in the United States (Wassem and Collver, 2001).

The Department of Labor also has the authority to investigate and impose sanctions on the employers of H-2A workers when they do not fulfill contractual obligations. Among other sanctions are denying certification to any employer for violating H-2A visa contract obligations; taking administrative measures to retrieve unpaid wages, imposition of the application of contractual obligations and establishment of fines for those who commit violations (Wassem and Collver, 2001) However, in practice it is difficult to carry out these functions adequately, given that on many occasions the agricultural lands are located in places a long way from the cities, the number of DOL inspectors is insufficient to carry out the inspections, and the law does not provide adequate ways for workers to go to the authorities when their rights are violated (Holley, 2001).

THE VULNERABILITY OF H-2 WORKERS

Although, according to the conditions stipulated in the legislation, the situation of the workers hired with this type of visa is much better not only than that of undocumented workers, but also of native workers, especially in the case of H-2A workers, the way in which these visas operate has given rise to numerous violations and abuse by employers and contractors who take advantage of the lack of supervision on the part of the authorities, the isolation of some work centers and the limitations on workers to defend themselves, to go to the authorities or to the consular representatives of their own country.

As it is impossible to know how extended these practices are, due to lack of information on the part of the United States government offices or follow-up by the Mexican authorities, I will try to illustrate them with cases that have been documented in academic research, lawyers' reports, and by legal firms and non-governmental organizations, as well as in journalistic reports in Mexico and the United States. However, all these examples deal with specific cases which can in no way be generalized.

WAYS THAT THE LABOR AND HUMAN RIGHTS OF H-2 WORKERS ARE ABUSED

Recruiters, Intermediaries, and Moneylenders in Mexico

In contrast to what happened with the Bracero Program, which originated as the result of an agreement between the United States and Mexican governments, in the H-2 visa program the process has been left in the hands of the employers, who in turn, rely on companies, organizations, and recruiters. Many of them have established wide-reaching contacts in numerous villages in the Mexican Republic who sell their services, both to business owners and to candidates for recruitment (Waller, 2006:8). Unfortunately, there is no official information on the number of agents who are operating, on the places where they work, or on the activities they carry out, although, according to Mexican legislation, the government is obliged to verify obligatory working periods, respect for human rights, and migrants' repatriation costs, as well as that the agencies for the collective hiring of Mexican workers are only set up with the authorization of the Mexican government.[12]

One of the most prominent is the organization set up by the powerful North Carolina Growers' Association (NCGA), which hires most H-2A workers specially to work in the tobacco fields.[13] Cano and Nájar (2004) point out that their network reaches dozens of Mexican villages through subcontractors coordinated with their subsidiary Manpower of America (MOA), a company established in Monterrey. It has representatives in Durango, Zacatecas, San Luis Potosí, Hidalgo, Guanajuato, Nayarit, Oaxaca, Puebla, Jalisco, Veracruz, and certain other states, and handles some 13,500 visas a year. Although its main clients are the farmers of North Carolina, it also has others from Georgia, Indiana, Mississippi, Texas, and Ohio. The manager of this agency obtains benefits from both the United States and from Mexico. In the former, the farmers pay $500 per worker. Meanwhile, the Mexican candidates say that they pay MOA between $400 and $500; the consulate keeps $200 and MOA $105 for doing all the applications in the consulate and other expenses, while the recruiters (*enganchadores*) in the states receive a commission of $40 dollars per worker. In this way, every agricultural cycle, MOA earns 1.3 million dollars, without taking into account the bribes (*mordidas*) that many applicants pay to be included on the lists. Some critics point out that it is common for them to pay much more because they have to bribe the recruiter in order to be considered. The recruiter also demands a promissory note to ensure that the workers keep their word and leave them in the lurch (Cano and Nájar, 2001).

The NCGA has also set up other "associated" businesses like NTEX Transit that provide transport for workers from North Carolina to the border. According to an ex-contractor, "They put them into the trucks jumbled up, cheek by jowl." The same happens with the money-transfer company Amerimex, which is imposed on the workers, supposedly because it "pays the best price for the dollar" (Cano and Nájar, 2001).

Although this is the most notorious case due to the number of people it handles and the control exerted over the workers, in the report referred above, other names are mentioned, such as that of Jorge Sicsik from Durango.[14]

Amongst the local recruiters, the same authors highlight the case of Elisa Lozano from Pachuca, Hidalgo, who charges 3,800 pesos to check over documents and put workers in contact with the main organization. However, there are many complaints from agricultural workers who wait, after having paid, for more than a year without getting a permit (Cano and Nájar, 2001).

With respect to H-2B visas, there are also similar examples. In the reports by Chris Guy (2005) of the Baltimore Sun on the U.S. crab fishing industry, reference is made to the company Del Al Associates of Virginia, with an office in Monterrey and, as in the cases already mentioned, also a network of subcontractors in other localities.[15] The Southern Poverty Law Center (SPLC, 2007) points out that it is common for these recruiters to charge workers fees to cover transport, visas, and other costs, including their own earnings. For example, Decatour Hotels, through a company called Accent Personnel Services, Inc., obtained 290 guest workers to fill positions in its hotels that became vacant due to the Hurricane Katrina evacuations. The company owner testified that Accent earned $1,200 for each person ($300 from Decatour Hotels and $900 from recruiters working in Peru, Bolivia, and the Dominican Republic). In total, each worker had to pay between $3,500 and $5,000 in order to cover recruitment, transport, and visa fees.

According to the sources mentioned, most workers had to get into debt in order make the payment demanded by the recruiters and for this had to offer as a guarantee the few goods and properties they possessed. Generally, the moneylenders charged high rates of interest that were are added to the original loan, and although the legislation establishes the obligation on the part of the employer to refund travel costs and the cost of the visa, the Southern Poverty Law Center (2007) has found that in practice, they are rarely paid back.

However, it is important to point out that there are also many cases of workers who simply make verbal agreements with their bosses, either directly when they are working there or through a relative, although there is no information on the way in which they handle their visas in the United States consulate, nor even on whether they avoid the use of intermediaries and coyotes.

Violations of H-2 Workers' Rights by Employers in the United States

The flouting of the law occurs in very varied forms, of which I will mention the ones which occur most repeatedly.

Avoidance of the Agreed Payments on Different Pretexts, Including the Non-Payment of the Established Wage for Overtime

In a report in the New York Times, a group of workers hired on H-2B visas to plant trees in Arkansas complained that they were paid only $4.30 dollars an hour, when the rate for H-2B tree-planters *(pineros)* should be $8.43 an hour.[16] In addition, even though they regularly worked seventy hours a week, they never received time-and-a-half. Officials of the Department of Labor itself confirmed that it was common for the companies to evade taking into account hours worked, as they only registered the hours in which the workers were planting trees and not the time they spent carrying and transporting the plants to their final destinations. However, the big companies denied responsibility, blaming the recruiters. The lawyers who took the case argued that the corporations are joint employers and cannot evade their responsibilities (Greenhouse, 2001).[17]

A farmer in North Carolina recognized that employers cheated the workers by docking two hours from a 10-hour day to reduce workers' pay from 6.98 dollars an hour to 5.58 (Yeoman, 2001).

One of the ways of paying lower wages is to use piece work, which implies accelerated rhythms of work and exhausting hours. However, Guernsey (2007:294) mentions that this mechanism is not taken into account by the DOL as it has not developed an adequate methodology for converting piece work into hourly wages, for which reason the Office of Foreign Labor Certification (OFLC) has not approved productivity standards either.

The Southern Poverty Law Center (2007) also refers to the case of female workers in the crab packing plants, as the bosses, taking advantage of their vulnerability, submit them extreme competition to fulfill quotas and obtain the pay they were offered.

There are also accusations of non-payment of travel and hiring expenses and/or of docking a short time which reduces the wages expected.[18]

Hiring of More Workers and for Times Longer Than Necessary

Many employers have resorted to these practices for fear that some workers will leave and that it will be impossible to fulfill the requirements of harvesting perishable products. However, for the workers, the fact that they can only work for a few hours, and for that reason receive wages well below those offered, is a serious blow to their economy as they cannot get enough money together to pay their travel expenses, let alone to save. Cano and Nájar (2001) point out that the Bell company for example, inflated the number of workers required and the period during which there would be employment for them in order to ensure that their associates would never lack workers. When the rhythm of the harvests slackens, the companies simply offer the workers the option of signing their "voluntary resignation."

Yeoman (2001) quotes a document from the *General Accounting Office* which mentions that farmers apply for workers for longer periods of time than really needed. When the work comes to an end, the men are forced to return home early in order to save paying for the return journey and other benefits. He found this same situation in different reports. Billy Green, who monitored the H-2A program for the North Carolina Employment Security Commission, wrote in a memorandum to the Department of Labor in 1998 that the 10,000 workers brought in by the employers were four times more than the number required (Yeoman, 2001).

The Mexican women in the crab industry also complain that the number of women hired has increased, which has resulted in the reduction in the number of hours worked, and thus income (Griffith, 2002).

Housing, Hygiene and Transport to the Workplace

A report published in *El Universal* (Gómez Quintero, 2007) in relation to the tobacco fields controlled by the NCGA states: "Next Saturday the first 169 temporary workers will arrive . . . . The luckiest will live in a communal dwelling with five rooms and capacity for a minimum of twenty people, which apparently has all the services. Others will sleep in a trailer, with seven other people . . . ." Barry Yeoman (2001) mentions the bad conditions found during his investigation at different farms. The employers refused to give their H-2A workers water in the fields and housed them in ruinous dwellings infested with rats and with the drains in a bad state. The kitchen was dark, with low-voltage bulbs and undrinkable water. In another company, the mattresses were so old and deformed that the workers preferred to sleep on the concrete floor. In one camp, not far from the previous one, thirty-two men shared a house with no bathroom and were forced to go to an outhouse of low quality that only contained four toilets, with no partitioning. In still another, a dozen men slept in a two-bedroom house so deteriorated that rats and raccoons got in through holes in the walls (Yeoman, 2001).

Accidents at Work, Illnesses Caused by Working
Conditions, Medical Insurance

Owing to the types of jobs that they do, as well as the exhausting rhythms and hours, accidents at work are very frequent. The most dramatic case is that of the "pineros" hired to do maintenance work in the forests and national parks, whose activity is considered one of the most dangerous in the American Union. The journalists Knudson and Amezcua (2005) state: "They are gashed by chain saws, bruised by tumbling logs and rocks, verbally abused and forced to live in squalor . . . . Rainstorms pummel them. Cold winds sweep over them. Hunger stalks them. And death claims them. Across Honduras and Guatemala, fourteen guest workers lay in tombs, victims of the worst non-fire-related workplace accident in the history of U.S. forests."

There have also been accusations of cases where bosses obstruct or impede workers access to adequate medical services, which are made more serious by the isolation in which some of them live. Yeoman (2001) denounced the fact that some employes deny the workers the necessary medical care after having been exposed to pesticides and refers to the case of one worker who was poisoned when cutting tobacco with no protective clothing; his boss refused to take him to a clinic. He mentions that at another farm (Jimmy Pike), also in North Carolina, according to a state report, a worker called Juan Araujo complained, "Sometimes blood comes out of our feet, and even like this, the boss wants more work done." Another argued that, due to the contact with chemicals, "my hands get very white and my fingers thin and weak, as if acid had spilled on them." Meanwhile, his employer admitted that he had not given them protective clothing and had not even installed portable toilets (Yeoman, 2001).

When workers complain about health conditions, some owners send them back to their own country, as in the case found by Ventura Gutiérrez, president of a the group of agricultural workers Unión Sin Fronteras (Yeoman, 2001). When this happens, the workers do not manage to get together the money they had hoped to earn, and they do not have their return journey paid for them.

Cano and Nájar (2004) say that although the owners have the obligation to offer the workers health insurance, in general they do not use it because they say that if they report the accidents the premium for the next year is higher. For this reason they prefer to have them treated on the spot or take them to a rural clinic, regardless of the severity of the accident or illness. If the worker complains or demands better attention, he or she runs the risk of getting fired and being put on the so-called "blacklist." The workers thus prefer to carry on working, although the wound stops them from working normally (Cano and Nájar, 2004).

Isolation, Employer Control, the Intermediary or the Overseer (Blacklists)

Sometimes, control is exerted by the recruiters who have diversified their activities. They are in charge of imposing almost military discipline in which abuse and insults form part of the way the work is organized and the blacklist is held up as a constant threat against any sign of indiscipline, lest workers lose their chance of returning (Cano and Nájar, 2004).

On top of this, workers' documents are confiscated from the moment they arrive, according to the employers, to prevent them from leaving and there being an insufficient workforce. But in practice, this turns into a letter of deportation which allows them to force the workers to accept the conditions imposed on them and to systematically violate what is stipulated in the contract (SPL, 2007). And since the worker got into debt to get work and needs to save money to pay back the loan, let alone earn his own keep and that of his family, he needs to work at least the forty hours promised for most of the period he was hired for, a situation that is becoming less and less common.

On occasions, these systems imposed by the recruiters and employers on both sides of the border have given rise to conditions of extreme exploitation and vulnerability similar to the old system of control in the Mexican hacien-das, the company store (*tienda de raya*), since because of the debts contracted in their place of origin, the workers are forced to stay and put up with abuse from their employers.

In some cases this could be considered "human trafficking," when the workers are deceived about the job, the working conditions, and/or the pay and, once they are inside the United States, are physically deprived of their freedom, subject to acts such as confiscation of their documents and threats of handing them over to the immigration authorities.[19]

There are extreme cases like those documented by Georgina Olson in the newspaper *Excélsior* (2008), of workers with H-2A visas who lived near New Orleans in two trailers, in terrible conditions, with poor food, extreme hours of work at minimal pay, threatened with a shotgun by their boss, Charles Bimbo. This employer had retained their passports and kept them under control with threats. Thanks to the help of two non-governmental organiza-tions, the workers were rescued and presented accusations of federal crimes such as forced labor, human trafficking, involuntary servitude, and payment of low wages.

Another case is that of the thirty workers from Veracruz hired on H-2B visas by an agent of the company Logimex to work in the Southwest Ship Yard, in the port of Channelview in Texas. They got into debt more than $1,500 to pay for their visas and passage. In addition to the terrible condi-tions, one of them had a heart attack due to the heat and lack of ventilation in the workplace; when they escaped, they were found by a company representa-tive who forced them to return at pistol point because he had their passports and their visas, which only allowed them to work for this particular business. As they needed to pay the debts they had acquired before leaving Veracruz, they were thinking of staying for at least the time necessary to recoup their investment in the journey (González, 2007).

Incompetence or Reluctance on the Part of the Authorities

Despite what is established by law, neither the DOL nor the DHS assume responsibility for verifying before hiring, wage conditions, hours, labor responsibilities, and other terms that the employers offer workers and, if nec-essary, to deny certification to those who abuse workers' legally established rights; nor do they carry out affirmative investigations to ensure that the employers are keeping their promises and pursue violations on the basis of explicit complaints by workers (Brenan Center, 2007).

The DOL claims to have neither the personnel nor funds needed, to which we should add lack of interest, above all when dealing with companies a long distance away. On the rare occasions that attention is given to workers' complaints, the department acts slowly and without finding solutions (Brenan Center, 2007).

Access to Justice

Individual workers, above all many on H-2B visas, are not able to defend their rights by going to the courts, as there is no federal law that lets them sue to ensure the fulfillment of the terms of their contract; nor, as we have already said, do they have the right to get aid from the Legal Services Corporation (Brenan Center, 2007).

In general, without access to lawyers with the experience and willingness to represent them, most workers are unable to take legal action, since they do not know English, do not understand the U.S. legal system, live in isolated areas, and have to leave the country when their contract ends, despite the fact that their situation violates the North American Agreement on Labor Cooperation (NAALC) (Abel, 2007).[20]

With respect to the federal courts, in contrast to domestic workers and undocumented workers who are protected by the *Migrant and Seasonal Agricultural Workers' Protection Act* (AWPA), the H-2A workers do not have this protection, nor do they have access to the federal court (although the government authorized, facilitated, and supervised their stay). Holley (2001) points out that the federal courts themselves have concluded that the H-2A figure was not created to benefit foreign workers, but only to protect domestic workers.

Under these conditions, all they can do is to sue in a state court, which often takes a partial attitude, partly because it is common for officials to be on good terms with local agro-businessmen, and partly in accordance with wide-reaching anti-Latino migrants sentiments, above all in the southern states (Holley, 2001).

Lastly, Holley concludes, "The H-2A worker is the latest incarnation of the juridically handicapped—i.e. handicapped by laws and legal institutions— farmworker in American society. Effectively, the current generation of guest workers has been deprived of a voice to protect themselves" (Holley, 2001:613).

CONCLUSION

The United States has a long tradition of immigration. For many years it opened its doors to numerous contingents from different European countries. However, its attitude changed in relation to its southern neighbors. It saw them as a seasonal workforce to do the heavy jobs, principally in agriculture, and easy to get rid of due to the common border. This is why Mexicans were exempted from the conditions that the law imposed on immigrants from other countries.

Pressure from employers, mainly in agriculture, demanding that the law fit in with their need for cheap labor, has been decisive. Due to them, the figure of temporary worker was accepted and included in the immigration legislation from the 1940s onward.

Recently an interest in hiring workers has increased not only in the United States, but also in a growing number of countries with the illusion of keeping their countries closed to the influence of outside groups. And they do not only resort to foreign workers only in the case of low-qualified workers; in recent decades they have searched for different mechanisms to attract, on a temporary basis, highly qualified labor to complement the local supply at a time when high technology has become one of the main motors of the economy.

Although they are found at both the higher and the lower ends of the social scale, temporary contracts give rise to a fragmentation of the labor market, and the treatment received, both in the legislation and in daily life, is very different.

In the United States, highly qualified temporary workers can change employers, travel with their families and aspire to permanent residence; H-2 workers, however, are offered a small number of visas and are not allowed to change jobs or aspire to permanent residence.

As well as the legal restrictions, the conditions in which H-2 visa holders live and work facilitates numerous forms of abuse of both their labor and human rights. At the same time, their access to instances that can prevent abuse and redress damage suffered is restricted.

In the face of the reluctance on the part of attracting societies, and specifically the United States, to end to this type of contract rejected by different social actors, in various forums mechanisms have been proposed to reduce the abuse that workers suffer at present, among which I could mention

1. Bilateral and more transparent handling of contracts to avoid the existence of unscrupulous recruiters.
2. Workers' retention of their freedom of movement and their right to change employers if agreed-upon conditions are not fulfilled.
3. Permission, if workers wish, to travel with their family, as is case with qualified workers.
4. Federal and state agencies' fulfillment of the functions they have been assigned, which would benefit not only temporary workers but also local workers by maintaining the wage levels and working conditions that they are supposed to defend.

5. Legal measures taken so that when government officials fail to solve work related problems, workers can lodge complaints before the legal system, both while they are in the United States and when they return to Mexico.

6. The possibility for those who wish it to be offered a way of getting permanent residence.

NOTES

1. H-2 visas were created to satisfy the demand for agricultural work in the east of the country, mainly for the apple and sugarcane harvests (Holley, 2001; Wassem and Collver, 2001). Mexican workers were not included, as the "Bracero Program" existed for them. However, the H-2 visa program always functioned with lower numbers.

2. This would complement the supply of labor from the almost 3 million persons already legalized.

3. However, as we know, this expectation was not fulfilled as, from then onward, the foreign population living in the country, mainly undocumented, grew at a higher rate than in previous decades.

4. "A nonimmigrant is a foreign national seeking to enter the United States temporarily for a specific purpose. Nonimmigrants are admitted for a temporary period of time and, once in the country, are restricted to activities related to the purpose for which their visa was issued" (Grieco, 2006:2).

5. Since March 1, 2003, the U.S. Citizenship and Immigration Service (USCIS) became one of the three components inherited from the INS to form part of the Department of Homeland Security (DHS). The USCIS is in charge of fundamentally transforming and improving the handling of immigration and citizenship services at the same time as improving national security (http://www.uscis.gov/graphics/aboutus/index.htm).

6. This is not surprising, as only H-3 visa existed although, if we consider J-1 and L-1 visas, the proportion is reduced to only 8 percent, as the J-1 visas totaled 139,354.

7. However, the proportions are very different, because while Mexican citizens occupy 90.9 percent of the H-2A visas (with 79,000 visas) and 67 percent of the H-2B visas (with 105,000 visas), the Jamaicans obtain 4.5 percent and 9.7 percent (with 4,000 and 15,000 visas, respectively).

8. The salary should be the highest among the adverse effect wage (AEWR), the prevailing wage, and the minimum federal or state wage for the region where the work will be done (French, 1999). The AEWR is determined annually by the DOL in each region of the country to avoid the employment of workers adversely affecting the salaries of Americans in similar jobs.

9. This document should contain (1) the starting and finishing dates and terms of employment, (2) working conditions and even information on transportation costs,

housing, and food that the employer has to pay for, (3) working hours, (4) frequency and classification of pay, (5) the nature of the employment (for example, the type of crop they will work with), (6) the tools and equipment required (to be provided by the employer free of charge), and (7) an announcement that there will be indemnification insurance with no cost to the worker (Commission for Labor Cooperation: 2002).

10. The Legal Services Corporation (LSC) is independent and has the authority to provide financial help to some legal aid programs. In rural areas these programs are devoted exclusively to representing agricultural workers and carry out awareness campaigns on their legal rights. However, they cannot offer help in criminal or immigration cases and are prohibited from representing their clients in cases involved in obtaining fees for them (Commission for Labor Cooperation, 2002).

11. However, family members do not have the right to work in the United States if they do not get some sort of work visa.

12. The provisions with respect to this are found in Section XXVI of Article 123 of the Constitution of the United States of Mexico, in articles 79 and 80 of the general law on population, and in Article 213 of the regulations of the general law on population.

13. According to information from the DOL (2005), in 2003, 9,506 workers from North Carolina were certified, these being 21.6 percent of all certifications, belonging to 25 percent of all certified companies (http://workforcesecurity.doleta.gov/foreign/h-2a_atlanta.asp).

14. Jorge Sicsik started working informally, due to fact that he spoke English, and gradually established contacts and mechanisms to attract potential migrants: he also has an active political life; he was municipal president (from 1995–1998) and the defeated PAN candidate in the 2000 elections. On the ground floor of his house there are a shoe store and his recruiting office, although he now works on a smaller scale thanks to the contacts he made over more than a decade (Cano and Nájar, 2001).

15. There are a large number of testimonies about the agents who operate in Mexico on behalf of American companies. As well as those mentioned above, there is the case of the workers who plant trees, who are promised that they will be able to earn enormous sums of money, which in practice turns out to be well below their expectations (Greenhouse, 2001).

16. Although, as I have mentioned, the regulations on H-2B visas do not require AEWR pay or the provision of benefits and implements, legally workers have the right to the minimum wage established for each state, as well as the right to overtime At this time, the minimum federal wage in Arkansas was $5.15 (Greenhouse, 2001). See also *Rural Migration News* (19–1-05), which states that Gillam Farms of Arkansas were sued by thirty-eight H-2A workers because they did not receive the minimum wage fixed in 2002 for the blueberry harvest.

17. We find the same problem with the employers of the "pineros," described in a report by Knudson and Amezcua of the Sacramento Bee (2005) and by Cano and Nájar (2001) in relation to the NCGA. In both cases they comment that when there are problems, nobody is the responsible employer.

18. See above on the report by the Southern Poverty Law Center (2007:8–9).

19. The Traffic Victims Protection Act (TVPA) " . . . defines victims of severe forms of trafficking as those persons subject to (1) sex trafficking in which a commercial sex act is induced by force, fraud, or coercion, or in which the person induced to perform such acts is under age 18 or (2) the recruitment, harboring, transportation, provision, or obtaining of a person for labor or services, through the use of force, fraud, or coercion, for the purpose of subjection to involuntary servitude, peonage, debt bondage, or slavery" (GAO, 2006:5).

20. The North American Agreement on Labor Cooperation (NAALC) is a labor agreement derived from NAFTA the objectives of which include "'promot[ing] compliance and effective enforcement by each Party of its labor law' and . . . 'foster[ing] transparency in the administration of labor law'" (Abel, 2007:2).

Chapter 9

Measuring Migration Connections across Latin America

Jonathan Hiskey and Abby Córdova

Coinciding with Latin America's political and economic liberalization process, Latin Americans over the past thirty years have been emigrating from their native countries at record levels, making the region one of the leading sending areas in the world by the beginning of the twenty-first century. The more than 20 million migrants who lived outside their native countries as of 2008 are seen by many as potentially critical agents in the economic and political development prospects of their home countries, yet systematic empirical work has only begun to uncover how and to what extent these migrants are influencing the economics and politics of their native countries. A central challenge to this research concerns the question of how to systematically measure the breadth and depth of migrants' connections with those they left behind in their home communities. Though these questions of how migrants influence events and individuals back home has a long tradition in the disciplines of sociology and anthropology (e.g., Levitt, 2001; Waldinger and Fitzgerald, 2004; Cohen, 2001; Kearney, 1995, 1986), scholars have yet to develop measures or gather data that allow for the assessment of migrants' impact on their home countries across multiple cases.

More generally, with few exceptions, the domain of migrant studies has been dominated by single country or community studies that make identification of generalizable patterns difficult. Massey and Durand's path-breaking Mexican Migration Project and the Latin American Migration Project offer two of the few sources of data that allow for the development and testing of propositions across multiple contexts. In the following pages we introduce a growing collection of survey data from the Latin American Public Opinion Project that we employ in order to develop a series of measures of migration connections among more than 30,000 Latin American respondents across more than twenty countries. Though it is certainly not without flaws, we argue that such a survey-based measurement strategy needs to be a central part of the growing research agenda on the question of how the most recent wave of migration has shaped the contours of Latin America's political and economic transition of the past three decades.

MIGRANT CONNECTIONS AND THEIR CONSEQUENCES

Work on the economic and sociological impact of migration is perhaps the most developed in terms of understanding the connections between migrants and their home communities. In the field of sociology, the vast amount of recent scholarship on migrant ties with their home communities, whether defined as transnational or not, has provided valuable insights into the potential areas of impact that migrants can have on their home communities (Basch et al., 1994; Cohen, 2001; Florini, 2000; Fox, 2005; Levitt, 1998, 2001; Portes, 2003; Schiller, 1999; Smith, 2006; Vertovec, 2003). We also have an extensive body of research on the economic effects of remittances at both the micro and macro levels (Brown, 2006; Fajnzylber and López, 2007; IADB, 2004; Jones, 1998; Keely and Tran, 1989; Munzele and Ratha, 2005; Orozco, 2002a, 200b, 2006). Money sent back home by migrants has become a critical source of foreign exchange for many countries, as well as a much-needed safety net for migrant families and an essential source of local economic activity for the many high-migration communities scattered across the region (de la Garza and Lowell, 2002). Conversely, the unequal distribution of these remittances among households and communities, the "remittance haves" and "remittance have-nots," has the potential for an exacerbation of the inequality divides that run through many Latin American societies (Jones, 1998).

Even more unclear are the political consequences of migration in Latin America. With the upsurge of migration occurring alongside a region-wide democratization trend, a host of potential tradeoffs suggest themselves with respect to the impact migration may have on such issues as the stability, longevity, and vitality of the region's many emerging democracies.

One potential influence of migration on Latin America's democratization process begins with the proposition that individuals who migrate will tend to be more risk-accepting than their non-migrating neighbors. If this is the case, then the high levels of migration experienced by some countries may have resulted in a "political brain drain" such that those individuals most inclined to participate in politics are opting to leave instead. More broadly, given the governance inadequacies of many of Latin America's new democracies, the fact that an increasing number of citizens chose to "exit" their systems during the turbulent, crisis-filled political transition years may have provided these political systems a political participation pressure release that enhanced their chances of survival (Hirschman, 1970, 1978, 1993).

Indeed, we have scattered theoretical, empirical, and anecdotal accounts of just such a dynamic taking place under authoritarian regimes of various sorts where leaders release or expel those individuals most likely to challenge them. Castro's policy of allowing the selective exit of individuals as a means to dissipate political voice within Cuba offers but one example of this. Though clearly distinct from a democratic regime, the key point is that whether through expulsion, exile, or individual choice, the systematic exit of a certain type of individual seems likely to have an impact on the degree of citizen participation in politics. Notwithstanding these potential connections between migration and democracy in Latin America, very few scholars have pursued this line of inquiry.

Research is beginning to emerge on another possible set of political consequences brought by the high levels of migration found in numerous Latin American countries in recent years. We know quite a bit on the aggregate political effects of various diasporas around the world, and more recently, on the policy and development impact that migrant groups (e.g., Mexico's "hometown associations"—HTAs) can have on their home communities (Florini, 2000; Goldring, 2004; Orozco, 2002b; Smith, 2006). What has remained underexplored until recently has been the question of how migrants themselves influence the political attitudes and behaviors of those family members and friends they leave behind. The core idea underlying this research is that through the many interactions migrants have with their family members and friends back home, a set of what Levitt (2001) refers to as "social remittances" are exchanged, and leads to changes in the political attitudes and behaviors of those on the receiving end of such exchanges.

With this thesis as the point of departure we can generate a variety of propositions relating the specific impact these social remittances might have. Some argue that recipients of social remittances will be more critical of their own system as they learn about how well other systems function. Others focus on the possible transmission of democratic values such as tolerance that may take place in these exchanges and will therefore lead to increasingly "better" democratic citizens in high-migration towns. Still other scholars have explored the potential impact that social remittances may have on levels of political participation among "those left behind." Goodman and Hiskey (2008) identify what they refer to as a process of "exit without leaving" where individuals with high levels of migration connections disengage from politics at home as they rely more and more on their migration connections. In this account, both economic and social remittances lead individuals to view with increasing skepticism, if not cynicism, their own political system and its ability to fulfill the basic tasks of government. Those with high levels of exposure to such remittances, then, will be less likely to participate in politics.

Two critical variables underlie research on migration connections and their various attitudinal and behavioral effects. The first such variable is the migrant's life experience in his or her host country. What a migrant experiences arguably will go a long way toward shaping the content of any social remittances that may be transmitted back home and, therefore, his or her subsequent impact on the attitudes and behaviors of those left behind. If, for example, a migrant enjoys unfettered access to electricity service in his or her host community, this may be contribute to a social remittance that highlights the contrast between the governance capabilities of the home and host country political systems. If, however, a migrant faces bureaucratic and financial obstacles to obtaining electricity in his or her host community, perhaps having his or her electricity cut off by the power company, the resultant social remittance may contain a decidedly different message. An assumption underlying at least some, if not most, of the social remittance framework is that the content of such remittances sent from migrants living in advanced industrial democracies will tend to place the host country in a favorable light when compared with the migrant's home country. While this may be an entirely plausible assumption, it still remains an assumption.

The second important factor underlying the social remittance framework is the actual content of the exchanges that take place between migrants and those left behind. Clearly what individual migrants talk about with their friends and family back home will vary quite a bit. Among the questions facing researchers are the degree to which the content of such conversations can be categorized into such topical areas as "financial matters" and "daily life issues," and whether any systematic patterns exist to help explain which types of migrants devote more time to certain types of "conversation categories." Being able to answer this question would offer a significant step forward in understanding the degree to which exposure to such remittances may influence the political attitudes and behaviors of those left behind.

Clearly, for both of these dimensions of the migrant's life—his or her life experiences in the host community and the content of his or her communications with those back home—the methodological challenges of gathering valid, reliable data on a representative sample of the target population are substantial. The fact that many migrants, particularly those without documents, seek to remain under the radar while in their host community makes an accurate assessment of the sampling frame difficult.

One of the leading Latino research organizations, the Pew Hispanic Center, has conducted extensive surveys of the U.S. Latino population but readily admits the challenges involved in targeting the undocumented migrant population, noting, "No researcher has attempted to conduct a survey of a nationally representative sample of the undocumented population that was drawn with the level of statistical certainty that is routine for large-scale polls . . ." (Pew, 2005:3). In its effort to record the attitudes and life experiences of this population, the Center instead deployed a purposive sampling strategy in a survey of close to 5,000 Mexican migrants carried out in 2004. Though done with tremendous methodological care under the direction of the University of Southern California's Annenberg School for Communication, the Center dispensed with standard probabilistic sampling techniques and instead administered the survey to willing participants found standing in line at seven Mexican consulates scattered across the United States over a period of five to ten business days (based on the size of the consulate city population). Though producing a sample that was roughly similar along certain demographic characteristics to the undocumented population estimates generated using the U.S. Census Bureau's Current Housing Population survey, the selection bias issues involved in the Pew's survey project make it difficult to know the degree to which its data are in any way reflective of the larger undocumented population.

Nonetheless, the approach represented one of the first systematic attempts to understand the life of the undocumented in the United States and their connections with those left behind. Findings from the survey reveal that close to 80 percent of respondents had sent some money back home on a regular basis, typically to a family member; 54 percent talked with family members back home on a regular basis; and 35 percent said they had communicated with family via email or some other form of digital technology. However intriguing these findings are, we are unable to know how well they map to the general population of Mexican migrants. Subsequent surveys by the Pew Center and others have relied on telephone surveys and employed various strategies to address the issues involved with telephone-based surveys of undocumented migrants, but sampling issues remain a problem.

While reliance on the oft-used phrase "best available data" is always an option, the simple reality is that we lack the capability at this point of generating survey data that are fully representative of the migrant side of migrant connections in most, if not all, receiving countries. In the United States, for example, with an estimated 12 million undocumented migrants (circa 2008) representing close to 30 percent of all foreign-born residents of the United States, it remains unclear whether it will ever be possible to gather representative data on even the most basic characteristics of such migrants' lives. Thus we remain dependent on more ethnographic-based approaches that provide rich, highly detailed accounts of the lives of migrants in their host

communities, but that are unable to provide sufficient cases or representativeness to allow for systematic evaluation of the various propositions related to
migrant connections.

We argue, therefore, that a more fruitful approach to the systematic assessment of the attitudinal and behavioral effects, if any, of migrant connections
is to turn our focus toward those friends and family members of migrants that
stayed behind in their native countries. While certainly not a perfect resolu-
tion of the methodological dilemma confronting the study of migrant connections, this approach carries with it several distinct advantages. First, the
population is far more accessible than the migrant population of most receiving countries. Second, the ability to gather nationally representative data for
this population enhances the analytical utility of the data. Third, by collecting representative attitudinal and behavioral data across an entire country,
we will be able to assess the effects *of varying levels of migrant connections*
across our sample population, rather than focusing only on those individuals
with high levels of connections to migrants. Through such an analysis, then,
we can get a far more robust sense of how migrant connections do or do not
influence attitudes and behaviors. In the remainder of this paper we introduce
this measurement strategy and the survey items we employ, and present the
results of our efforts to adequately measure and assess the impact of migration connections on those left behind.

THE OTHER SIDE OF MIGRATION CONNECTIONS

Our principal challenge is to adequately capture an individual's degree of
connections to migration in order to assess any potential effects such connections might have on, for example, the political attitudes and behaviors of
the person. Goodman and Hiskey (2008), for example, find that Mexicans
living in high-migration contexts tend to be more supportive of democracy
in the abstract but more critical of Mexico's political system than their counterparts in low-migration towns. In terms of political behavior, the authors
find a disengagement from formal politics among high migration individuals,
but an active involvement in community organizations. Similarly, Pérez-
Armendáriz and Crow (2010) find more critical assessments of Mexican
democracy among those individuals with migration connections, while also
finding higher levels of nonelectoral political activities (e.g., writing a letter to the editor) and involvement in organizations among these individuals.
In both of these recent studies, however, the data are confined to a single
country, Mexico, that is in many ways a highly unique case with respect to
migration, due to its long history with the United States. What we seek is to

develop a measurement strategy that allows for exploration of these ideas across a wide range of migratory histories.

In order to move beyond the single country studies of the past, we rely on recently released cross-national survey data that allows us to assess the range of migration connections across over 33,000 individuals living in myriad communities located in twenty-one Latin American and Caribbean countries with distinct migration histories. Such a wide range of countries offers the chance to assess not only the individual-level effect of migration connections, but also to incorporate into that analysis the contextual effects associated with high and low aggregate migration levels.

The problem, until recently, with a survey-based measurement approach to assessing migration connections has been the paucity of survey items related to migration in most cross-national survey efforts carried out in sending regions. Such long-running and wide-ranging projects as the Latinobarometer and Afrobarometer, for example, offer little help in assessing the degree of migrant connections among their survey respondents. Though the Latinobarometer has included items in recent rounds of its surveys that ask individuals about their migration intentions (if any)[1] and what they think about how emigrants from their country are treated in receiving countries, the survey includes no items that ask individuals about their connections with migrants living abroad. Only with the release of the 2006 and 2008 rounds of the Latin American Public Opinion Project's (LAPOP) AmericasBarometer survey do we have nationally representative data on the migration connections of individuals across most Latin American countries. In the following section we offer an overview of these data and the various ways they might be used to begin to assess the impact of migration connections on the political attitudes and behaviors of those left behind.

Relying on the three core migration connection items included in the both the 2006 and 2008 AmericasBarometer survey instruments, our first approach toward assessment of migration links is through the development of what we refer to as a "migration connection index" (MCI). Though not specifically constructed for such an index, we view these items as tapping various dimensions of respondents' connections to a migrant network and thus amenable to the construction of an index that provides a range of migration connection values. The three survey questions are as follows:

1. Do you have plans to leave the country to work or live during the next three years?[2]
2. Do you have any relatives currently living in another country that previously lived in this household?
3. Do you receive remittances?

Moving from the first to the third item we see each as tapping a progressively more in-depth involvement with a migration network. Though our first item offers no direct indication of an individual's connection with migrants abroad, we view an individual with intentions to emigrate as being indirectly connected to a migration network through the evident awareness and acceptance of emigration as a viable life option. This awareness may have many sources, but one likely way is through contact with others who have had more direct experiences with migration. Though we make no claims to knowing this for certain, we posit with some degree of certainty that those individuals thinking about emigration, all else being equal, are more likely to have these types of connections to migration than those who have no such migration intentions. Indeed, in many ways our ideas relating migration intentions to broader migration connections rest in part on research on the cumulative causes of migration that highlight the role existing migrant networks play in prompting individuals to consider migration (Taylor, 1986; Massey et al., 1987; Massey, 1990, 1998).

In order to test the plausibility of this line of reasoning, we offer a brief exploration of the correlation between respondent migration intentions in Mexico and the level of community migration intensity in which they live. If intentions to emigrate do suggest, ceterus peribus, a greater probability of exposure to migration networks, then we should expect to find a higher percentage of respondents expressing such intentions in towns with higher aggregate migration activity. Combining the 2006 and 2008 LAPOP surveys for Mexico, close to 15 percent of respondents expressed an intention to emigrate within the next three years, the vast majority of whom indicated that the United States was the planned destination. When broken down by migration context, however, these migration intention rates change significantly. Among the 1,176 respondents (of 3,048 total respondents) who lived in "very low"–migration contexts,[3] only 11.3 percent expressed intentions to emigrate. Conversely, of the 288 respondents who lived in "high"- or "very high"–migration contexts, over 18 percent reported plans to emigrate. In analysis of variance tests, these differences in means emerged significant at the $p<.001$ level. Though we must recognize the bluntness of such a test, it does offer some indication that those individuals with emigration plans do have a greater probability of having had some exposure to migration networks, thus justifying the item's inclusion in our measure of "migration connections."

Our second item offers a far more direct means of assessing the degree of connections one might have with a migration network, asking respondents whether they have relatives currently residing in another country. Though this item, again, does not offer definitive evidence of an individual having an active connection with migration, as the respondent may have lost touch with the migrant family member, it does offer an indicator of individuals with a much greater probability of having such connections when compared to those respondents with no relatives living abroad.

Our final item asks respondents if they currently receive remittances, providing the one firm indicator that a respondent has active connections to a migrant abroad. Though this connection may involve little or no regular communication between the remittance sender and receiver, at a minimum the remittance recipient is connected to a migration network through the economic ties such funds create. We also posit, though, that remittance recipients will be more likely to communicate on a more regular basis with migrants than those who do not receive remittances. The likelihood of such enhanced forms of connections between the remittance recipient and migrants is the basis for our treatment of this item as the most concrete indicator of migrant connections.

As with migration intentions, we can offer an exploratory test of this proposition with the 2008 LAPOP data due to the inclusion of an additional item in that year's instrument that asked respondents who reported having migrant family members how often they communicated with those family members. By comparing the frequency of communications between respondents and their migrant family members among those who did and did not report receiving remittances we can get a sense of the degree to which receipt of remittances taps a deeper connection with migration than simply having family members abroad does. Among those respondents who received remittances, over half (50.6 percent) reported talking with their migrant family members at least once or twice a week. Among those respondents who did not receive remittances, only 22.3 percent communicated with their migrant family members on a weekly basis. What these differences suggest is what we might intuitively expect—those individuals who receive remittances tend to be more directly connected to migration than those who do not receive remittances.

Taking into account the varying theoretical links that our three items have with migration connections, we construct an index that attaches increasing weights to each of the three components:

1. Respondents with intentions to leave the country receive a score of .5; all others receive a score of 0.
2. Respondents with relatives living abroad receive a score of 1; all others receive a score of 0.
3. Respondents receiving remittances receive a score of 1.5; all others receive a score of 0.

Thus, the range of the index is 0 to 3. Our weighting system reflects the theoretical import of each item in terms of its relationship to our concept of central interest—the degree to which a person is connected to a migrant network. The measure then represents an attempt to capture, albeit not completely, the range of possible levels of connection an individual may have with migration. Table 9.1 displays the distribution of MCI scores across the more than 33,000 respondents from twenty-one Latin American and Caribbean countries.[4] Immediately apparent should be the general absence of any migration connections among a majority of the respondents. These individuals then offer a useful baseline for assessing the impact increasing levels of contact with a migrant network may have on one's political (or any other of interest) attitudinal and behavioral profiles. In addition, the substantial number of individuals with no discernible migration connections highlights the highly variable nature of migration patterns across Latin America, making all the more intriguing attempts to understand how migration has affected political and economic development patterns in high-migration localities and, as a consequence, how distinct these communities are from the majority of low migration towns and cities across Latin America.

Table 9.1.   Migration Connection Index Across Latin America and Selected Countries

Migration Connection Index Scores	Total Sample*	Mexico	El Salvador	Argentina
0	18,545 60.5%	1,020 66.2%	645 41.8%	1,120 80.6%
.5	4,101 13.4%	129 8.4%	172 11.1%	151 10.9%
1	2,815 8.2%	206 13.4%	230 14.9%	59 4.2%
1.5	1,637 4.7%	64 4.2%	141 9.1%	25 1.8%
2.0	262 .8%	2 .1	29 1.9%	2 .1%
2.5	1,740 5.0%	87 5.6%	221 14.3%	23 1.7%
3.0	1,548 4.5%	32 2.1%	105 6.8%	10 .7
Total	30,648 100%	1,540 100%	1,543 100%	1,390 100%

Source: AmericasBarometer, 2008. Total sample frequencies and means calculated using a weight to obtain equal number of cases per country. Country specific frequencies are unweighted.

In looking at the frequency of MCI values displayed in Table 9.1, one problem with the measure becomes immediately apparent. For the most part, the distribution of respondents across the seven possible values of the MCI performs as we would expect, with the number of respondents declining as the MCI value increases. What such a progression suggests is that our index is successful in capturing successively greater degrees of migration connections. So while 13.5 percent of the respondents expressed intentions of emigrating, but had no other apparent connections to migration, only 4.3 percent of our respondents received an MCI value of 3, indicating that they expressed a desire to emigrate, had at least one migrant family member, and received remittances. The only category that does not fit this "Guttman-like" progression of values is the group of respondents who received a value of 2.0. The only way for a respondent to attain a value of 2.0 is for her to express intentions to emigrate and receive remittances, but not have any migrant family member. This group of respondents represented less than 1 percent of the survey sample, and appears to us as problematic perhaps due to the wording of the family member survey item. Though it is certainly possible that one could receive remittances from someone other than a family member, most research on this question suggests that remittances are almost exclusively exchanged between family members (e.g., husband and wife, daughter and mother, etc.). The wording of the survey item specifically asks about whether a family member who *"previously lived in this household."* We suspect that in some cases, individuals were receiving remittances from family members who had not lived in the respondent's household, and thus appear as though they have no family members living abroad. In order to address this issue, we offer a second, "adjusted MCI" that simply assumes that all remittance recipients also have a migrant family member. Though we recognize this assumption almost certainly does not hold for all 275 respondents who fall into this category, we are confident that it does for most. The range for this "adjusted MCI" then remains 0–3.0 but simply does not have any respondents fall in the 2.0 category. Because so few cases were involved, though, the difference in the mean values of the two measures is negligible. More generally, though, this issue raises questions about the advisability of our overall index strategy and the decision to attach differential weights to the three items. Though we contend that such a decision is theoretically defensible, there are alternative approaches to using these survey items to measure migration connections that merit exploration.

Our second approach to measuring migrant connections addresses not only the item weighting decisions we used for the MCI but also the issue of the inclusion of the "migration intentions" item. Though we do see such intentions as an indication of at least minimal exposure to a migrant network of some sort, the fact that one set of dependent variables used in work on migration connections (e.g., Goodman and Hiskey, 2008) includes attitudes toward the political system, an endogeneity issue arises where migration intentions may be a consequence of system dissatisfaction. Though we still contend that expression of migration intentions serves as a useful proxy for at least some degree of connections with migration, we recognize the strong theoretical case, one that begins with Hirschman's work, for why the causal arrow may run from system dissatisfaction to a desire to leave that system. Thus, in order to more confidently parse out the unique effects of migration connections on individuals living in Latin America, we proceed with a second analytical strategy that drops the "migration intentions" item from our measure.

Using only the migrant family member and the remittance items, we offer two ways to approach their use in analyses of migration connections. The first, most straightforward approach is to simply include each item as a separate dummy variable. If, as we suspect, the vast majority of respondents who report receiving remittances also have migrant family members, then the remittance dummy variable would represent the category with the strongest degree of migration connections. Indeed, in most research on remittance senders and receivers, there is little mention of individuals receiving remittances from non-family members (Pew, 2003). We therefore choose to place those 275 respondents into our second migrant category below:

Baseline group: Those with no migrant connections (no migrant family members; no remittances) (N = 25,367; 73.5 percent of total)

Migrant Connection Category #1: Those with migrant family connection (migrant family member, but does not receive remittances. N = 5,486; 12.5 percent of total)

Migrant Connection Category #2: Those with remittance connections (receives remittances) (N = 3,668; 10.6 percent of total).

With these categories, we can use dichotomous variables as mentioned above, or again rely on an additive scale similar to the MCI approach, creating an ordinal measure where the baseline group receives a value of 0, Category #1 receives a value of 1, and Category #2 receives a value of 2. When taking the latter approach, we produce the distribution of scores displayed in Table 9.2. As can be seen, the same general story emerges from this second approach, with the frequency distributions for the overall sample and the three countries of Mexico, El Salvador, and Argentina all telling the same stories as told in Table 9.1.

What the sum total of these measurement strategies suggests to us is that by using this multipronged approach we can begin to gain confidence in

Table 9.2.   Migration Connection Categories Across Latin America and Selected
Countries

Reduced MCI Scores	Total Sample	Mexico	El Salvador	Argentina
0	26,269	1,165	819	1,362
	76.15%	74.7%	52.9%	91.7%
1	4,838	275	404	90
	14.0%	17.6%	26.1%	6.1%
2	3,393	120	326	34
	9.8%	7.7%	21%	2.3%
Total	34,500	1,560	1,549	1,486
	100%	100%	100%	100%

Source: AmericasBarometer, 2008

the utility of these survey items to tap migration connections across Latin America, both at the individual and country levels. We now turn to a brief descriptive review of variations in these migrant connections across Latin America and a series of construct validity tests of the measures at different levels of aggregation. These tests first explore how well our measures of migration connections correspond to other country and local-level measures of migration activity in the region, and then how well they correspond to other concepts that theoretically should relate to varying degrees of migration connections. We then conclude with a discussion of the utility of these measures in future analyses of the impact migration connections may have on such areas as the political attitudes and behaviors of individuals living in Latin America as well as the broader economic and political development processes taking place in the region.

EVALUATING MEASURES OF MIGRATION CONNECTIONS

Figure 9.1 displays the country ranking of the mean MCI, adjusted MCI, and Migration Connection Category scores. As is clear, all paint the same picture of a region with highly distinct levels of migration connections, ranging from the extensive connections in Haiti, Jamaica, and El Salvador to the negligible connections in Chile, Venezuela, and Brazil. Only in two cases, Peru and Colombia, do the aggregate rankings of the countries change when using the Migration Connection Categories approach. Since this measure dropped the Migration Intentions item completely, it is encouraging that we find such similar aggregate results. This suggests that the three items do indeed tap the idea of migration connections in similar ways. One slight concern that

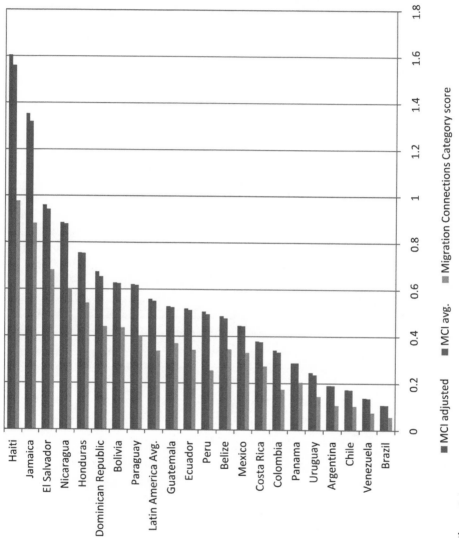

Figure 9.1.

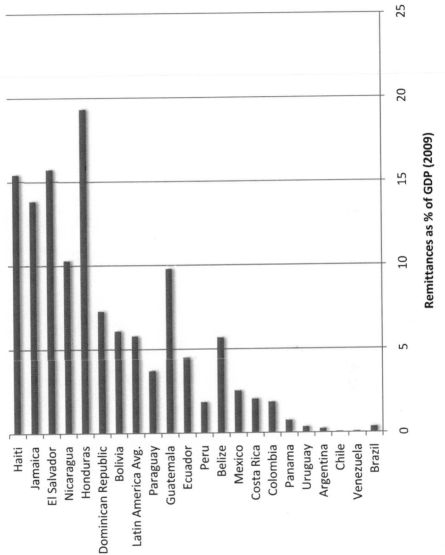

Remittances as % of GDP (2009)

Figure 9.2.

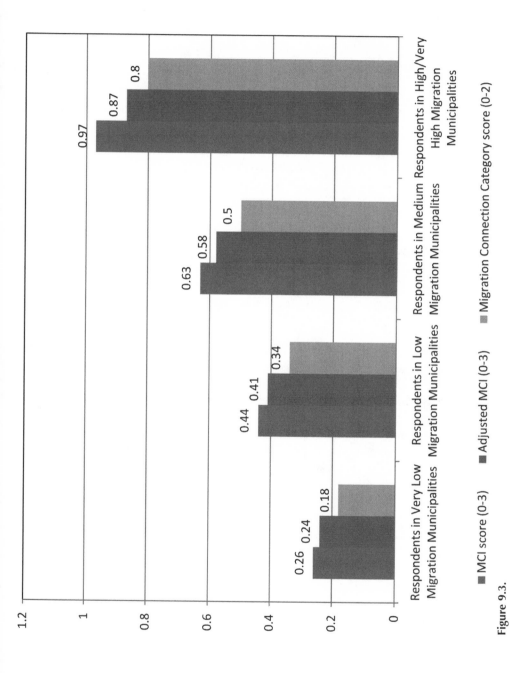

Figure 9.3.

arises from the country rankings is the appearance of some sensitivity of all the measures to population size, with the larger countries lining up at the bottom of the chart while many of the smaller countries are at the top. The fact, however, that Costa Rica, a country with a population of 4.1 million and very little migration activity, ranks behind Mexico (pop. 109.9 million) for all three measures suggests that at least at the country level these measures are indeed offering a useful indicator of migration connections across Latin America.

Another test of the utility of these country-level measures of migration connections is to compare them with another measure of migration unrelated to the survey items. In Figure 9.2 we offer a graphical display of the fairly strong relationship between our MCI country rankings (as displayed in Figure 9.1) and the amount of remittances received by countries in 2007 as a percentage of their GDP. While Figure 9.2 only displays a bar for the remittance measure, the order of the countries from top to bottom in the chart reflects the MCI rankings in Figure 9.1. With few exceptions, the country MCI ranks based on our survey based items are remarkably similar to the country rankings based on relative remittance rates. Though cases such as Honduras and Belize stand out due to their unusually high rate of remittances relative to the size of their economies, the majority of the twenty-one countries fall in or around the same position.

We now move to the municipal level to assess how well our Migration Connection measures map to other measures of migration activity at a lower level of aggregation. Returning to LAPOP's Mexico 2008 survey data, we again employ CONAPO's Migration Intensity index as a basis of comparison for our migration connection measures. The expectation here is that the average Migration Connection score will correspond to the CONAPO Migration Intensity categories of "very low," "low," "medium," and "high/very high." As is evident in Figure 9.3, this expectation is strongly supported, with a consistently significant increase in the mean respondent scores of all three Migration Connection measures across the four municipal migration contexts. All of the differences in means across these four categories are significant at the $p<.001$ level. At one level this strong association between municipal migration context and mean Migration Connection scores is intuitive: respondents living in high migration contexts should have higher levels of connections to migration. However, the fact that a set of measures based on survey data correlates so strongly with municipal migration scores developed by a Mexican government agency using 2000 census data is an encouraging sign that our measures are indeed effectively tapping the concept of migration connections and capturing meaningful variations in levels of such connections across country, community, and, we hope, individuals.

It is to the individual level that we turn now, in an effort to at least offer an initial assessment of whether our Migration Connection measures are indeed producing valid differentiations in citizens' levels of connections with migration across a wide range of contexts. We employ here a standard approach to testing the validity of a measure by examining its construct validity or the extent to which it is related to another set of variables with which it should be theoretically related. To some extent the previous discussion of our measures' aggregate relationship with country and municipal level measures of migration intensity represent an effort to assess the construct validity of our measures at those aggregate levels. We contend that at both levels, the measures emerge as valid indicators of their intended concept. But it is at the individual level that we are most concerned with our measure tapping the concept of migration connections, for it is at the individual level that we are most interested in uncovering the effects of migration connections.

As noted earlier, both Goodman and Hiskey (2008) and Armendáriz and Crow (2010) find strong evidence for individuals with migration connections to exhibit higher levels of non-electoral forms of participation. Though the latter authors focus on alternative forms of political participation, and the former find that those living in high-migration contexts exhibit higher levels of community-level civic participation, the similarity in the two sets of findings is striking. We capitalize on the theoretical and empirical links established by these authors in offering our final test of the construct validity of our migration connection measures. Using local participation questions included in the AmericasBarometer 2008 survey we expect our measures of migration connections to exhibit behavior consistent with the prior research that suggests that higher levels of connections to migration will be associated with higher levels of local forms of civic and political participation. Thus if we categorize respondents into the three Migration Connection Categories, for example, we should find increasingly higher levels of community participation as we move from those respondents who have no migration connection to those who have migrant family members and receive remittances. Table 9.3 displays the mean participation scores for these three groups of respondents across the following four types of local participation activities:

1. Over past twelve months tried to help solve a community problem (1 = Never; 2 = Once or twice a year; 3 = Once or twice a month; 4 = Once a week)
2. Over past twelve months participated in committee to improve the community (1 = Never; 2 = Once or twice a year; 3 = Once or twice a month; 4 = Once a week)

Table 9.3   **Migration Connection Categories and Local Participation Levels**

Migration Connection Categories	Solve Community Problem	Parents Association Meeting	Religious Organizations	Town Council Meetings
0	1.52**	1.66**	2.22**	.101**
1	1.64*	1.73**	2.43**	.123*
2	1.69*	1.83**	2.66**	.13*

Source: LAPOP AmericasBarometer 2008. Number of asterisks* denotes the number of statistically significant differences (at p<.05) exist between one group mean and the other five groups using bothTamhane's
T2 and Dunnett's T3 pairwise comparison tests with equal variances not assumed. For example, the group
of respondents with a score of) in the Adjusted MCI have a group mean 1.50 for the "Solve a community
problem" item. This mean is statistically distinct from all five other MCI categories' means for this item.
For the first three participation items, the value range is 1–4 where: 1 = Never; 2 = Once or twice a year;
3 = Once or twice a month; 4 = Once a week. For the "Attended community meeting" item, the values
are: 0 = No; 1 = Yes.

3. Over past twelve months attended meetings of religious organizations (1 = Never; 2 = Once or twice a year; 3 = Once or twice a month; 4 = Once a week)
4. Over past twelve months attended town meeting of any sort (0 = No; 1 = Yes)

This assessment of the construct validity of the Migration Connections Categories measure offers consistent support for the contention that the measure at least is capturing a basic distinction between those respondents with no migration connections and those with some type of connection. Across all four participation variables, the mean score for the "no Migration Connections" category of respondents is consistently and significantly less partici-patory than the two other Migration Connections categories. Thus whether in the form of attendance at religious meetings or town council meetings, those with no migration connections were, on average, far less participatory than their migration-connected counterparts. Where this test of the construct validity of our migration measure runs into a bit of difficulty is in the lack of significant differences between the group means of the two categories of respondents with some form of migrant connection. Only for attendance at religious meetings are the mean scores of these two groups significantly dis-tinct from one another. In fact, for the other types of local participation, there is a striking similarity in the mean scores for these two groups.

When we carry out the same analysis of means on the Migration Connection Index (both full and adjusted), we find even stronger support for the validity of these measures and their utility in tapping the level of connec-tions to migration individuals across Latin America have. Though not all group means are significantly different from each other, in virtually all of the

Table 9.4.   Adjusted Migration Connection Index and Local Participation Levels

Adjusted MCI Scores	Solve Community Problem	Parents Association Meeting	Religious Organizations	Town Council Meetings
0	1.50*****	1.71*	2.25****	.094*****
.5	1.57***	1.71*	2.21****	.115*
1.0	1.63*	1.73*	2.43****	.122*
1.5	1.63*	1.73*	2.44****	.124*
2.5	1.67**	1.75*	2.60****	.126*
3	1.69**	1.88*****	2.70****	1.87*

Source: LAPOP AmericasBarometer 2008. Number of asterisks* denotes the number of statistically significant differences (at p<.05) exist between one group mean and the other five groups using bothTamhane's
T2 and Dunnett's T3 pairwise comparison tests with equal variances not assumed. For example, the group
of respondents with a score of) in the Adjusted MCI have a group mean 1.50 for the "Solve a community
problem" item. This mean is statistically distinct from all five other MCI categories' means for this item.
For the first three participation items, the value range is 1–4 where: 1 = Never; 2 = Once or twice a year;
3 = Once or twice a month; 4 = Once a week. For the "Attended community meeting" item, the values
are: 0 = No; 1 = Yes.

comparisons we see an increased level of average participation rates among
the groups with higher levels of connections to migration. Only for the town
council participation variable does the MCI not appear to capture any meaningful differences among respondents. Conversely, for attempts to solve a
community problem, we see a seamless progression of increased activity with
each increase in the MCI category. Though certainly not perfect across all of
the variables examined here, this exercise in construct validity tests offers
sufficient support for a continued, and more nuanced, exploration of the various ways that migration connections may be affecting political attitudes and
behaviors among those left behind across Latin America.

CONCLUSION

Our goal in this paper has been to introduce a new and, we hope, productive way of thinking about and measuring migration connections across the
Americas. Though much work has been carried out on the basic question of
how migration affects the economic and political development prospects of
sending countries around the world, we know of few if any works that have
focused these efforts on the reported connections to migration of citizens of
these sending countries. We have tremendously valuable ethnographic studies of the various effects of migration on sending communities and countries
and equally important work on the economics and demographic effects of
migration on sending communities.

We put forth our systematic, individual-based measures of migration connections not as a replacement for these other methodological and disciplinary approaches, but rather as merely one more step in trying to answer the wide range of questions related to the fact that in some communities, in some countries, in some regions of the world, millions of people are leaving their homes, friends, and family members behind, but continuing to maintain contact with them through the ever-expanding and evolving communication technologies. The impact these journeys have on the migrants themselves is well documented, though still not entirely understood. The impact these journeys, and the individuals who take them, have on those left behind is still an area with more questions than answers. Our hope is that through a more systematic assessment of migrant connections, we can begin to make progress in this area of research.

NOTES

1. These items revolve around the question of whether the respondent has any plans to emigrate in the near future.

2. This is the one item included in the Latino barometer surveys that can potentially tap the beginning of a person's connection with migration, as we explain below.

3. As defined by the Mexican government's Population Council in its "Migration Intensity Index" that relies on 2000 census data to assess the migration levels across the over 4,000 municipalities in Mexico (CONAPO, 2005).

4. LAPOP carried out nationally representative surveys in the following country: Mexico; Guatemala, El Salvador, Honduras, Nicaragua, Costa Rica, Panama, Colombia, Ecuador, Bolivia, Peru, Paraguay, Chile, Uruguay, Brazil, Venezuela, Argentina, Dominican Republic, Haiti, Jamaica, and Belize. The total number of respondents for the 2008 round of the AmericasBarometer was 34,521. Surveys were also carried out in the United States and Canada, but those data are not included in this work. For more information on the sampling procedures used for the surveys and other background information on the project, see the project's website at http://www.vanderbilt.edu/lapop/.

Chapter 10

Remittances as an Economic Development Engine

Regional Evidence from Mexico

Pia M. Orrenius, Madeline Zavodny, Jesús Cañas, and Roberto Coronado

Remittances play a critical role in the Mexican economy.[1] Mexicans living in the United States sent a record $25 billion back home in 2008, putting remittances third after oil and maquiladora exports as a generator of foreign currency for Mexico. Remittance flows exceeded foreign direct investment into the country. Further, remittances were equal to about 3 percent of the value of Mexico's gross domestic product that year, with their relative importance having more than doubled since 2000.

Remittances are an important source of funds not just for Mexico but for many developing countries. Remittance flows to developing countries reached $328 billion in 2008, up 15 percent from 2007, with India, China, and Mexico the top three recipients.[2] The tremendous volume of remittances raises the question of what role remittances play in economic development. Do remittances foster economic growth, as developing countries surely hope, or do they instead encourage more out-migration and discourage economic activity among those who remain behind?

Mexico is an ideal country for examining these issues. Understanding how remittances affect economic development within Mexico is crucial for policymakers both in Mexico and its neighbor to the north, the United States. Mexico has experienced a staggering outflow of labor—about 8 million workers, or over 15 percent of the Mexican-born labor force, have migrated to the United States in recent years. While migration and the accompanying remittance flows are sizable for the country as a whole, they are quite varied geographically. A handful of Mexican states are responsible for the bulk of migrants and remittances.

Data enabling researchers to study the effects of remittances on economic development at the Mexican state level have recently become available.

Although there is a large and growing literature on the effects of remittances at the household and national levels, relatively few studies examine effects at the state level. State-level analysis offers important advantages. National effects can mask large regional disparities while household level analysis struggles with the fact that households which receive remittances may differ substantially from households that do not, making meaningful inferences about the effects of remittances more difficult. State-level analysis allows us to form a panel data set with both temporal and spatial variation while still getting at the general equilibrium or multiplier effects of remittances.

This chapter presents an overview of recent trends in Mexican remittances. It then reviews the literature on the economic impacts of remittances to Mexico and summarizes our recent research findings on the effects of remittances on several aspects of economic development, including employment, unemployment, wages, wage inequality, and school enrollment rates. Based on Mexican state-level data from 2003–2007, the results discussed here indicate that remittances improve labor market conditions — formal employment rises and unemployment rates fall when remittances increase in high-migration states. Remittances also appear to shift the wage distribution to the right by reducing the fraction of workers in a state who earn the minimum wage or less. However, we do not find any remittance effects on school enrollment rates.

RECENT TRENDS IN MEXICAN REMITTANCES

Remittances to Mexico rose steadily from the mid-1990s until the onset of the global downturn in 2008. Based on data from Banco de México, inflation-adjusted remittances to Mexico grew at an average annual rate of 15.9 percent during 1995 to 2002; the growth rate rose to 24.3 percent during 2003 to 2006. However, with the onset of the recession in the United States, remittances to Mexico were down about 1 percent in 2007 from the previous year and fell an additional 7.2 percent in 2008. As of August of 2009, remittances to Mexico were down 13.7 percent from twelve months prior (see Figure 10.1).

What drove the rapid growth of remittances to Mexico? This question has puzzled researchers because the most likely economic and demographic forces do not seem to have changed at the same pace at which remittances increased. Fundamental factors, such as the size of the Mexican migrant population, their incomes and the strength of their ties to Mexico, did not grow as fast as remittances during this period.[3] For example, real remittances almost doubled from 2000 to 2005 while the Mexican-born population in the United States grew by only 20 percent. Estimates indicate Mexican migration

Thousands of 2009 dollars

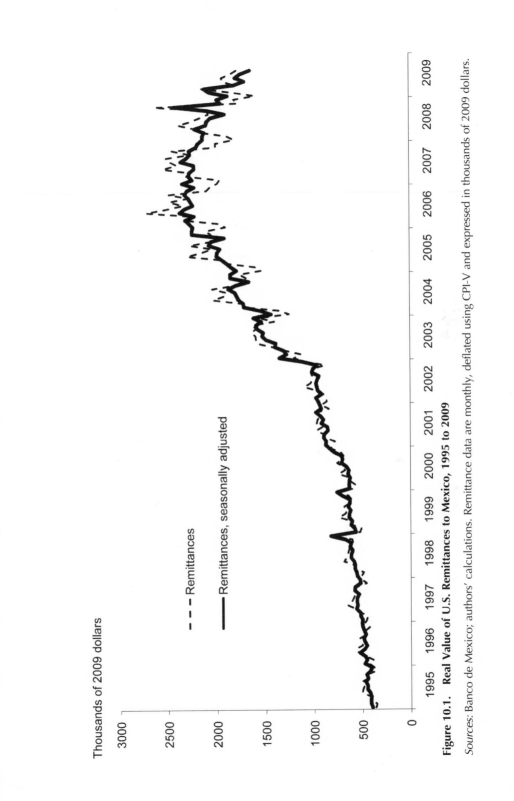

Figure 10.1. Real Value of U.S. Remittances to Mexico, 1995 to 2009

Sources: Banco de Mexico; authors' calculations. Remittance data are monthly, deflated using CPI-V and expressed in thousands of 2009 dollars.

flows—legal and illegal—actually fell during 2001 to 2003 as the United States experienced a recession followed by a weak labor market recovery.[4] Migration flows from Mexico to the United States in 2004 and 2005 were still well below 2000 levels. Meanwhile, real median weekly earnings among Mexican immigrants in the United States rose less than 7 percent during 2000 to 2005, and the dollar appreciated only 7.4 percent vis-à-vis the peso during that time.[5]

The biggest change among remittance drivers during the early 2000s was in the average transaction cost of money transfers. The cost of sending funds to Mexico fell more than 50 percent between 2000 and 2006.[6] One major cause of this decline was greater competition. More than 100 money-transfer organizations served Mexico in 2005, compared with only five in 1995.[7] Costs also fell due to technological change, such as increased use of debit and credit cards and the creation of transfer options, such as the Federal Reserve System's Direct a México automated clearinghouse system. As costs declined, large numbers of migrants switched from carrying money home to using electronic transfers. Banco de México estimates that electronic transfers rose from 53 percent of remittances in 1996 to 86 percent in 2003 and reached 93 percent by 2006.[8]

Electronic money transfers are easier to keep tabs on, and some of the displacement of informal remittances has contributed to increases in overall transfers. In this way, better measurement has contributed significantly to the high rate of remittance growth in recent years. In addition, Banco de México overhauled its procedures for collecting and recording remittance data. In October 2002, Banco de México issued rules under which all banks and wire-transfer companies had to register with the central bank and report monthly remittances by Mexican state of destination. These changes led to a more accurate measure of remittance flows (and made state-level research possible).[9] All together, lower transaction costs, the increase in the use of formal transfer mechanisms and the new measurement system, not changes in fundamental economic factors, likely account for most of the growth in remittances in the 2000s.

Remittance flows are not evenly distributed throughout Mexico. Not surprisingly, remittances go primarily to states that are the main sources of international migrants. These states tend to be relatively rural and poor. Remittances represent as much as 15 percent of economic activity (gross state product, or GSP) for those states. As shown in the map (Figure 10.2), the central–western states attract most of these financial flows, with Michoacán at the top with almost $2.5 billion in 2006, or 16.1 percent of GSP. Guanajuato follows at $2.1 billion (14.8 percent), then Jalisco at $2 billion (2.4 percent) and Estado de México at $1.9 billion (6.3 percent). As a share of GSP,

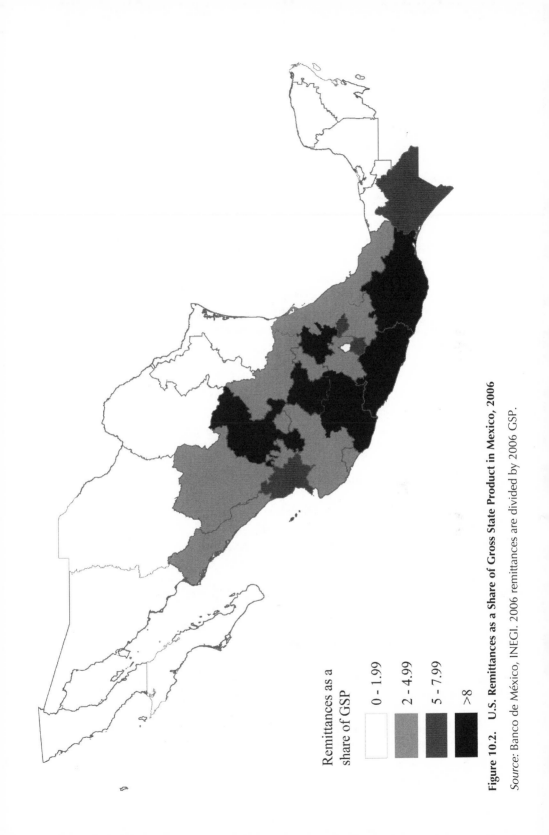

Figure 10.2. U.S. Remittances as a Share of Gross State Product in Mexico, 2006

Source: Banco de México, INEGI. 2006 remittances are divided by 2006 GSP.

Remittances as a
share of GSP

0 - 1.99

2 - 4.99

5 - 7.99

>8

remittances are also significant in Guerrero, Zacatecas, Oaxaca, and Nayarit. In contrast, the northern Mexican border states of Baja California Norte, Sonora, Chihuahua, Nuevo León, Coahuila, and Tamaulipas are among those with the lowest remittances, both in levels and as a share of GSP. Together, they received less than $1.7 billion in remittances in 2008, which represented only 0.9 percent of their joint GSP.

Remittances vary across states and time. Figure 10.3 shows the real value of remittances to four very different transfer-receiving states, Michoacán, Guanajuato, Estado de México, and Oaxaca. The major reason for the differences in levels is, of course, the number of migrants from that state, which in turn reflects population size, income, economic development, and history. The central-western states in Mexico, such as Michoacán and Guanajuato, have been sending migrants to the United States since the Mexican Revolution. U.S. migration was predominately made up of seasonal agricultural workers for decades, so the workers who migrated were farm workers at home as well. Once migrant networks were in place and the Mexican economy took a turn for the worse in the 1970s, 1980s, and mid-1990s, northward migration intensified.[10] Migrants in the United States began to spread into non-farm industries, such as construction, manufacturing, and services. The source areas became increasingly diversified as well. Relatively new sending states in Mexico included Estado de México and Oaxaca.

Growth patterns also differ by state. Year-to-year changes are driven by the volume of migration outflows, by the characteristics of migrants, by the industries in which migrants are employed, and by changes in economic growth in the destination. Figure 10.4 displays remittances indexed to their 2003 level in order to better show growth over time and across states. The effect of the 2008–2009 recession is apparent, as all states experienced declines in remittances starting in 2007 or earlier. Newer sending states appear to have faster remittance growth while older, mature sending states have slower growth. There may be several reasons for this, including the fact that migrants from newer sending states tend to go to new destinations in the United States, which typically have faster-growing economies.[11] Also, research suggests that recent migrants are the most active remitters and that remittances decline with years in the United States.[12] Michoacán accounts for more remittances than any other state but experienced the slowest growth during this period, with the downturn beginning in 2006. Michoacanos tend to go to the Midwest, where the economic decline started earlier than in other parts of the United States, which likely contributed to the poor performance of migrants' remittances. But Michoacanos are also well established and settled in the United States and, over time, their families have joined them, weakening their ties to Mexico.

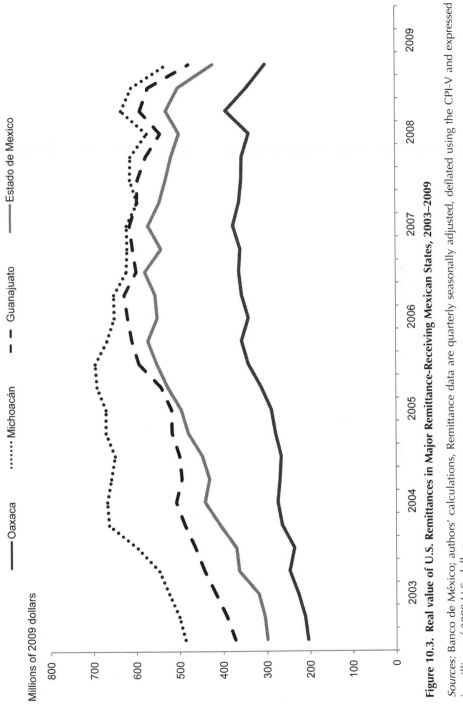

Millions of 2009 dollars

——— Oaxaca •••••• Michoacán – – Guanajuato ——— Estado de Mexico

Figure 10.3. Real value of U.S. Remittances in Major Remittance-Receiving Mexican States, 2003–2009

Sources: Banco de México; authors' calculations, Remittance data are quarterly seasonally adjusted, deflated using the CPI-V and expressed in millions of 2009 U.S. dollars.

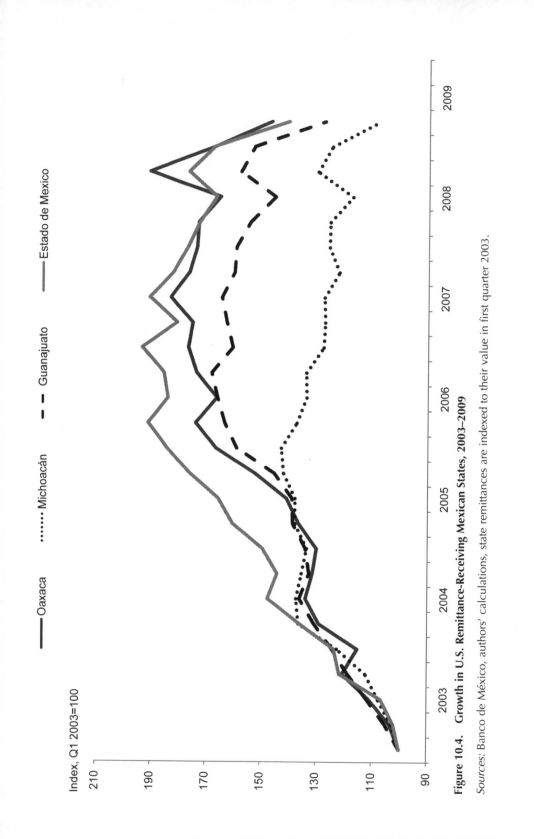

Figure 10.4. Growth in U.S. Remittance-Receiving Mexican States, 2003–2009

Sources: Banco de México, authors' calculations, state remittances are indexed to their value in first quarter 2003.

For the Mexican states, remittances are an important source of income and economic stability. Money transfers from family members in the United States are crucial to maintaining living standards and sustaining local economies, particularly in relatively poor states. Over 1.4 million Mexican households, including more than 12 percent of rural households and almost 4 percent of urban households, receive remittances.[13] How exactly do remittances affect the families that receive them and the broader community?

PREVIOUS RESEARCH ON EFFECTS OF MEXICAN REMITTANCES

Because remittances have become a major source of income for many developing countries, there is a large and growing economics literature on the determinants and effects of remittances. Most of these studies concentrate on the economic impacts that such flows have on receiving, or home, countries. For Mexico, a growing body of research examines the effect of remittances on poverty, schooling, labor force participation, inequality, and the financial sector. We begin by briefly summarizing the expected economic effects of remittances from a theoretical point of view and then what empirical research reveals about the effects of remittances in Mexico.

From a theoretical standpoint, remittances can have both positive and negative economic consequences. Households that receive remittances are made better off because they have higher income, which boosts either their consumption or savings or both. These households may be able to make investments that they previously could not, including sending children to school. Both of these effects should spur economic development. Investment helps secure households' future income stream while higher consumption usually generates multiplier effects throughout the economy that help all households, not just those receiving remittances.

On the downside, remittance-receiving households may reduce their labor supply because they now have a source of funds other than their own labor income, hence they can consume more leisure. Remittance inflows and the associated higher consumption levels can lead to price increases and exchange rate movements that further undo some of the positive economic effects. Such price and exchange rate changes affect consumption not only among households that receive remittances but also among those who do not. Remittances can exacerbate income inequality by widening gaps between those households that receive funds and those who do not. Income inequality may be ameliorated, however, if remittances lead to improvements in employment and earnings among non-recipient households. Whether remittances boost economic development on net thus depends on a host of factors. In addition, short-run effects may differ from long-run effects.

Turning to empirical evidence, remittances appear to reduce poverty among recipient households in Mexico. Esquivel and Huerta-Pineda (2007) report that receiving remittances reduces a household's probability of being in poverty by about 6–10 percentage points, a sizable reduction given poverty rates that range from 16 percent to 44 percent of households, depending on how poverty is measured. López-Córdova (2004) shows that the fraction of households receiving remittances is negatively associated with the poverty rate across all Mexican municipalities in the year 2000.

Most research on Mexico finds evidence of a positive effect of remittances on educational outcomes. Hanson and Woodruff (2003) suggest that living in a household with a U.S. migrant increases years of schooling among girls whose parents have low education levels. Remittance inflows raise household income and relax credit constraints, which perhaps enables families to pay school fees and delay girls' entry into the labor force. Borraz (2005) finds a positive but small effect of remittances on schooling, with the impact only occurring for children living in cities with fewer than 2,500 inhabitants and whose mothers have a very low level of education. López-Córdova (2004) shows that the fraction of households receiving remittance income is positively associated with school attendance rates and negatively associated with child illiteracy rates across Mexican municipalities in year 2000.

The effect of remittances on labor supply is less sanguine for Mexico, although studies to date have focused only on recipient households. Hanson (2007) finds, after controlling for observable characteristics, that individuals are less likely to participate in the labor force if their household has sent migrants abroad or has received remittances from abroad.[14] He also finds that, during the 1990s, women from high-migration states became less likely to work outside the home than women from low-migration states. This suggests that remittances might reduce labor supply among those remaining in Mexico, although the effect could be due to migration instead. Cox-Edwards and Rodriguez-Oreggia (2009) find no systematic difference in labor force behavior between households that receive remittances and those that do not.

Previous research suggests that remittances increase income inequality in Mexico. Mora-Rivera (2005) shows that international remittances increase the Gini coefficient—a measure of inequality—in rural Mexican communities. However, he concludes that domestic remittances, which are from workers moving within Mexico, reduce the Gini coefficient. These differing impacts could be driven by migrant selection. If domestic migrants are from the lower end of the income distribution, their migration should boost incomes among poor households, reducing income disparities rather than increasing them.

Remittances appear to have played a key role in the development of the financial sector in certain areas of Mexico. Remittances have spurred financial intermediation in small communities that might otherwise have little access to banks. Demirgüç-Kunt et al. (2007) show that remittances have a positive impact on bank deposits, number of bank accounts and bank branches at the municipal level in Mexico. In addition, migration and ensuing remittances may boost investment and alleviate capital constraints (economic parlance for the inability to borrow funds for productive uses). Based on a survey of more than 6,000 self-employed workers and small firm owners located in forty-four urban areas of Mexico, Woodruff, and Zenteno (2007) find that migration is associated with higher household investment levels, especially in automobiles, tools, and inventories. Taylor and Wyatt (1996) report that remittances boost livestock ownership among rural Mexican households. Migration and remittances thus can help fund investment among families who are unable to borrow funds for productive uses, thereby fostering economic development.

Previous research thus suggests that remittances have a positive effect on economic development in Mexico, on balance. Much of the research discussed above is based on comparing households that receive remittances with those that do not. We next turn to further evidence on the effects of remittances, but at the state level rather than the household level. This is done in order to mitigate two concerns. The first is that households that receive remittances may differ from households that do not in ways that are not readily observable. The second is that household-level surveys tend to capture about one-third of the official volume of international remittances as measured by Banco de México. A state-level analysis can use a more complete measure of remittances. It also can capture indirect effects of remittances on non-recipient households, the so-called multiplier effects or positive spillovers that may result.

EVIDENCE ON THE EFFECT OF REMITTANCES ON ECONOMIC DEVELOPMENT IN MEXICO

We examined the relationship between remittance levels and several indicators of economic development at the state level in Mexico during 2003 to 2007.[15] We merged quarterly data on remittances with quarterly data on formal-sector employment, median wages per day (in real pesos, deflated using the regional Mexican CPI) and the unemployment rate. At the annual level, we examined the effect of remittances on school enrollment and the wage distribution. The measures of enrollment are the fractions of age-appropriate children enrolled in primary, secondary, and technical (or vocational) schools, and universities, in the state. The measures of the wage distribution are the fractions of workers earning less than or equal to the national minimum wage, one to two times the minimum wage, two to three times the minimum wage, three to five times the minimum wage, and more than five times the minimum wage.

We regressed each quarterly or annual state-level measure of economic development on the level of real remittances received in that state. The regressions included controls for real foreign direct investment, net international migration flows, and size of labor force. They also included state and time-fixed effects. The state effects control for unobservable differences that are fixed over time, such as distance from the U.S. border, while the time-fixed effects control for changes that are common to states, such as changes in the U.S. or Mexican economy. Because the effects of remittances are likely to be larger in high-migration states, we only included high-migration states in some specifications. We addressed endogeneity concerns by using U.S. wages as an instrumental variable for remittances and the relative sizes of male birth cohorts by state in Mexico from 1973–1977 as an instrumental variable for net migration flows.[16]

The results indicate that remittances generally have a positive effect on economic development in Mexican states. Higher remittances are associated with better outcomes in labor markets, although these effects are difficult to discern in states where migration is less common. In high-migration states, wages and employment rise with remittances while unemployment rates fall. For instance, our analysis suggests that an additional $100 million in remittances to a state in a quarter will increase formal-sector employment by 15 percent and reduce the unemployment rate by 2.78 percentage points. Table 10.1 provides a summary of these results, both for all states (column 1) and for high-migration states (column 2).

Regarding the impact of remittances on the wage distribution, remittances appear to reduce the fraction of workers earning at most the minimum wage by almost 2 percentage points and boost the share which earns three to five times the minimum wage by 0.84 percentage points. In the sample of high-migration states, remittances have an even larger negative effect on the share of lowest-wage workers (–2.42 percentage points) and are associated with an increase of 1.25 percentage points in the share of workers who are in the middle of the wage distribution (those earning two to three times the minimum wage).

However, the analysis does not reveal a causal relationship between remittances and schooling in all states or in high-migration states. Given the

Table 10.1. Estimated Effects of Remittances on Mexican States, 2003–2007

	All States	High-Migration States
Labor Market Measures		
Employment	0.35	0.15*
Wages	0.12	0.06
Unemployment rate	−2.95	−2.78**
Wage Inequality		
Share of workers earning ≤1 times MW	−1.94**	−2.42**
Share of workers earning 1–2 times MW	0.57	0.71
Share of workers earning 2–3 times MW	0.70	1.25*
Share of workers earning 3–5 times MW	0.84**	0.70
Share of workers earning >5 times MW	−0.18	−0.24
School Enrollment		
Enrollment rate in primary school	−0.17	0.08
Enrollment rate in secondary school	0.51	0.30
Enrollment rate in university	−0.03	−0.03
Enrollment rate in technical school	−0.11	−0.11

Note: Shown are estimated coefficients on remittances from two-stage least squares regressions. Each row is from a separate regression. Significance levels are denoted * $p < 0.1$ and ** $p < 0.05$. See text and Orrenius et al. (2009) for details on other variables and data sources.

complexity underlying enrollment rates, including demographic composition, more detailed data may be needed to identify the true effect of remittances on schooling. Further research on the effect of remittances on enrollment is particularly important given that increases in educational attainment are likely the best source of long-term economic growth for developing countries like Mexico.

CONCLUSION

Remittances can have myriad benefits for developing countries. Studies have shown that migrants' transfers home can reduce poverty, increase children's schooling, finance household investments, and increase access to financial services. Remittances have become a significant source of income for Mexico, especially for states in the central-west part of the country. This makes it important to study the trends behind such a large flow of funds and the role those funds play in economic development. A growing literature that attempts to fill this gap generally finds positive effects on economic development, although it suggests that income inequality may increase in at least the short run. Our analysis at the state level in Mexico complements previous research by showing that remittances improve regional labor markets by increasing employment and lowering unemployment rates. In contrast to prior work, our analysis indicates that remittances shift the wage distribution to the right by reducing the fraction of workers who earn the minimum wage or less. Our analysis provides little evidence that remittances boost aggregate school enrollment rates.

The role of remittances in economic development is likely to only grow in importance. The years 2008 and 2009 marked a decline in U.S.–Mexico migration and remittances, but both are likely to resume previous trends once the U.S. economy begins to grow again. In the meantime, how the decline in remittances and the return of migrant workers from the United States affected Mexican incomes, consumption and economic development is an important question not only for Mexico—and other developing countries in similar situations—but also for the United States as a destination for millions of Mexican immigrants.

NOTES

1. The views expressed here are those of the authors and do not necessarily reflect those of the Federal Reserve Bank of Dallas or the Federal Reserve System. This chapter is based on previous research by the authors (Cañas et al., 2007; Orrenius et al., 2009).

2. Ratha and Xu (2008).

3. See Cañas et al. (2007).

4. Passel and Suro (2005).

5. The change in Mexican immigrants' earnings is based on authors' calculations from the Current Population Survey Outgoing Rotation Group data.

6. Orozco (2006a).

7. Mascaró (2007).

8. Cervantes (2007).

9. Banco de México data indicate both higher levels and faster growth in remittances than other data sources, including estimates from the U.S. Department of Commerce and from individual- or household-level surveys of senders and recipients. For a discussion, see Cañas et al. (2007).

10. Massey et al (1987).

11. Massey (2008).

12. Lucas (2008).

13. Demirgüç-Kunt et al. (2007).

14. Amuedo-Dorantes and Pozo (2009) find that labor supply also responds to the volatility in remittances.

15. This section is based on Orrenius et al. (2009).

16. Endogeneity bias is a concern because remittances increase in response to economic hardship. In other words, states with lower levels of development or lower growth rates might receive more remittances. Similarly, out-migration may have impacted the economic variables under consideration here. In addition, migration effects can confound the impacts of remittances. Controlling for endogeneity bias requires having an instrumental variable that is correlated with remittances but not with other Mexican economic development indicators and that varies within Mexican states over time. See Orrenius et al. (2009) for more details and data sources.

Chapter 11

Is It Remittances or Is It Tickets to America?

A First Look at Financial Transfers among New U.S.-Legal Immigrants Born in Mexico

Guillermina Jasso

There are two main stories about Mexicans who go to the United States.[1] One is about Mexicans in difficult economic circumstances who go north for sojourns of varying duration, work hard, send money home to their families—spouse and children, as well as parents and siblings—yearn for their homeland, build new homes in their villages, and return home for periods of varying duration until the final idyllic homecoming. There are songs to go with this story, and movies as well. Who can forget the haunting strains of *Canción Mixteca*, which has played on radio stations in the ever since it was written in 1912 by the Oaxacan José López Alavez (1889–1974)? Originating during the Mexican Revolution of 1910, at a time of great social and political upheavals, when soldiers and others were far from home, it soon became the anthem of Mexicans abroad.

In the second story, Mexicans, whatever their economic circumstances, go to the United States, fall in love with the American way of life—the Constitution, the customs—some marrying Americans of diverse ancestral origins, some changing their names, adopting George Washington and Abraham Lincoln, reading endlessly the letters of Abigail and John Adams, and disappear into the American population, surfacing several times a year to remember their heritage, and, of course, eating avocados and hot peppers every day of the year. There is no song for this story, and no movies. At least not yet. And there is not even good information about these quintessential Americans, for they may not check the Hispanic box on Census questionnaires and social surveys.

In between these extremes, there are many variations. In particular, there are many variations for the first and sometimes the second generation. Some Mexicans move permanently to the United States but remain lifelong Mexicans.

They re-create in the United States the neighborhoods of Mexico, from struggling rentals to plush gated communities. The corresponding merchants and social institutions sprout to serve them—corner groceries and expensive private schools. Some become insular, not too different from the Amana Colonies or the Amish. Others remain Mexicans but live in integrated neighborhoods and form warm friendships with Americans of many ancestral origins. And there is even a new pattern, reminiscent of summers in the American northeast in the days before women went to work, in which a Mexican family buys a vacation home in the United States, and before two Christmases and two Easters have passed, the wife and children are living full-time in the United States and the husband commuting on weekends from Mexico.

These diverse patterns are linked to transfers behavior. Remittances are an integral part of the first story, but, except for the occasional gift or care package to townspeople in the old country, disappear from the other stories.[2]

The literature on remittances highlights the part they play in improving life for individuals and families in the origin country. But, besides remittances, there is a second type of financial transfers—designed to improve life for individuals and families in the origin country by helping them to leave the country. This is the legendary type of transfer from the turn of the twentieth century, as hundreds of thousands of men left Europe to start a life in the United States and saved enough money to send to their wives for the passage to America.

The contemporary counterpart of this second type of financial transfer has three components: (1) money for the passage, (2) money for preparation for the passage in terms of investment in health and education, and (3) money for preparation for the passage in terms of obtaining documents (birth certificates, marriage certificates, police records, medical examinations) and filing forms in the origin country—that is, money for the visa process. Put simply, the second type of financial transfer is a *ticket to America.*

Of course, the ticket to America involves not only financial transfers to the origin country but also expenditures in the United States, the latter not only expenses associated with helping the new immigrant get settled, but also expenses related to the visa process. For example, an earlier migrant who now sponsors a spouse and children must also file forms in the United States (in particular, the I-130, Petition for Alien Relative, which starts the visa process). Further, the sponsor assumes financial responsibility for the immigrant, if it becomes necessary, via the contractually binding affidavit of support (Form I-864 and related forms), until the immigrant becomes a U.S. citizen or achieves forty quarters of qualified work.

Both types of financial transfers—remittances and tickets to America— have the potential to not only improve the lives of individuals but also to have significant subsequent development effects for the origin country, as the literature on remittances as well as recent accounts of new enterprises in China and India suggest.

The migrant stories above and their distinctive transfers patterns are intimately linked to the migrant's legal status in the United States. A priori we may conjecture that in the first story remittances are regular and stable. However, if a previously circular migrant decides to remain in the United States, the character of financial transfers may gradually change from remittances into a ticket to America and then disappear altogether, except for remittances to parents and occasional care packages. This change may occur while the migrant is unauthorized but will almost always have already occurred when the migrant achieves legal permanent residence in the United States and becomes a full-time U.S. resident.

This chapter contributes to the understanding of transfers behavior by examining financial transfers among persons born in Mexico who are new legal immigrants in the United States. Data are drawn from the first round of the New Immigrant Survey (NIS), a longitudinal survey of immigrants admitted to U.S. legal permanent residence in 2003. The paper is organized as follows: the second section provides some brief background on the U.S. immigration context. The third section describes the data. The fourth section presents a portrait of adult Mexico-born U.S. immigrants in the 2003 cohort. The fifth section describes the transfers behavior of the Mexico-born immigrants, contrasted to the entire cohort; introduces a new way to think of transfers between select pairs of immigrants and their transfers partners; and then focuses on one important subset—immigrants who acquire a visa as the parent of a U.S. citizen. The sixth section concludes.

U.S. IMMIGRATION CONTEXT

As shown in Table 11.1, under current U.S. immigration law, foreign-born persons in the United States include legal permanent residents (LPR), LPRs who have become naturalized citizens of the United States, persons in a variety of legal temporary statuses, and persons in an illegal status.

Importantly for present purposes, both legal temporary residents and unauthorized migrants may be further characterized according to whether they are already on the LPR track, aspire to LPR, or do not aspire to LPR. Transfers behavior will differ across these subtypes. For example, migrants who do not aspire to LPR may regularly send remittances home, while those already on

Table 11.1. Types of Foreign-Born Persons in the United States

1 Legal permanent residents (LPR)
2 LPRs who have naturalized
3 Legal temporary residents (nonimmigrants)
3.1 On LPR track
3.2 Aspiring to LPR
3.3 Not aspiring to LPR
4 Unauthorized
4.1 On LPR track
4.2 Aspiring to LPR
4.3 Not aspiring to LPR

the LPR track or aspiring to become LPRs may have begun the shift away from remittances and toward the ticket to America.

The United States admits about a million persons a year to LPR (Table 11.2).[3,4] The system of visa allocation provides numerically unlimited visas to the spouses, minor children, and parents of adult U.S. citizens (a set collectively called "immediate relatives of U.S. citizens"). Numerically limited visas are granted to three main categories of immigrants: (1) family immigrants, comprised of the adult children and siblings of U.S. citizens (a set collectively called "close relatives of U.S. citizens" to distinguish them from "immediate relatives of U.S. citizens") and the spouses and children of LPRs, (2) employment immigrants, comprised of five subcategories, and (3) diversity immigrants (winners of the lottery visas designated for persons from countries underrepresented in recent immigration—defined as countries whose nationals received less than 50,000 LPR visas during the preceding five years). Two additional categories of LPR visas have subsets of both numerically limited and numerically unlimited type: (4) humanitarian immigrants (including refugees, asylees, and parolees), and (5) legalization immigrants—that is, illegal immigrants who are becoming legal, including registry-provision immigrants (who qualify in virtue of length of illegal residence) and cancellation-of-removal immigrants, plus immigrants targeted by special legalization legislation (such as the Immigration Reform and Control Act of 1986, or IRCA, and the Nicaraguan Adjustment and Central American Relief Act of 1997, or NACARA).[5]

The person who qualifies for an immigrant visa (e.g., the spouse or other relative of a U.S. citizen, or the prospective employment-visa worker) is known as the *principal*. Many of the visa categories also provide immigrant visas for the spouses and minor children of the principal. Major exceptions include visas for the spouses, parents, and minor children of U.S. citizens.

Mexico became the top origin country of U.S. legal permanent residents in the 1961–1970 decade, and has remained in first place to this day. Earlier,

Table 11.2. Recent and Current Annual Flows of New Legal Permanent Residents to the United States

| Fiscal Year(s) | All Immigrants | Born in Mexico | |
		Number	Percent
A. Average annual flow			
1991–1995	781,848	89,436	11.4
1996–2000	771,307	151,367	19.6
2001–2005	980,388	175,365	17.9
B. Annual flow			
2006	1,266,129	173,749	13.7
2007	1,052,415	148,640	14.1
2008	1,107,126	189,989	17.2
2009	1,130,818	164,920	14.6
2010	1,042,625	139,120	13.3

Notes: Flows of new legal permanent residents (LPR) represent all persons granted legal permanent residence during the period. In most years, over half of all new LPRs are already living in the United States. Through FY 2000 figures refer to the total, non-IRCA-legalization number of new LPRs. This number was reported as "total non-legalization" in Table 4 of the INS and DHS *Yearbooks* through the 2004 *Yearbook* and could be obtained for Mexico from Table 8 through the 2000 *Yearbook*. Starting in FY 2001 figures refer to the full total, including a very small number of IRCA legalizations. IRCA legalizations declined from a high of over a million in 1991 to less than a thousand in every year since 1998, with a low of 8 in 1999 and totals of 263, 55, 39, 128, 188, 217, 93, 116, and 83 in Fiscal Years 2001 thru 2009, respectively (DHS *Yearbooks*, Table 4 through 2004, Table 7 thereafter). Mexico-born IRCA legalizations in the period 1991–2000 totaled 1,047,351.

in the 1921–1930 decade, it had been in second place, behind Canada. But the European upheavals sent Mexico to fifth place in the 1931–1940 decade. From there it began its ascent, to fourth place in the 1941–1950 decade, and third place in the 1951–1960 decade. In the three decades from 1931 to 1960, Germany was in first place—due, of course, to the large number of refugees from the Nazi era.[6]

As shown in Table 11.2, the proportion Mexico-born among new legal immigrants hovered in the 18–20 percent range in the 1996–2005 period, and has fluctuated between 13 percent and 17 percent since then. Thus, persons born in Mexico are a substantial component of the annual flow of new legal immigrants. Indeed, no other country even comes close in the share of LPR visas granted to its nationals. In 2008–2010, for example, China, in second place, had shares of 5.7–7.3 percent (DHS *Yearbooks*, 2008–2010).

Many people around the world are ineligible to receive a visa to visit the United States because they are poor; they fall under the public charge ground of ineligibility. The process of applying for an immigrant visa is arduous, time-consuming, and expensive. Persons waiting for numerically limited

Table 11.3.   Legalization of Illegals: U.S. Immigration Registry Law

Year of Act	Entry Date	Years in U.S. Required	
		Shortest	Longest
1929	1 July 1924	5	15
1939	3 June 1921	18	19
1940	1 July 1924	16	34
1958	28 June 1940	18	25
1965	30 June 1948	17	38
1986	1 January 1972	14	39

visas may have to wait many years. The current upper extreme (as of June 2011) is over twenty-three years for persons from the Philippines approved for visas as the siblings of U.S. citizens; at the other extreme, visas in some of the employment-based categories (such as that for priority workers, including world-renowned scientists, artists, and executives) are available immediately (U.S. Department of State, *Visa Bulletins*).

Because many persons who wish to come to the United States are not eligible for a visa—not even to visit—and many others can visit but must wait many years before advancing to LPR, a population of unauthorized immigrants has accumulated. Table 11.3 summarizes the registry provisions of U.S. law, provisions which enable persons who have lived for many years in the United States to become legal permanent residents. Not surprisingly, registry provisions made their appearance in 1929, soon after numerical restrictions were imposed on U.S. immigration in 1921. As shown in Table 11.3, the requisite duration of U.S. residence has ranged from 5 years in 1929 to thirty-eight years in 1986, before passage of IRCA reduced it to fourteen, and now thirty-nine, years.

Besides the wait for numerically limited visas, all visa applications take processing time. In general, the visa process lasts from the date when the first application is filed (known in numerically limited visa cases as the "priority date") to the date that legal permanent residence is granted.[7]

NEW IMMIGRANT SURVEY

Data analyzed in this chapter are drawn from the NIS 2003 cohort. The sampling frame consists of all new LPRs whose records were compiled in the seven-month period May–November 2003. On average, interviews were conducted approximately four months after admission to LPR; mean (median) time elapsed between LPR and interview was seventeen (fourteen) weeks. All respondents were interviewed in the language of their choice—a total of ninety-five languages. The analyses reported in this paper pertain to immigrants born in Mexico who are in the Adult Sample (age 18 and older). These immigrants ($n = 1,164$) are a subset of the main sampled immigrants ($N = 8,573$) in the Adult Sample (age 18 and older). The response rate for the main sampled immigrants in the Adult Sample was 68.6 percent. They were re-interviewed in 2007–2010 and will continue to be re-interviewed periodically.[8]

Interviews were conducted not only with the main sampled immigrants but also with their spouses, if they were married and the spouse was living in the household. Additionally, assessments were carried out on children age 3–12 according to an age-eligibility schedule, and up to two children 8–12 in the household were also interviewed.

Information was obtained on a large number of topical domains, including education, employment, marriage and fertility, health, language, and religion. The following are some features of the data which affect the questionnaire items analyzed in this paper.

1. Because the sampling frame was the official administrative record, the data base includes information from both the administrative records and the survey interviews.
2. Immigrants who upon being contacted reported they were overseas received only a short questionnaire, and their spouses were not interviewed. The size of this subset is 321 in the Adult Sample.
3. Although the survey was designed as a face-to-face interview, a majority of the interviews in the Adult Sample became telephone interviews. This occurred for two reasons: (1) some immigrants requested telephone interviews due to their work schedules or family responsibilities, and (2) some immigrants requested to be interviewed in languages for which no trained bilingual interviewers or interpreters could be found in the area.
4. Spouses living in the household with the sampled and interviewed (non-overseas) immigrant were invited to participate. A total of 4,334 did so.
5. Main sampled immigrants with spouses in the household were given the choice to designate self or spouse as the financially knowledgeable person to be administered all the financial portions of the questionnaire.
6. Some questions were asked only of randomized subsets of respondents.

Finally, the Adult Sample was stratified by type of visa. All descriptive characteristics reported below (except those in Appendix Table 11.13) are based on data weighted to adjust for the sampling stratification.

A few notes on the data are collected in an appendix. As well, Appendix Table 11.13 reports the basic survey characteristics of the Mexico subset and the full Adult Sample.

A PORTRAIT OF NEW LEGAL IMMIGRANTS BORN IN MEXICO AND ADMITTED TO LPR IN 2003

Immigrant Class of Admission

If all immigrants from Mexico had numerically restricted visas, the flow from Mexico would be constrained to under 30,000 visas a year (7 percent of the annual worldwide limit, which fluctuates somewhat). In Table 11.2,

Table 11.4. Immigrant Class of Admission, New U.S. Legal Immigrants Born in Mexico: NIS-2003

Class of Admission (Percent)	Born in Mexico			All Immigrants
	Men	Women	All	
Spouse of NB U.S. citizen	26.7	19.3	22.3	16.2
Spouse of FB U.S. citizen	25.8	23.7	24.6	17.9
Parent of U.S. citizen	15.4	20.6	18.5	11.9
Minor child of U.S. citizen	8.50	3.60	5.55	3.38
Adult single child of U.S. citizen	3.73	3.69	3.71	3.28
Adult married child of U.S. citizen	1.26	1.19	1.22	1.72
Spouse of adult child of U.S. citizen	.84	1.20	1.06	1.51
Sibling of U.S. citizen	1.65	2.02	1.87	3.94
Spouse of sibling of U.S. citizen	.41	.55	.50	2.49
Spouse of LPR	1.38	13.5	8.66	2.44
Child of LPR	3.52	2.81	3.09	2.81
Employment principal	3.60	.61	1.80	6.02
Employment spouse	.46	.75	.63	3.63
Diversity principal	0	0	0	5.53
Diversity spouse	0	0	0	2.58
Refugee/asylee/parolee principal	0	0	0	5.35
Refugee/asylee/parolee spouse	.24	0	.09	1.22
Legalization principal	6.52	6.49	6.50	7.98
Other	0	0	0	.05
Number of Immigrants	457	707	1,164	8,573

Note: Percentages based on weighted data.

we saw that for fifteen years the annual total has been five to six times as high. Accordingly, the numbers of immigrants from Mexico with numerically unrestricted visas—spouses, parents, and minor children of U.S. citizens—must be quite large. And so they are, as shown in Table 11.4, which provides the distribution of major immigrant visas, by sex.

In particular, as has been often remarked, persons born in Mexico seem to be exceptionally attractive mates for U.S. citizens. Indeed, almost 47 percent of all Mexico-born adult immigrants are admitted to LPR as spouses of U.S. citizens. Another 18.5 percent gain LPR as parents of U.S. citizens. And another 6 percent acquire LPR as minor children of U.S. citizens.

A large majority of U.S. immigrants born in Mexico—approximately 91 percent—have family visas. Besides the 71 percent admitted with numerically unrestricted immediate relative visas, another 8.36 percent are relatives of U.S. citizens and 11.8 percent are relatives of LPRs. That leaves 2.43 percent with employment visas and 6.5 percent with legalization visas.

Sex Ratio

Most U.S. legal immigrants from Mexico are women—60.2 percent in 2003 (Table 11.5). U.S. immigration in general is predominantly female and has been so since 1930. Data compiled by the U.S. Immigration Commission (1911) for the period 1820–1867 and incorporated into the series based on official immigration statistics in the U.S. Census Bureau's (1975) *Historical Statistics of the United States*, combined with figures from the INS and DHS *Annual Reports* and *Yearbooks* for the years since 1970, indicate that the percentage male was greater than 50 percent in every year before 1930 (except, trivially, in 1922) and generally less than 50 percent afterward (except during the years of IRCA legalizations and, trivially, in 1984 and 1985).

Female predominance in legal immigration may be due to two factors. The first is the provision of U.S. law by which spouses and parents of U.S. citizens may be admitted to LPR in unlimited numbers. Thus, brides may be more common than grooms, given the historically greater U.S. male presence in travel and military service abroad (which may be diminishing), and widowed mothers may be in greater supply than widowed fathers. The second is the very nature of restrictive immigration law. Before there were numerical restrictions on U.S. immigration, the inflow would include a large number of temporary sojourners—including young people (mostly males in the time before gender equality) who are in the migration stream to seek their fortune or for the adventure. Now

Table 11.5.   Basic Characteristics of New U.S. Legal Immigrants Born in Mexico: NIS-2003

| Characteristic | Born in Mexico | | | All Immigrants |
	Men	Women	All	
A. Gender and Age				
Percent female	NA	NA	60.2	56.5
Age at admission to LPR (years)	36.1	39.7	38.3	38.9
B. Location in Mexico's Stratification Structure: Family Income at Age 16				
Far below average	21.6	21.0	21.2	9.93
Below average	28.0	24.9	26.1	18.8
Average	39.7	42.6	41.4	53.1
Above average	6.68	8.34	7.67	14.5
Far above average	4.05	3.23	3.56	3.65
C. Educational Attainment and History				
Average schooling (years)	9.31	8.54	8.84	11.9
Any schooling in U.S. (if years of schooling > 0)	25.3	21.3	22.9	19.2
Years schooling in U.S. (if years of schooling in U.S. > 0)	6.27	5.86	6.04	4.46

Note: Estimates based on weighted data.

that immigration is restricted, as well as costly in time and money, the fortune-hunting and adventure-seeking segment of temporary sojourners may be diminished.

Age

Male immigrants from Mexico are almost four years younger, on average, than female immigrants from Mexico. This, too, appears to be an artifact of immigration law and visa status, as there are proportionally more spouses of U.S. citizens among men and more parents of U.S. citizens among women (Tables 11.4 and 11.5).

Figure 11.1 provides a closer look at age by presenting the quantile functions associated with the age distributions. The quantile functions depict age as a function of relative rank and thus simultaneously enable a look at both the position (quantity and rank) of particular individuals as well as the whole distribution. Thus, female immigrants from Mexico not only have a higher average age than male immigrants; they are also older than men in the region from the percentage rank of 3 to the percentage rank of 94.6. As a group, the

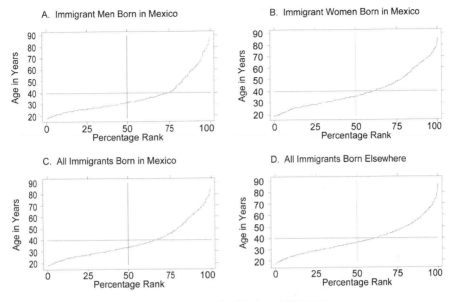

Figure 11.1. Quantile Function of Age Distribution: NIS-2003

Mexico-born are younger than those born elsewhere from close to the origin to about the 79.7 percentage point.

Family Income at Age 16

The NIS survey asked respondents about their family income when they were age 16, compared to families in the origin country. Five response categories were provided: far below average, below average, average, above average, and far above average. Table 11.5, panel B, reports the percentage distributions, by sex, and Figure 11.2 graphs the responses. As with the cohort overall (Jasso, 2011), there is little difference between the two sex-specific distributions. However, there is a marked difference between the Mexico distribution and that in the cohort overall. While over half of the cohort reported average family income (53.1 percent), the figure for Mexico was almost 12 percentage points lower: 41.4 percent. And while the left tails are fatter than the right for the cohort overall, with 28.7 percent reporting income below or far below average versus 18.2 percent reporting income above or far above average, the asymmetry in the cohort pales beside the asymmetry among the Mexico-born, with 47.3 percent reporting income below or far below average and 11.2 percent reporting income above or far above average. Indeed, the proportion below and far below average exceeds the proportion average by almost 6 percentage points. Note that the proportion in the far above average category is virtually the same for the Mexico-born and the cohort overall.

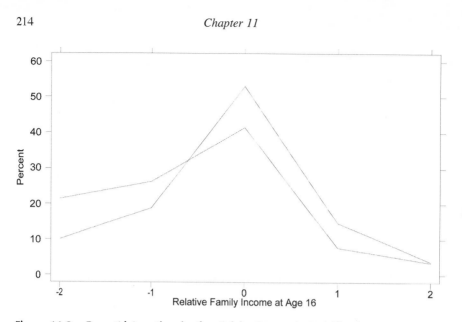

Figure 11.2. **Parental Location in the Origin Country's Stratification Structure, All Immigrants and the Mexican Born: NIS-2003. The full Cohort's Distribution has the Higher Mode**

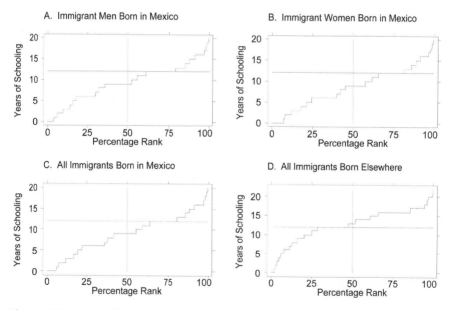

Figure 11.3.   Quantile Function of Schooling Distribution: NIS-2003

Schooling

As shown in Table 11.5, panel C, average completed years of schooling among the Mexico-born are 9.31 years among men and 8.54 years among women. Figure 11.3 provides the quantile functions for the schooling distributions. The graphs indicate that men have higher schooling than women throughout the entire range until about the 97th percentile.

Average schooling is lower among the Mexico-born than in the full cohort—by almost three years (Table 11.5). The quantile function for the non-Mexican subset dominates that for the Mexico-born throughout the entire distribution (Figure 11.3). Within visa class, average schooling is still lower among the Mexico-born. For example, average schooling among spouses of native-born U.S. citizens is 10.8 years among the Mexico-born and 14.4 among the rest; among spouses of foreign-born U.S. citizens, the Mexico-born average 10.5 years and the non-Mexico-born average thirteen years; in the parent-of-U.S.-citizen category, the Mexico-born average 3.51 years and the others 9.06 years. However, there are two exceptions to this pattern of lower schooling among the Mexico-born. Among immigrants admitted as the minor children of U.S. citizens (age between 18 and 21), average schooling is 11.7 years among both immigrants born in Mexico and immigrants born elsewhere. And among spouses of LPRs, the Mexico-born have a higher average schooling—10.5 years—than the others, who register 6.31 years. There may be other important differences between the Mexico-born and the non-Mexico-born that could help account for the schooling differences.

Of course, the content (and effects) of years of schooling differ across countries. Completion of six years of schooling, for example, may signal quite different "education" in the Mexico of thirty years ago and the United States of today. Additionally, the link between ability and schooling may differ as well; dropping out of high school in the United States signals something quite different from having lower schooling because there were no schools available or because, say, girls were not allowed to go to school.

Among immigrants from Mexico, 5.86 percent report no schooling whatsoever, as do 2.48 percent of those born in the rest of the world.

Within the set of immigrants born in Mexico who have some completed schooling, 23 percent report schooling in the U.S. This figure is higher than the 19 percent in the full cohort. Nevertheless, both figures are high, suggesting substantial time spent in the United States prior to LPR. Probing further, among those who report some U.S. schooling, the average number of years is higher among the Mexico-born—6 years—than among the full cohort—4.46 years.

Visa History and Visa Process

New Arrivals and Adjustees

Most new legal immigrants are already living in the United States and adjust their status from a temporary (or unauthorized) status to LPR. The proportion adjustees averaged 55.8 percent in the 1996–2005 period, and since then registered 64.7 percent, 59.0 percent, 57.9 percent, 59.1 percent, and 54.3 percent in fiscal years 2006 to 2010, respectively (INS and DHS *Yearbooks*). Immigrants born in Mexico are no exception to this trend and, in fact, far exceed the averages for the cohort. As shown in Table 11.6, the proportions adjustee among Mexico-born men and women were 80.7 percent and 73.6 percent, respectively, among the adults surveyed in the NIS-2003.

Previous U.S. Experience

The proportion adjustee underestimates the proportion already living in the United States, for two reasons: First, employment-based immigrants who

Table 11.6. Visa History and Visa Process among New U.S. Legal Immigrants Born in Mexico: NIS-2003

Characteristic	Born in Mexico			All Immigrants
	Men	*Women*	*All*	
Duration of visa process (years)	4.50	4.99	4.80	4.43
Percent adjustee	80.7	73.6	76.5	57.4
Documents lost, new arrival principals	10.0	3.06	5.22	7.56
Documents lost, adjustee principals	15.5	14.2	14.7	13.7
Documents lost, new arrivals	9.40	2.98	5.04	7.27
Documents lost, adjustees	15.3	14.0	14.5	13.5
Visa depression	14.4	22.3	19.1	17.4
Visa depression, new arrivals	9.43	20.8	17.0	15.5
Visa depression, adjustees	15.4	22.7	19.6	18.7
Identifies as principal, men principals	NA	NA	69.4	83.0
Identifies as principal, women principals	NA	NA	66.6	75.6
Identifies as principal, men nonprincipals	NA	NA	22.3	33.3
Identifies as principal, women nonprincipals	NA	NA	12.5	22.2

Note: Estimates based on weighted data.

are already in the United States may elect consular processing. Second, new-arrival immigrants may already be living in the United States, in an undocumented status, and return to their origin country for visa processing.

Of course, even more new arrivals have previous U.S. experience. For example, among the FY 1996 immigrants surveyed in the NIS-Pilot, 55 percent were adjusting status and an additional 14 percent had been in the United States before, for a total of 69 percent with U.S. experience.

Have new legal immigrants from Mexico who are new arrivals been in the United States before? Given the proximity of the countries, it is not implausible that all of them have U.S. experience.

Duration of Visa Process

The time between the filing of the first document in the visa process (e.g., Form I-130, Petition for Alien Relative) and admission to LPR averaged 4.5 years for male immigrants from Mexico—similar to the average of 4.43 years for the cohort overall–but almost five years for female immigrants (Table 11.6). From approximately the 24th to the 91st percentile, visa process among the Mexico-born is longer for women than men (Figure 11.4). Thus, the duration of the visa process for all Mexico-born exceeds that for immigrants born elsewhere, on average (Table 11.6), as well as throughout the distribution except between the 87.6 and 99.8 percentiles (Figure 11.4).

Within visa category, the shortest average duration of the visa process was 1.11 years for new-arrival wives of native-born U.S. citizens (Jasso, 2011)—a piece of information which will be helpful in interpreting financial transfers below.

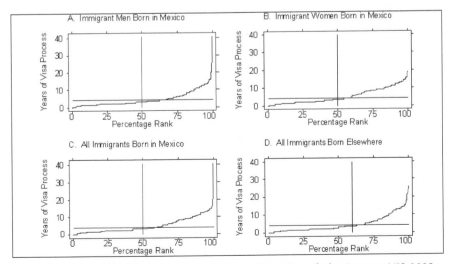

Figure 11.4. Quantile Function of Distribution of Duration of Visa Process: NIS-2003

Lost Documents

As discussed on Internet immigration blogs and forums, sometimes immigration offices lose documents. For prospective immigrants, lost documents are more than an irritation. Lost documents can prolong the visa process, wreak havoc on carefully made plans for housing (at origin and at destination) or for children's schooling (at origin and at destination), and, indeed, jeopardize the entire immigration process. Lost documents contribute to what Levine, Hill, and Warren (1985:3) call the "emotional costs" of migration. As in the full cohort, the incidence of lost documents is greater in immigration offices in the United States than in U.S. consulates and embassies abroad (Jasso, 2011). The rate of lost documents among Mexico-born immigrants, shown in Table 11.6, is almost three times as high for adjustee principals (whose cases receive more processing in immigration offices in the United States)— 14.7 percent—as for new arrival principals (whose cases have more processing in the U.S. embassy and consulates in Mexico)—5.22 percent.

There is also an intriguing gender difference. While the rates of lost documents in offices in the United States are similar for Mexico-born men and women principals (15.5 percent and 14.2 percent, respectively), in Mexico-based offices, the rate is over three times as high for men as it is for women (10 percent versus 3.06 percent). Further research may reveal the relevant gender dynamics.

Of course, while documents are lost in "cases," everyone in the case is affected—not only the principal but also the accompanying spouse and children. Thus, Table 11.6 also shows the rates of lost documents experienced by NIS respondents, whether or not they were the principal.

Visa Depression

The survey asked respondents whether, during the past twelve months, they had "ever felt sad, blue, or depressed because of the process of becoming a permanent resident alien." As shown in Table 11.6, 19 percent of the Mexico-born immigrants answered in the affirmative, slightly higher than the 17.4 percent in the cohort overall. Adjustees are expected to have higher visa depression than new arrivals, because adjustees endure two distinct stressful processes simultaneously—learning to live in a new country and the visa process—while new arrivals endure the visa process in the comfort of their origin country and only after admission to LPR do they begin the process of accommodating to the United States (Jasso, Massey, Rosenzweig and Smith, 2005). Among immigrants from Mexico, men display the expected pattern, adjustees reporting a higher proportion of visa depression than new arrivals (15.4 percent versus 9.43 percent). Women, however, do not; they report rates that are high and very similar—20.8 percent among new arrivals versus 22.7 percent among adjustees. A possibility that future work might explore is that some of the women new arrivals are really already living in the United States illegally and going through the visa process as if they were living in Mexico.

Declaring Oneself the Principal

As noted above, the person who qualifies for an immigrant visa is known as the principal. The NIS asked respondents whether they were the principal. As shown in Table 11.6, among principals, 69.4 percent of the men born in Mexico and 66.6 percent of the women born in Mexico correctly identified themselves as the principal—less than the 83.0 percent and 75.6 percent among men and women, respectively, in the cohort overall. The pattern is similar among nonprincipals: Men are more likely than women to claim to be the principal, and non-Mexicans are more likely than Mexicans to claim principal status. The Mexico effect may be a further manifestation of the language or social status mechanisms discussed in Jasso (2011).

Interestingly, the gender differential among principals is smaller among immigrants from Mexico than in the cohort overall.

Previous Illegal Experience

Previous illegal experience can be estimated by combining information from the official administrative record and from the survey (Jasso, Massey, Rosenzweig and Smith, 2008; Jasso, 2011).

The main sources of information about previous illegal experience based on the administrative record are as follows: If admission to LPR is based on legalization, the immigrant class of admission provides this information; as shown in Table 11.4, approximately 6.5 percent of the NIS-2003 immigrants born in Mexico have legalization visas. Additionally, even if admission to LPR is based on one of the usual visa classes—such as family or employment—if the immigrant is adjusting status, the immigrant record includes the nonimmigrant class of admission and the most recent date of admission with that nonimmigrant visa. For example, the nonimmigrant visa, a temporary visa, may be an F-1 academic student visa, an L-1 intracompany transferee visa, or an H1-B specialty occupation visa. Immigrants who had entered the United States without entry documents—technically "entered without inspection"—are given the code EWI (sometimes abbreviated WI) in the nonimmigrant visa field of the immigrant record. In recent years, a new code has appeared, a code for unknown (UU or, sometimes, UN), as well as a tendency to leave the field blank. It is widely believed that both the UU code and missing data are a euphemism for illegal status. Finally, if the nonimmigrant visa is a visitor for pleasure visa (B2) and the most recent recorded entry is six years prior to LPR, it is reasonable to believe the person has overstayed the visa (Warren, 2003, unpubl.).

The main sources of information based on the survey are the questions in the trip history, which ask what kind of documents were used on each trip to the United States.[9]

Table 11.7 reports the proportions by component of the estimate together with the total combined estimates. As shown, immigrants born in Mexico have larger proportions than the cohort overall in every component except two. Not surprisingly, these are the legalization visa—given that some legalization programs, such as NACARA, are designated for persons born in certain countries not including Mexico—and the Warren overstay measure—given that immigrants from countries other than Mexico may not have the option to cross a land border without documents and thus fly in with a tourist visa.

An intriguing finding is the sex difference in the survey measures—while 64 percent of men born in Mexico report entering without documents, only

Table 11.7. Previous Illegal Experience among New U.S. Legal Immigrants Born in Mexico: NIS-2003

| | Born in Mexico | | | All |
Source of Information	Men	Women	All	Immigrants
Immigrant legalization visa	6.52	6.49	6.50	7.98
Nonimmigrant code EWI/WI	14.5	12.7	13.4	3.76
Nonimmigrant code UU/UN	37.2	26.6	30.8	12.4
Nonimmigrant code missing	22.0	22.6	22.4	14.4
Warren measure	3.62	5.39	4.68	5.12
Survey measures	64.0	45.7	53.0	21.6
Total based on legalization visa or EWI/WI code	19.8	18.1	18.8	11.4
Total based on record alone	77.4	67.3	71.3	35.7
Total including survey measures	85.4	72.4	77.6	39.6

Notes: The information based on immigrant and nonimmigrant visa is from the official administrative immigrant record. The four components based on nonimmigrant visas are mutually exclusive. The Warren measure refers to having a nonimmigrant tourist visa (B2) and reporting the most recent entry six years or more earlier. The two other components — the immigrant legalization visa and the survey measures — may be combined with any of the other codes, so that, for example, a given respondent may be included in both the legalization visa figure, one of the nonimmigrant visa figures, and the survey measures. Thus, the total estimate is less than the sum of the components. The total estimate may be an underestimate, as it may miss new-arrival immigrants who were already living in the United States, having entered without inspection, and do not report it in the survey measures; as well, the total estimate may miss persons who had been working without authorization.

45.7 percent of the women do so. This difference is larger than the sex difference based on the record alone, which is about 10 percentage points. Overall, 85.4 percent of the men are estimated to have previous illegal experience and 72.4 percent of the women.

These estimates may underestimate true previous illegal experience, as they may miss unauthorized employment as well as some reporting of illegal entry among new arrivals.

Persons born in Mexico who have achieved legal permanent residence in the United States have worked hard to attain a piece of the American dream. With lower family income during childhood and less formal education, on average, than their peers born in other countries, they have endured the hardships of illegality and the stresses of the visa process. We will now explore their transfers profile.

FINANCIAL TRANSFERS: REMITTANCES AND TICKETS TO AMERICA

The transfers portion of the questionnaire was administered as follows: First, it was administered to all main sampled respondents who did not have a spouse in the household or who were overseas. Second, in the case of non-overseas married main sampled respondents with the spouse in the household, the transfers questionnaire was given to those who said they were financially knowledgeable and to the spouses declared as financially knowledgeable. Of the financially knowledgeable spouses, 293 did not participate in the survey. Thus, the sample size for the cohort in the transfers section is 8,280 (=8573–293).

Estimating the Proportion of the Cohort Involved in Transfers

Approximately one-fifth of randomly chosen respondents—1,687—were asked a global question, "During the last twelve months, did you (or your spouse) give or receive any financial assistance (such as gifts, transfers, bequests, or loans) to or from your (or your spouse's) relatives, friends or employer?" Cases not involved in transfers were skipped out of the section on financial transfers.

If all respondents in the 20 percent randomized subsample understood the global question as encompassing all transfers, including transfers to spouse, parents, and children, then the global question provides a reasonable estimate of involvement in transfers. The estimate, based on weighted data, is

12.9 percent. However, if some immigrants involved in transfers with their spouse, parents, or children did not think of these persons as "relatives" and answered, "No," then the estimate is a lower-bound estimate.[10]

To construct a more reasonable estimate, we sum responses in the affirmative to all the questions tapping transfers with particular kinds of relatives, as well as with friends and employer. The two estimates do not correspond exactly. While the global question imposes no residence restriction on relatives and friends and no country of residence on the employer, the specific questions restrict transfers with relatives and friends to periods when they were "not living with you in the same house" and transfers with employer to "employer in the United States." Thus, except for the meaning of "relatives," the global question should yield a larger estimate than the sum of the specific questions.

There are two potential problems with the data on specific transfers, both of which are or will be addressed in the second and future rounds of data collection and the second of which can be overcome in specific analyses of special subsets. First, due to a programming error, the questions on transfers with siblings and siblings' spouses were not asked of the financially knowledgeable spouses of main sampled immigrants; thus, estimates of transfers with siblings are incomplete. Second, there is some ambiguity concerning the referent in the transaction when the information was obtained from the financially knowledgeable spouses. For example, the question tapping transfers from a U.S. employer asks, "Did you (or your spouse) receive financial assistance in the form of a loan or a gift from your current employer in the United States?" The referent employer may not be the same when the main sampled immigrant answers as when the spouse answers; indeed, the main sampled immigrant may be employed but not the spouse, and vice-versa. Similarly, children "not living with you in the same house" may not be the same children when the main sampled immigrant answers and when the financially knowledgeable spouse answers.

To estimate the proportions involved in each specific transfer, information obtained from the main sampled immigrants and from financially knowledgeable spouses was combined cognizant of symmetries. For example, to estimate transfers from a sampled immigrant to spouse, we combined information from sampled immigrants on transfers *to* their spouse and information from financially knowledgeable spouses on transfers *from* their spouse. Similar rules were defined for parents and spouse's parents, and so forth.

A final data matter. Recall that respondents who fell in the 20 percent randomized subsample for the global transfers question were skipped out of the specific transfers questions if they answered "No" to the global question. Accordingly, the specific questions were not asked of respondents in the

20 percent subsample who may have been involved in transfers with spouse, children, or parents but did not construe them as relatives, thereby reducing the proportion of the full cohort reporting involvement with specific transfers. To overcome this, we estimate the specific transfers involvement on the 80 percent subsample who did not receive the global question. Except for reduction in sample size, these 80 percent subsample estimates are good estimates of the corresponding proportions.

Table 11.8 presents estimates of involvement in all the specific transfers for which the NIS provides information, separately for men and women born in Mexico, all immigrants born in Mexico, and the entire NIS-2003 cohort. All estimates are based on the entire 80 percent of the sample or subsample who received the transfers questions (excluding only respondents whose financially knowledgeable spouses did not participate in the survey); these are 8,280 in the full sample, of whom 1,687 are in the 20 percent subsample and 6,593 in the 80 percent subsample. Thus, these estimates do not distinguish between individuals who are or are not "at risk" of particular transfers. Our intent here is to provide a portrait of the cohort and the Mexico-born subsample. Obviously, behavioral analyses will carefully define particular subsets—exploring transfers from employers only among those employed, transfers with parents only among those with at least one parent still living, transfers with spouses only among the married, and so forth.[11]

Table 11.8, panel A, reports the results of the global question asked of the 20 percent subsample. As shown, the Mexico-born have a lower involvement rate than the cohort as a whole—7.65 percent versus 12.9 percent. Within the Mexico-born, men have a higher involvement rate than women—10.5 percent versus 5.78 percent. These are, as discussed above, lower-bound estimates.

Table 11.8, panel C, reports the corresponding estimates of transfers involvement based on the specific transfers. The numbers are substantially larger than the global-question estimates—31 percent for the cohort overall versus 12.9 percent. Among Mexico-born women, the global and specific estimates differ even more—5.78 percent in the global estimate versus 25 percent in the specific-transfers estimate.

Evidently, the global question did not operate as intended; spouses, parents, or children were not seen as "relatives." Sampling fluctuation alone would be unlikely to account for these large differences between the two sets of estimates. Moreover, as discussed above, the global question is less restrictive than the specific questions, so that these differences may understate the misconstrual of "relatives." Accordingly, we rely in this paper on the 80 percent subsample estimates.

Based on the 80 percent subsample estimates, 26.7 percent of the men and 25 percent of the women from Mexico were involved in transfers during the

Table 11.8.   Transfers To and From New U.S. Legal Immigrants Born in Mexico During the Previous Twelve Months: NIS-2003

Variable	Born in Mexico			All Immigrants
	Men	Women	All	
A. Global Question Asked of Randomly Selected Subsample of 20 Percent				
Involved in transfers with relatives, friends, employer	10.5	5.78	7.65	12.9
Number of observations	91	143	234	1,687
B. Specific Transfers Questions, Based on Randomly Selected Subsample of 80 Percent				
Transfers to spouse	1.64	.44	.93	1.78
Transfers from spouse	0	3.38	2.02	2.90
Transfers both to/from spouse	0	.37	.22	.23
Transfers to own parents	10.2	6.00	7.72	8.83
Transfers from own parents	2.04	1.24	1.56	4.34
Transfers both to/from own parents	.08	0	.03	.25
Transfers to spouse's parents	4.24	3.45	3.77	4.53
Transfers from spouse's parents	.39	.65	.54	1.57
Transfers both to/from spouse's parents	0	0	0	.20
Transfers to children under 17	3.52	2.82	3.10	4.11
Transfers to children 17+	2.29	3.05	2.74	3.51
Transfers from children 17+	3.22	4.77	4.14	2.34
Transfers both to/from children 17+	.41	.50	.46	.20
Transfers to own siblings	1.38	.71	.98	2.28
Transfers from own siblings	.70	.56	.62	1.34
Transfers both to/from own siblings	0	0	0	.05
Transfers to spouse's siblings	.22	.20	.21	.61
Transfers from spouse's siblings	.08	.20	.15	.33
Transfers both to/from spouse's siblings	0	0	0	.01
Transfers to other relatives	.74	.80	.78	2.10
Transfers from other relatives	.92	1.44	1.23	1.06
Transfers both to/from other relatives	0	0	0	.02
Transfers to friends	0	0	0	.32
Transfers from friends	0	0	0	.11
Transfers both to/from friends	0	0	0	.01
Transfers from U.S. employer	0	.29	.17	.41

Table 11.8. **Transfers To and From New U.S. Legal Immigrants Born in Mexico During the Previous Twelve Months: NIS-2003** *(Continued)*

	Born in Mexico			All
Variable	Men	Women	All	*Immigrants*
C. Summary of Transfers, Based on Randomly Selected Subsample of 80 Percent				
Transfers to others	19.3	14.5	16.5	20.3
Transfers from others	7.34	11.5	9.83	12.4
Transfers both to/from others	.49	.87	.72	.94
Any transfers involvement	26.7	25.0	25.7	31.0
Number of observations in B and C	360	536	896	6,593

Note: Estimates are based on weighted data. Estimates in panels B and C are reported as percentages of the 80 percent randomized subset which was asked the transfers questions, whether or not respondents are married, have children, etc. All items in panel B except the employer item request information on transfers while the possible transfers partner was not living in the same house with the respondent. Data for transfers with siblings are incomplete.

year preceding the interview, somewhat less than the 31 percent in the cohort overall. On average, the interview occurred seventeen weeks after admission to LPR; thus, the referent period for transfers spanned, on average, approximately eight months prior to LPR and four months afterward.

The estimates in the summary panel C of Table 11.8 also show that there is movement of financial assistance both to and from the new legal immigrants. We will explore this in Section 11.4.3, below, but for now we note that there seem to be few specific-transfers cases in which the same individual participates in both giving and receiving assistance, that the proportion giving in any specific transfers exceeds the proportion receiving in any specific transfers not only in the full cohort—20.3 percent versus 12.4 percent—but also within the sex-specific Mexico-born sets—19.3 percent and 14.5 percent versus 7.34 percent and 11.5 percent, among men and women, respectively—and that, interestingly, the proportions giving and receiving are very close among Mexican women.[12]

As shown, new legal immigrants from Mexico have modest rates of financial transfers to others—19.3 percent among men and 14.5 percent among women. Clearly, they are not conforming to the first story with which we began. They have gotten their own tickets to America, paid their dues, so to speak, waited a long time, endured the hardships of illegality, and suffered visa depression, and now are building a new life. Moreover, even those who sent transfers may have been sending, not remittances, but rather tickets to America.

Estimating Involvement in Specific Transfers

Table 11.8, panel B reports estimates of giving, receiving, and both giving and receiving in each specific type of transfer. Careful study requires examination of the subset at risk of each kind of transfer. For example, the questions on transfers with spouse pertain only to sampled immigrants who were married and only to periods, within the last twelve months, when the two spouses were living apart. Estimates (not shown) indicate that within the Mexico-born, 6.88 percent of the men and 10.3 percent of the women reported having lived apart during the preceding year (16.3 percent in the entire cohort). The set who had lived apart obviously has small sample sizes for the Mexico-born. Ignoring for the moment the low sample size, what is noteworthy is that, not unexpectedly, the two sexes differ importantly in the direction of transfers. While 29.7 percent of the men report transfers to spouses, none of the women do so; and, in the only estimate based on more than fifteen observations, 43 percent of the women report transfers from spouses. Again, this signals distinctive patterns of giving and receiving, not only by gender but also by immigrant visa class.

Among the Mexico-born, the largest rates of specific transfers are transfers to own parents—10.2 percent among men and 6 percent among women. The second largest rates of specific transfers are transfers to spouse's parents, among men, while among women, transfers from children age 17 and older (which will be explored below).

The Mexico-born report no transfers involvement with friends or with relatives beyond spouse, parents, children, and siblings. In the cohort overall, the proportions engaging in such transfers are tiny.

Exploring and Interpreting Transfers to and from New Legal Immigrants and Particular Kinds of Transfers Partners

The estimates in Table 11.8, panel C indicate that there are nontrivial transfers to the legal immigrants themselves. Earlier we saw in Table 11.4 the distribution of new immigrants by visa type. It seems reasonable to expect that particular types of pairs of immigrant and transfers partner may exhibit distinctive transfers configurations. Accordingly, we construct a matrix with rows corresponding to immigrant visa type and columns corresponding to transfers partners. Table 11.9 presents the matrix and highlights nine cells in which the new immigrants received a ticket to America from the transfers partner.

In the three cells of the matrix in Table 11.9 in which the transfers partner is a spouse, there is one and only one transfers partner of that type. However, in the other six cells, there could be multiple partners of that type—for example, two biological parents and possibly a stepparent as well, more than one employer, and several children and siblings.[13]

In all nine cells, the immigrants may receive financial transfers from the transfers partners. In the cells with multiple potential transfers partners, the

Table 11.9. Transfers Matrix, by Immigrant Visa and Transfers Partner, Highlighting Special Pairs Where Immigrant Receives a Ticket to America from the Transfers Partner

Immigrant Visa	Transfers Partner						
	Spouse	Parent	Minor Child	Adult Child	Sibling	Friend	Employer
Spouse of NB US Citizen	Receive Ticket						
Spouse of FB US Citizen	Receive Ticket						
Parent of US Citizen				Receive Ticket			
Minor Child of US Citizen		Receive Ticket					
Adult Child of US Citizen		Receive Ticket					
Sibling of US Citizen					Receive Ticket		
Spouse of LPR	Receive Ticket						
Child of LPR		Receive Ticket					
Employment Principal							Receive Ticket
Diversity Principal							
Humanitarian Principal							
Legalization Principal							

financial transfers may involve either/both the sponsor for the visa and the other possible partners.

As noted, the information on financial transfers obtained in the NIS pertain to the year preceding the interview. Given that the average time between the date of LPR and the interview was four months and that the shortest visa process lasted 1.11 years (among new-arrival wives of native-born U.S. citizens), financial transfers received by the new immigrants in the nine cells were received while the visa process was ongoing and immediately afterward. Accordingly, financial transfers received by the new immigrants may be a component of the ticket to America, whether received in the origin country—such as funds for obtaining birth certificates, marriage certificates, military records, police records, school transcripts, medical examinations, vaccinations, and so forth—or in the United States (such as funds for security deposits on a lease or utilities), or may be a classic remittance for the immigrant's subsistence before traveling to the United States.

Note that financial transfers received by spouses of native-born U.S. citizens (the top left cell in Table 11.9) have a dual character. They both are and are not classic remittances. They resemble classic remittances if they are sent to another country. However, because the giver is not a migrant, they are not classic remittances. This duality extends to research. The literature on remittances does not analyze behavioral patterns associated with U.S. natives sending remittances abroad; yet macro studies, based on country-level financial accounts, do not distinguish between migrant and non-migrant senders. Note also that such transfers are not inconsistent with the usage of "remittance" in the classic care packages.

Thus, the immigrants in the foregoing nine special pairs have received a ticket to America, possibly including a financial component, and may also have received remittances in the past year. Those same immigrants may also have received financial transfers from the other transfers partners in the matrix; for example, a new parent immigrant may have received transfers from an employer, and a spouse of U.S. citizen may have received transfers from a sibling or friend. Indeed, those other partners may have contributed to the ticket to America.

Finally, all immigrants, of all types, may be simultaneously engaged in sending remittances. The spouse of a U.S. citizen, who received a ticket and possibly remittances from the U.S. citizen spouse, may be sending remittances to parents, children, siblings, and friends. And so also may every other immigrant type, including diversity, humanitarian, and legalization immigrants. Anecdotal evidence also suggests that, at least in the case of siblings, the new immigrant may be sending funds to the sponsor to cover all the sponsor's expenses (such as filing Form I-130). It is even possible to consider the extreme case in which the new immigrant handsomely compensates the sponsor, in effect purchasing the ticket to America. For now, however, it is probably safe to assume that at least in seven of the nine cells of Table 11.9—except those for immigrants admitted as siblings of U.S. citizens and as employment principals—the new immigrants have received a ticket to America.

Table 11.9 provides a way to assemble information about transfers involvement in the period leading up to the new immigrants' admission to LPR, highlighting the tickets to America they have received. Soon, however, the new immigrants of Table 11.9 will themselves be sending family members in the origin country tickets to America, generating a second phase and a second table. For example, Jasso and Rosenzweig (2010) examine new legal immigrants who have children abroad, exploring their decision, in the first few years after admission to LPR, whether to send remittances or instead send tickets to America.

Table 11.9 suggests that it may be substantively appropriate to analyze particular pairs of immigrants and transfers partners. We turn now to carry out exactly such an exercise.

Transfers and Housing Assistance among New Legal Immigrants Admitted as Parents of U.S. Citizens

Immigrants Achieving LPR as Parents of U.S. Citizens

The visa category for parents of U.S. citizens is the second most popular category for new immigrant visas, after that for spouses of U.S. citizens. In the years 2006–2010, for example, the number of immigrants admitted as parents of U.S. citizens was 120,441, 116,734, 121,470, 120,155, and 116,208, respectively, comprising 9.5–11.1 percent of the annual cohorts (DHS *Yearbooks*, 2006–2010). During the years between 1921 and 1965, the immigration of parents of U.S. citizens was unlimited for natives of the Western Hemisphere (like all immigration) and restricted for natives of the Eastern Hemisphere (first preference after 1924, second preference after 1952). Passage of the 1965 act placed the whole world under numerical restriction but exempted parents of adult U.S. citizens (along with spouses and minor children) from numerical restriction. The large flow of older immigrants via the parent visa has stimulated interest in new studies on this population, as they contribute to understanding of aging dynamics in the United States (Hauser, 2009).[14]

As shown in Table 11.4, Mexico follows the same pattern; the parent category is the second most popular visa category. The proportion of new immigrants admitted as parents of U.S. citizens was 15.4 percent among men and 20.6 percent among women. We now restrict attention to this subset. In the full Adult Sample ($N = 8,573$), there are 996 parents, and in the Mexico subsample ($n = 1,164$), there are 270 parents. Earlier we noted that the Mexico-born constitute the largest share of new legal immigrants (Table 11.2), and among the adults of the 2003 cohort they represent 17.5 percent (Jasso, 2011). But that share pales when compared to the Mexico-born share of parent-immigrants: 27.2 percent, almost 10 percentage points higher. The countries in second through fifth place are China (10.3 percent), India (8.93 percent), Philippines (7.91 percent), and Haiti (3.52 percent).

No consideration of parent immigrants would be complete without a brief look at the nativity of the sponsor-child. Among the 996 parent immigrants, 8.26 percent were sponsored by a now-adult child who was born in the

United States. The corresponding percentage among the Mexico-born parent immigrants is over twice as high — 18.1 percent. Viewed differently, among the parent immigrants sponsored by a (now-adult) child who was born in the United States, 59.5 percent were born in Mexico. The next highest share was 5.84 percent, who were born in Nigeria. Not surprisingly, gender and previous illegal experience play a part. Among the Mexico-born immigrants sponsored by children born in the United States, 77.7 percent are women, and among these mothers, 83.2 percent have previous illegal experience. A logit regression (not shown) of the probability that the parent-immigrant's sponsor is born in the United States reveals strong and highly significant positive effects of previous illegal experience and birth in Mexico, as well as a highly significant negative effect of age. The pooled model finds no effect of gender. However, in sex-specific logit regressions, we replicate the negative effect of age and positive effect of previous illegal experience among both sexes but a statistically significant Mexico effect only among women. We leave to future work further analysis of the sponsor-child's nativity, as well as of the parent immigrants' marital, fertility, and migration histories.

Excluding immigrants whose financially knowledgeable spouses did not participate in the survey leaves 969 parents, of whom 265 were born in Mexico. As above, for the transfers analysis, we examine the randomized 80 percent subsample. As shown in Table 11.10, panel A, this special sub-sample totals 784 parents, with 217 born in Mexico.

In the cohort overall, parent immigrants are twenty-five years older, on average, than the entire cohort (63.7 years versus 38.9 years, Tables 11.10 and 11.5). They are more predominantly female — by about 10 percentage points (66 percent versus 55.8 percent). As would be expected given what is known about changes over time in educational systems around the world, average schooling completed is four-and-a-half years less than in the cohort overall (7.44 years versus 11.9 years). Parent immigrants differ dramatically from the cohort in their adjustee rates and previous illegal experience. While 57.4 percent of the cohort adjusted to LPR while already living in the United States, only 30.9 of the parent immigrants did so; and while 39.6 percent of the cohort is estimated to have previous illegal experience, only 26.8 percent of the parents do so. Of course, it is possible that parent immigrants may be overrepresented in that elusive segment which is in the United States illegally but goes through the visa process as if they were living abroad, traveling back to the origin country to conclude the visa process and receive the immigrant visa.

The figures for the Mexico-born in Table 11.10 indicate that their schooling is even lower, on average, than that of other parent immigrants — 3.57 years versus 7.44 years. As would be expected, previous illegal experience is higher

Table 11.10.   Summary Characteristics among Immigrant Parents of U.S. Citizens, by Mexico Birth: NIS-2003

Variable	Parent-Immigrants Born in Mexico			All Parent-Immigrants
	Men	Women	All	
A. Based on 80 Percent Random Subsample				
Average age at LPR (years)	65.0	60.9	62.3	63.7
Percent female	–	–	65.2	66.0
Average schooling (years)	3.80	3.44	3.57	7.44
Percent adjustee	32.7	34.6	33.9	30.9
Previous illegal experience	53.3	43.3	46.8	26.8
Self-assessed health at interview	2.84	3.05	2.97	3.19
Percent born in Mexico	–	–	–	27.6
Number of observations	73	144	217	784
B. Based on Respondents Asked Housing Questions within the 80 Percent Subsample				
Average age at LPR (years)	65.0	60.5	62.2	63.8
Percent female	–	–	63.2	65.7
Average schooling (years)	3.89	3.55	3.67	7.53
Percent adjustee	37.0	42.7	40.6	32.9
Previous illegal experience	57.0	45.5	49.7	27.4
Self-assessed health at interview	2.80	3.08	2.97	3.18
Percent born in Mexico	–	–	–	25.4
Number of observations	65	117	182	713

Note: Estimates are based on weighted data. The sample consists of respondents who are in the randomized 80 percent subsample and who were administered the housing questions. The self-assessed health measure is a 5-point scale, with 1 indicating "Poor" and 5 indicating "Excellent".

among the Mexico-born by 20 percentage points—46.8 years versus 26.8 years—and higher among men than women by 10 percentage points—53.3 percent versus 43.3 percent. However, these figures are substantially lower than among the entire Mexico-born subset, for which we estimate that 85.4 percent and 72.4 percent of men and women, respectively, have previous illegal experience (Table 11.7).

In multivariate analyses below, we will also consider the parent immigrants' self-assessed health. As shown in Table 11.10, panel A, the health measure registers an average of about three for the parents overall and for the Mexico-born subset, where 1 indicates "Poor" and 5 indicates "Excellent." This contrasts with averages of 3.86 in the entire cohort and 3.55 among the Mexico-born. Thus, parent immigrants appear to be somewhat more similar to each other in matters of health than their fellow LPRs in other visa classes.

Transfers between Immigrant Parents of U.S. Citizens and Their Children

Our focus is on transfers between these parents and their children age 17 and older. Table 11.11, panel A reports the proportions of the parent immigrants involved in transfers to, from, and both to and from with their adult children. As shown, the big story is that of transfers from the children, and these proportions are higher among the Mexico-born than in the cohort overall— 20.6 percent versus 15 percent. Within the Mexico-born, almost 20 percent of the men and 21 percent of the women receive transfers, plus 2.50 percent and 1.40 percent of men and women, respectively, who both give and receive transfers.

Table 11.11. Transfers Given and Received by Immigrant Parents of U.S. Citizens To and From Children Age 17 and Older, During the Previous Twelve Months: NIS-2003

Variable	Born in Mexico			All Immigrants
	Men	Women	All	
A. Specific Transfers Questions, Based on 80 Percent Random Subsample				
Transfers to children 17+	5.02	3.10	3.77	3.75
Transfers from children 17+	19.8	21.0	20.6	15.0
Transfers both to/from children 17+	2.50	1.40	1.78	.79
Number of observations	73	144	217	784
B. Housing Provided to Immigrant Parents of U.S. Citizens by Their Children, Based on Respondents Administered Housing Questions				
In full sample	57.8	53.6	55.0	67.0
Number of observations	74	147	221	878
In 80 percent random subsample	58.0	51.3	53.8	67.4
Number of observations	65	117	182	713
C. Summary of Transfers, Based on Respondents Administered Housing Questions Who Are in the 80 Percent Random Subsample				
Transfers to children, no housing	2.08	1.82	1.92	1.65
Transfers to children, housing	1.51	.82	1.08	2.09
Transfers from children, no housing	1.38	7.96	5.54	4.14
Transfers from children, housing	16.4	14.5	15.2	10.7
Transfers to/from children, no housing	0	.82	.52	.26
Transfers to/from children, housing	2.83	0	1.04	.46
No transfers, no housing	38.5	38.1	38.3	26.6
No transfers, housing	37.2	35.9	36.4	54.1
Receive transfers or housing	59.4	60.1	59.8	71.8
Number of observations	65	117	182	713

Note: Estimates are based on weighted data.

These same parents have also received tickets to America. Their children have sponsored them for an immigrant visa, filled out paperwork (like the Form I-130 which started the visa process) and assembled documents like birth certificates and marriage certificates, and they have assumed financial responsibility should their parents be unable to support themselves, for as long as ten years.

These parents, then, have received tickets to America and, possibly to prepare, some 20–21 percent have received financial assistance. Yet that is not all. Many of these parents also receive housing assistance from their children.

Housing Assistance Received by Immigrant Parents of U.S. Citizens from Their Children

To assess housing assistance, we examine information collected in the NIS on home ownership. The housing questions were in Section H of the questionnaire, covering assets. Section H was not presented to the 321 overseas respondents. It was presented to main sampled respondents who were financially knowledgeable and to financially knowledgeable spouses. Table 11.10, panel B reports basic characteristics for the subset who both were asked the housing questions and also fell in the 80 percent random subsample.

The home ownership question asked respondents whether they own or are buying, rent, or "live here for free." If the "live for free" option was chosen, a follow-up question, "Why is that?" was asked. The responses overwhelmingly mentioned who respondents lived with, for example, "live with daughter and her family" or "live with sister." A few responses mentioned lack of resources. Because we know from the visa category that the sponsor (an adult child of the immigrant) has assumed financial responsibility, responses calling attention to restricted resources were included in a category of support by children.[15]

Table 11.11, panel B reports the proportions in the full sample living in housing provided by their children. However, because this information will be combined with the information on transfers, we also report the proportions in the 80 percent random subsample. The estimates indicate that a large majority of parent immigrants live in housing provided by their children. The proportions are about 58 percent for Mexico-born men, 51–54 percent for Mexico-born women, and a substantially larger 67 percent in the cohort overall.

A Comprehensive Portrait of Financial and Housing Assistance Received by Immigrant Parents of U.S. Citizens from Their Children

Combining the transfers and housing information yields a comprehensive portrait (Table 11.11, panel C). We see, for example, that the dominant pattern in the cohort overall is receiving housing but no transfers (54.1 percent), while among the Mexico-born, this pattern is slightly edged by the pattern of no transfers and no housing (38.5 percent versus 37.2 percent among men, 38.1 percent versus 35.9 percent among women). Nonetheless, nontrivial proportions receive both transfers and housing from their children— 16.4 percent and 14.5 percent among the Mexico-born men and women, respectively. Given that the transfers questions pertain to periods when the immigrant was not living with the child, these figures must reflect either provision of housing costs (rather than living together) or receipt of housing assistance and transfers from different children.

Overall, a substantial majority of parent immigrants receive either financial transfers or housing assistance from their adult children—59–60 percent of the Mexico-born and almost 72 percent in the overall cohort.

Parent immigrants thus exemplify the ticket to America.

Multivariate Analyses

To explore more deeply the financial and housing assistance provided by adult children to their immigrant parents, we specify a logit equation in which the determinants are the immigrant's age (represented by linear and quadratic terms), sex, and years of schooling, whether the immigrant is an adjustee and has previous illegal experience, the immigrant's self-assessed health at the time of the interview (soon after LPR), and whether the immigrant was born in Mexico. The subsample for the regressions includes respondents in the 80 percent subsample who also received the housing questions (Table 11.11, panel C). Missing data on regressors reduce the sample size from 713 to 707.

In the first specification, the dependent variable is receiving either financial or housing assistance. As shown in Table 11.12, immigrant's age is highly significant; with the probability of receiving assistance increasing with age (the parabola peaks at almost 115 years). Adjustees and immigrants with previous illegal experience are less likely to receive assistance, net of each other (both are significant at the .05 level). Immigrants born in Mexico are also less likely to receive assistance (significance at the .01 level), a result not unexpected given the proportion in Table 11.11, panel C.

To probe more deeply, we specify two further equations whose dependent variables are the probability of receiving financial assistance and housing assistance, respectively. Recall that the transfers information pertains to periods when the immigrant parent is not living in the same house with the children providing financial assistance. Recall also that the proportion of immigrant parents receiving housing assistance far exceeds the proportion receiving financial assistance. Thus, a priori, the results in the first equation may be dominated by housing dynamics and may confound two very different processes.

Table 11.12. Determinants of Receiving Financial Transfers and Housing Assistance from Adult Children, Among U.S. Immigrants Admitted as Parents of U.S. Citizens: Logit Estimates, NIS-2003

Regressor	Receive Transfer and/or Housing	Receive Transfer	Receive Housing
Age	.176	.0900	.156
Age squared	−.000768	−.000543	−.000571
Joint test chi² (2 df)	52.53***	2.85	59.54***
Sex (1 = female)	.326	.303	.198
	(1.61)	(1.27)	(1.01)
Years of schooling	−.0273	−.0276	−.0258
	(1.34)	(1.19)	(1.33)
Adjustee	−.625	−1.044	−.462
	(2.54)*	(3.09)**	(1.93)+
Previous illegal experience	−.521	.358	−.704
	(2.02)*	(1.12)	(2.81)**
Health at interview	−.0479	−.208	.0126
	(.52)	(1.95)+	(.14)
Born in Mexico	−.658	.503	−.675
	(2.62)**	(1.92)+	(2.81)**
Constant	−6.272	−4.500	−6.179
	(1.76)+	(1.15)	(1.72)+
Log pseudolikelihood	−355.74	−291.09	−377.24
Number of observations	707	707	707

Notes: Absolute values of asymptotic t-ratio appear in parentheses under parameter estimates for numeric and binary variables.
$(+ p < .10, * p < .05, ** p < .01, *** p < .001$; two-tailed tests for single coefficients, one-tailed for joint tests)

In the transfers equation (Table 11.12, middle column), only one regressor is statistically significant, being an adjustee (at the .01 level). Adjustees are significantly less likely to receive financial transfers, suggesting that adjustees may be living with their children or may not need help beyond housing assistance. The healthier are also less likely to receive transfers (borderline significance at .051), as would be expected. Consistent with the higher proportions of Mexico-born receiving transfers (Table 11.11, panel A), the effect of being born in Mexico is positive (though achieving only borderline significance at .055).

The housing equation (Table 11.12, rightmost column) indicates age has a highly significant positive effect (the parabola peaks at 137 years), as would be expected. Previous illegal experience has a large statistically significant negative effect (at the .01 level), suggesting that illegal immigrants who survive the hardships of illegality acquire their own homes and do not have to rely on their children for housing assistance. Indeed, the data indicate that among parent immigrants with no previous illegal experience, only 7.82 percent own their home, while among those with illegal experience, more than twice as many do so—18.8 percent. Among adjustees, the figures are even more dramatic—while only 8.07 percent of those with no illegal experience own their homes at the time of interview, a large 22.8 percent of those with illegal experience do so. It is not surprising thus that adjustees also receive less housing assistance. Similarly, parent immigrants born in Mexico also receive less housing assistance, as they may also have less need of it.

What about the children providing assistance to their parents? They may be previous immigrants who naturalized. Or they may be in that elusive set of children born in the United States and citizens from birth whose parents were in the country temporarily to study or work and who as adults went to the United States to live. Both sets may exemplify the process of financial transfers morphing from remittances into tickets to America.

CONCLUSION

In the life of an individual migrant, financial transfers may mean different things at different points in the migrant trajectory. Transfers may begin as remittances to spouse, children, or other family members in the origin country, but morph into tickets to America. The migrant in the United States may help bring family members there. As has been widely conjectured, migrants who become legal permanent residents in the United States, and eventually citizens of the United States, are in the vanguard of this transnational activity.

This paper examined transfers behavior in the cohort of persons who became legal permanent residents of the United States in 2003, focusing particularly on immigrants born in Mexico. We provided a portrait of the Mexico-born contingent of new immigrants in the United States, and we found that new legal immigrants from Mexico have modest rates of transfers to others—19.3 percent among men and 14.5 percent among women. They also have nontrivial rates of receiving transfers—7.34 percent and 11.5 percent among men and women, respectively.

To explore more deeply the idea of financial transfers as tickets to America, we developed a new way to think about transfers involving legal permanent residents. Due to provisions of U.S. immigration law which require that most family and employment immigrants be sponsored, it is possible to identify select pairs of new immigrants and their sponsors in which transfers are likely to be *from* sponsors *to* immigrants.

We identified nine such select pairs, classifying them by the type of immigrant visa and the type of transfers partner:

1. Spouses of native-born U.S. citizens and their U.S. citizen spouse sponsors
2. Spouses of foreign-born U.S. citizens and their U.S. citizen spouse sponsors
3. Spouses of U.S. legal permanent residents and their LPR spouse sponsors
4. Minor children of U.S. citizens and their U.S. citizen parent sponsors
5. Adult children of U.S. citizens and their U.S. citizen parent sponsors
6. Children of U.S. legal permanent residents and their LPR parent sponsors
7. Parents of U.S. citizens and their U.S. citizen offspring sponsors
8. Siblings of U.S. citizens and their U.S. citizen sibling sponsors
9. Employment principals and their U.S. employer

In these nine cases, the new immigrant is receiving a ticket to America and may have received financial assistance in the origin country—either a financial component of the ticket to America or a classic remittance to help meet the immigrant's subsistence needs before traveling to the United States.

In a preliminary foray, we explored the case of parent immigrants and their adult children who sponsor the parents' immigration, give them financial assistance (including both remittances and a financial component of the ticket to America), and give them housing assistance in the United States. Parent immigrants are important to study as they are the second largest class of new legal immigrants and are exempt from numerical limitation. We found that about a fifth receive financial assistance from their adult children, and over half receive housing assistance in the United States after immigration. Approximately 59–60 percent receive either financial or housing assistance. Multivariate analyses indicate that parents who are younger and healthier are less likely to receive financial assistance from their adult children—beyond sponsorship for immigration. We also found that adjustees are less likely to receive financial assistance (presumably because they have had time to get settled in the United States), and that immigrants with previous illegal experience are less likely to receive housing assistance, presumably for the same reason.

There is much further work to be done, both in understanding transfers involving legal immigrants with parent visas and in understanding the other eight select pairs. With respect to parent immigrants, it will be important to distinguish different forms of housing assistance—forms in which, variously, parents live with children, or parents live separately but children pay the rent or pay the mortgage. Similarly, it will be important to distinguish between children who provide housing, children who provide financial assistance, and children who provide both. As well, it will be useful to take account of the parent's and children's gender, as well as the immigrant parent's marital status. Finally, it will be illuminating to distinguish by the presence of grand-children in the United States.

With respect to the broader set of new legal immigrants in the United States, this work underscores the need to study sponsors. Except in the case of native-born U.S. citizen sponsors, all sponsors are previous immigrants. Apparently, they are continuing a trajectory of assistance to family members, a trajectory which begins with classical remittances and then morphs into tickets to America, including financial assistance to prepare and make the trip, and continues with financial and housing assistance in the United States. The tickets to America they provide cost more than the amount received by the immigrants they sponsor, for they must also file sponsorship documents in the United States and assume financial responsibility, if necessary, for the new immigrants they sponsor for up to ten years.

Understanding the dynamics of providing assistance that begins as remit-tances and becomes tickets to America would appear to be a major challenge in the study of international migration in general and in the study of migration from Mexico to the United States in particular.

APPENDIX 11

Notes on the NIS-2003 Data

The sampling frame for the New Immigrant Survey was the electronic file containing the official government records on all persons who were admitted to legal permanent residence in the United States during the seven-month period between May and December 2003. The government record includes the immigrant's class and date of admission to LPR, country of birth, country of last permanent residence, country of nationality, and, for immigrants with numerically restricted visas, the country of chargeability. It also contains date of birth, sex, and marital status. Thus, there are several variables for which the data set contains two alternate pieces of information, one based on the government record, the other obtained during the survey. These include country of birth, date of birth, sex, and marital status. The information drawn from the two sources does not always agree. Both sources are vulnerable

Table 11.13. Basic Survey Characteristics of New U.S. Legal Immigrants Born in Mexico: NIS-2003

Characteristic	Born in Mexico			All Immigrants
	Men	Women	All	
Total in sample	457	707	1,164	8,573
Not overseas	435	651	1,086	8,252
Interviewed in person	265	384	649	3,429
Interviewed by phone	192	321	513	5,120
Months between LPR & interview	4.03	3.96	3.99	3.91

Notes: Figures represent raw cases with no sampling weights. Overseas cases were administered an abbreviated questionnaire, and their spouses were not interviewed.

to errors. For example, information on the government record could have been mispunched, information from the survey could have been erroneously entered by the interviewer, and so on.

In this chapter, we use a recent coding of country of birth which resolved discrepancies between the two sources of information by examining the other country information in the government record and the trip history in the survey. Similarly, we use a coding of sex prepared by NIS staff. For age, we use the date of birth from the government record.

NOTES

1. Paper prepared for the Conference on Migration and Remittances: Trends, Impacts, and New Challenges, sponsored by Centro de Investigación y Docencia Económicas (CIDE), Universidad Iberoamericana, and Georgetown University, held in Mexico City in February 2009. I gratefully acknowledge New York University for its intellectual and financial support.

2. The Cooperative for American Remittances to Europe (CARE), which was founded in 1945, initiated a program of food relief for the people of Europe, who faced starvation at the end of World War II. CARE Packages, which included beef, honey, raisins, coffee, and other foods, could be purchased for $10 and sent to specific individuals or, as the program continued, to specific localities. Later the program extended the contents of CARE Packages to special cultural diets and as well to nonfood items like blankets and tools, and extended distribution to Asia and other parts of the world. After two decades and delivery of more than 100 million CARE Packages, CARE phased out the CARE Packages, and evolved into an international organization supporting long-term development projects. It also changed its name twice, most

recently in 1993, when it became Cooperative for Assistance and Relief Everywhere. See Rangan and Lee (2009) and Strom (2011).

3. The acronym LPR is used for both lawful permanent resident and lawful permanent residence. The context should make clear whether reference is to person or status.

4. In Table 11.2, immigration figures through FY 2000 refer to the total, non-IRCA-legalization number of new LPRs. This number was reported as "total non-legalization" in Table 4 of the INS and DHS *Yearbooks* through the 2004 *Yearbook* and could be obtained for Mexico from Table 8 through the 2000 *Yearbook*. Starting in FY 2001, the figures in Table 11.2 refer to the full total, including a small number of IRCA legalizations. IRCA legalizations declined from a high of over 1 million in 1991 to less than 1,000 in every year since 1998, with a low of 8 in 1999 and totals of 263, 55, 39, 128, 188, 217, 93, 116, and 83 in Fiscal Years 2001 through 2009, respectively (DHS *Yearbooks*, Table 4 through 2004, Table 7 thereafter). Mexico-born IRCA legalizations in the period 1991–2000 totaled 1,047,351.

5. Persons born in Mexico are not eligible for diversity visas, as the number of visas granted to the Mexico-born exceeded 50,000 during the 5 years preceding every year since the diversity visa program started (Table 11.2).

6. For additional historical information and data sources, see Jasso and Rosenzweig (2006) and the references cited therein.

7. For further information about the U.S. immigration context, see Jasso (2011) and the references cited therein.

8. For succinct overview of the NIS project, see Jasso (2008); for fuller overview, see Jasso et al. (in press) and Jasso (2011) and the references cited therein. For data or documentation, see the project website (http://nis.princeton.edu).

9. While estimates of previous illegal experience based on survey measures obviously require a survey, estimates based on the government record can be undertaken for all immigrant cohorts since 1972 which are available for sale by the National Technical Information Service (NTIS). The U.S. government made the microdata available through the year 2000. Thus, a time series of previous illegal experience could be constructed for the years 1972–2000. If such data are also released for the years since 2000, the time series could be brought up to date. Comparison with survey-based estimates for the years 1996 and 2003 would shed light on illegal experience (Jasso, Massey, Rosenzweig and Smith, 2008).

10. Of the 1,687 respondents in the random 20 percent subsample, 27 did not respond. Here, and in the rest of this section, estimates are based on the entire cohort or subset who were asked a given question. If we calculate the percent involved in transfers based on the 1,660 responders to the global question, the weighted estimate is 13.1 percent.

11. For example, Jasso (2009) reports transfers estimates to and from spouse only for the subset who is married and lived apart at some point during the previous twelve months.

12. The proportions in the to, from, and to/from subsets sum to more than the proportion with any involvement, due to the fact that a given respondent may be give-only in one specific transfers, receive-only in another, and both in still another.

13. For specific rules on eligibility of step and adoptive parents and children as sponsors and/or prospective immigrants, see the instructions to Form I-130, "Petition for Alien Relative."

14. The U.S. citizen sponsor of a parent must be age 21 or older; thus, the "child" and "children" in discussions of parent immigrants are adults.

15. Housing assistance is of two kinds: (1) paying the immigrant parent's housing costs (rent or mortgage payment) and (2) inviting the immigrant parent to live with the son or daughter.

Chapter 12

Migradollars in Latin America

A Comparative Analysis

Douglas S. Massey, Jorge Durand, and Karen A. Pren

It has long been recognized that international migrants send considerable money back to friends and relatives in countries of origin, and often bring funds with them when they return home on visits. The importance of these foreign earnings to migrants, their families, and their communities of origin was noted early on by scholars such as Thomas and Znaniecki (1918–1919) and Gamio (1930); and recent research underscores the continued importance of migrant-generated transfers in nations throughout the world (Massey et al., 1998:222–274). Indeed, as the number of international migrants rose during the late twentieth and early twenty-first centuries, the volume of what Durand (1988) calls "migradollars" steadily rose to become a major source of foreign exchange and international liquidity for many migrant-sending nations (Terry and Wilson, 2005; Ozden and Schiff, 2005).

Despite the ubiquity and continued salience of migrant savings and remittances around the world, the research literature on migradollars is not that well developed. Anthropologists were the first among contemporary scholars to study the effects of migrant remittances and savings on origin communities, using qualitative methods to describe how funds were spent and the consequences of that spending for individuals, households, and community residents in general. These ethnographic studies found that migradollars were devoted primarily to current consumption and family maintenance, with relatively small amounts being channeled to productive ends. The general conclusion was that international migration simply represented yet another example unequal exchange that served to stifle local development and perpetuate poverty in the Third World (Kearney, 1986).

Economists initially paid little attention to migrant remittances because they were not predicted under neoclassical economic theory, which viewed migration as a means of maximizing lifetime earnings by moving permanently to a high wage labor market. The New Economics of Labor Migration, however, viewed migration as a means of overcoming local market failures and specifically predicted remittances as a result. Guided by its hypotheses, economists, sociologists, and demographers began to pay more attention to migradollars beginning in the 1980s; but as quantitative researchers took up the issue, they quickly faced roadblocks because of the scarcity of good data.

In order to overcome this constraint, the Mexican Migration Project (MMP) was launched. From its inception in 1982 it has systematically gathered information about the funds saved and remitted by migrants on their most recent U.S. trip, and also ascertained how these funds were spent (Durand and Massey, 2004). When the Latin American Migration Project (LAMP) was launched in 1998, the same questions were asked of migrants from other sending countries in the region (Donato et al., 2010). Together, the LAMP and MMP data provide the basis for large-scale comparative analyses of migrant decision-making with respect to remitting, saving, and spending throughout Latin America.

A growing body of work has accumulated using MMP data to study the use of migradollars in Mexico (see Amuedo-Dorantes and Pozo, 2007; Amuedo-Dorantes and Banzak, 2006; Amuedo-Dorantes, Banzak and Pozo, 2005; Arias and Durand, 1997; Durand, Parrado and Massey, 1996; Kanaiaupuni and Donato, 1999; Massey and Parrado, 1994, 1997; Massey and Basem, 1992; Quinn, 2005, 2009; Roberts and Morris, 2004; Sana, 2008). These studies generally find that migrant decisions to remit and save follow the precepts of the new economics of labor migration and that migradollars, though channeled primarily into consumption, do not inevitably perpetuate dependency. Instead, the likelihood of remitting and saving, the amounts remitted and saved, and the uses to which these funds are put vary with life cycle characteristics and with local and national economic circumstances. During life stages when family dependency is low and when economic conditions are favorable, the marginal likelihood of productive investment is often quite high.

Although a growing number of studies have also been done using LAMP data as well, the literature on migradollars in other Latin American nations is not as well developed as in Mexico. Often only one country is examined, or two or three settings are compared; and large-scale analyses on data from multiple countries have generally not been done. Nevertheless, the studies that have been done find that the likelihood of remitting and saving, the amounts involved, and the propensity to invest are tied to family circumstances and structural economic conditions that vary across time and space (see Amuedo-Dorantes and Pozo, 2007; Duany, 2010; Amuedo-Dorantes, Georges and Pozo, 2010; Duany, 2010; Sana, 2008; Sana and Massey, 2005). Given that at this point, the literature is dominated by studies done in Mexico, in the present analysis we expand the basis for theoretical and substantive generalization by considering remittance and savings decisions in six countries covered by the LAMP and the MMP.

THEORETICAL PERSPECTIVES

Early research on migradollars was mostly qualitative and dominated by dependency theory, whose leading hypothesis was that asymmetric power relations between developed and developing nations led to unequal terms of trade for most exchanges, including international migration (Frank, 1969; Furtado, 1970; Cardoso and Falleto, 1979). Although remittances raised consumption in sending communities and generated new commercial enterprises, these outcomes relied on the continued arrival of foreign earnings rather than autonomous local development and thus served to maintain migrant communities in a state of transnational dependency (see Reichert, 1981, 1982).

The New Economics of Labor Migration offered an alternative theoretical view that linked migration to local market failures and saw remittances as a way for households to diversify risks, accumulate capital, and overcome credit constraints, thereby offering more latitude for positive development effects (Stark and Bloom, 1985). In rural areas, especially, local markets for insurance, capital, and credit are typically ineffective or non-existent, and international migration offers a tractable means for low-income families to self-insure against risks stemming from crop failures, price fluctuations, and job loss, as well a way to self-finance productive investments in agriculture and non-agrarian business enterprises and to make consumer purchases in the absence of credit markets (Stark, 1991).

Under these circumstances, international migration and the arrival of migradollars need not lead inevitably to underdevelopment and dependency. Instead, by increasing household liquidity migradollars may allow households to survive local economic downturns, maintain consumption during periods of recession, and engage in productive investment when economic conditions improve. The key empirical issue is under what circumstances productive investment is likely to occur. In general, theory and research suggest that migradollars are channeled to consumption rather than investment during the early stages of household formation, when recently married migrants are seeking to acquire housing and satisfy the needs of a growing family. As children age and join the labor force, however, budget constraints are eased and it becomes more tractable to use foreign earnings as a source of investment capital.

Investment also depends on circumstances in the local and national political economy, of course. Communities that lack infrastructure and have little access to markets are unlikely to attract productive investments by migrants or anyone else; but communities that are well situated to exploit nearby markets and take advantage of good infrastructure might be very attractive targets for investment. Likewise, during periods of hyperinflation and currency devaluation, migrants will tend to keep their earnings in hard currencies rather than channeling them into assets valued in depreciating currencies. Under the new economics of labor migration, then, the role of government policymakers is to create economic circumstances conducive to investment and programs to facilitate productive spending, such as conditional cash transfer programs or investment matching programs (Valencia Lomeli, 2008; Orozco and Rouse, 2007).

DATA AND METHODS

In this analysis, we draw on data from both the MMP and LAMP to study migrant decision-making with regard to remitting, saving, and investing across six Latin American nations: Mexico, Costa Rica, the Dominican Republic, Nicaragua, Costa Rica, and Peru. The data were gathered using ethnosurvey methods to sample specific communities selected to provide social, economic, and geographic diversity to the database. The ethnosurvey combines representative random sampling and quantitative data collection with qualitative interviewing and ethnographic fieldwork to produce valid and reliable data on sensitive topics, such as undocumented migration.

This approach was developed and tested initially by Massey et al. (1987) in surveys of four Mexican communities done in 1982–1983. Since 1987 ethnosurvey methods have been applied each year to a new set of Mexican communities selected to enhance the diversity of the sample, yielding a large body of standardized data that is both reliable and valid on documented and undocumented migration to the United States (Durand and Massey, 2004). Beginning in 1998 the same methods have been applied each year to survey new communities in other Latin American nations under the aegis of the Latin American Migration Project (Massey and Sana, 2004; Donato et al., 2010).

Here we draw on surveys conducted in 7 communities in Costa Rica, 9 in Nicaragua, 3 in Guatemala, 5 in Peru, 7 in the Dominican Republic, and 124 in Mexico. Information about the sample is summarized in Table 12.1. Given that the MMP has been in the field every year since 1987 gathering data from a new set of Mexican communities, whereas the LAMP annually surveys different communities in different countries, the number of households

Table 12.1. Sample Sizes, Sampling Fractions, and Refusal Rates for Country-specific Samples Used in Analysis of Migrant Remittances and Savings

Country	Households	Refusal Rate
Mexico	20,847	0.075
Costa Rica	1,292	0.046
Dominican Republic	907	0.047
Guatemala	513	0.019
Nicaragua	1,598	0.059
Peru	826	0.299
Total	25,983	0.084

surveyed in Mexico (20,847) is much greater than in any other country (the range across the non-Mexican samples is 513 to 1,598). As can be seen in the table, the refusal rate was generally quite low, averaging just 0.084 across all countries. The major exception is Peru, where interviewing was concentrated in metropolitan Lima, an urban area that was characterized by high levels of urban violence at the time, which created suspicion and hostility that made it difficult to secure respondent cooperation.

In both the MMP and LAMP, household heads with U.S. experience were asked a battery of questions about their latest trip to the United States, including specific items on whether remittances were sent, the average amount sent per month, and the uses to which the remittances were put. Migrant household heads were also asked whether they had accumulated savings on their last U.S. trip, the amount they brought with them when they returned, and how these funds were used. These two series of questions provide data on the number and use of migradollars that we explore in some detail in the next section.

In multivariate analyses, we express patterns of remitting, saving, and spending as a function of selected independent variables that prior theory and research suggest influence migrant decision-making. These variables are listed and their mean values shown by country in Table 12.2. This and all subsequent tables refer to household heads who took at least one trip to the United States in each of the samples. Although countries in the LAMP often send migrants to multiple international destinations, here we focus only on migrants to the United States. The life cycle characteristics we consider include age and the number of minors under age 18 present in the household. In most countries, the average age fell within the narrow range of 33 to 35 years, except in Peru where respondents were somewhat older, with an average age of around 41 years. Migrants from Peru also exhibited lower levels of household dependency, with an average of just 0.9 minors per household, which is consistent with lower rates of fertility generally observed in urban settings. Across the other countries, household dependency ranged from an average 1.35 minors per household in the Dominican Republic to 2.26 in Mexico. We also measure the gender of the household head to control for family structure. A female head generally indicates a matrifocal household in which no adult male was present. As one would expect, the share of female heads is greatest in the Caribbean (31 percent), and lowest in Mexico (5 percent) (see Massey, Fischer and Capoferro, 2006).

Table 12.2.   Independent Variables Used in Analysis of Migrant Remittances and Savings

Independent Variables	Mexico	Costa Rica	Dominican Republic	Guatemala	Nicaragua	Peru
Life Cycle Characteristics						
Age	33.8	33.4	33.9	35.0	35.1	41.1
Female	5.0	15.3	30.6	6.6	24.4	10.0
Number of Minors	2.26	1.47	1.35	1.97	1.44	0.9
Human Capital						
Years of Schooling	5.6	8.2	9.9	7.5	10.3	14.0
Prior U.S. Experience	59.6	35.9	18.8	30.2	19.2	20.0
Physical Capital						
Land Owned	14.8	17.9	5.0	13.2	6.4	0.0
Business Owned	12.2	19.6	8.1	35.5	23.1	35.0
Home Owned	54.0	50.8	22.5	55.3	50.6	65.0
Legal Status						
Undocumented	76.7	93.1	40.0	92.1	90.5	65.0
Temporary	2.5	2.1	0.6	7.9	1.2	10.0
Legal	20.4	3.7	58.8	0.0	8.3	20.0
Citizen	0.4	1.1	0.6	0.0	0.0	5.0
Trip Characteristics						
Duration of Trip	36.3	45.6	138.2	45.5	97.9	23.2
Accompanied by Spouse	14.2	14.2	20.6	6.5	31.4	5.0
Accompanied by Children	6.6	7.9	23.1	0.0	22.4	10.0
Net Monthly Earnings	1,150	1,685	853	985	1,450	1,406
Federal Taxes Withheld	61.1	28.5	60.0	53.9	57.1	0.0
Community Infrastructure						
Paved Road to Highway	82.9	100	100	100	100	100
Bank in Community	81.1	62.9	90.0	100	66.7	100
Sample Size	*5,954*	*189*	*160*	*76*	*156*	*20*

We consider the influence of two measures of human capital on the repatriation and use of migradollars. General human capital is measured by years of schooling, which range from a low of 5.6 years in Mexico to 14 years in Peru. Like migrants from Mexico, those from Costa Rica and Guatemala generally have low levels of education (around eight years), whereas those from Nicaragua and the Dominican Republic are higher (around ten years), though not as high as in Peru. Thus migrants from Peru and the Dominican Republic are generally from the middle or lower middle classes, whereas those from the other countries tend to be campesinos or unskilled urban laborers. Migration-specific human capital is measured by cumulative U.S. experience prior to the last trip. Given the long history of migration from Mexico, migrants from that country display the greatest accumulated time in the United States (around 60 months). Migrants from Costa Rica and Guatemala lie in between, at 30–35 months, and those from the Dominican Republic, Nicaragua, and Peru are lowest, at 19–20 months.

Our multivariate models include three dummy variables to indicate a migrant's access to physical capital: whether or not the household owned farmland, whether or not it owned a business, and whether or not it owned a home. The rate of land ownership ranged from 0 percent in the very urban Peruvian sample to 18 percent in Costa Rica, followed by 15 percent in Mexico, 13 percent in Guatemala, 6 percent in Nicaragua, and 5 percent in the Dominican Republic. In contrast, the rate of business ownership was greatest in Peru and Guatemala, where around 35 percent of migrants operated a household business, compared with a value of just 8 percent in the Dominican Republic and 12 percent in Mexico. Costa Rica and Nicaragua again were in between, with rates of 20 percent and 23 percent, respectively. Except in the Dominican Republic, home ownership rates were generally high—in the range of 50–55 percent for Mexicans, Costa Ricans, Guatemalans, and Nicaraguans. Peruvians displayed the highest rate of ownership at 65 percent, whereas Dominicans were lowest, at just 23 percent.

We observe a great contrast in the distribution of migrants by legal status across countries. As one would expect, Mexicans are predominantly undocumented, at 73 percent, though a significant minority share are legal. Likewise, Guatemalans are overwhelmingly undocumented, at 83 percent, reflecting the reluctance of U.S. authorities to accept them as official refugees. In contrast, for political reasons Dominicans were given privileged access to legal status in the early 1960s (Riosmena, 2010) and thus display the highest rate of documentation, with around 59 percent being legal residents and 1 percent being U.S. citizens. Owing to their higher class status and greater education, Peruvian migrants are also relatively likely to be legal residents (20 percent) or citizens (5 percent). Most Nicaraguan migrants (79 percent) are undocumented, though a few (8 percent) are legal residents.

We also observe considerable variation in the circumstances surrounding the trip to the United States. Whereas Mexican migrants historically have migrated using temporary or recurrent strategies that involve multiple trips and great circularity (Massey et al., 1987), Dominicans quickly established a pattern of long-term, settled migration (Riosmena, 2010). Thus whereas the average Mexican trip lasted 36 months the duration was 138 months for Dominican migrants. Nicaraguans also tend to take a small number trips of long duration, averaging 98 months, whereas Peruvian trips were quite short at just 23 months. Costa Ricans and Guatemalans were intermediate, with average trip durations of around 36 months each.

In terms of family members' being present on the trip, across all countries, most respondents migrated without spouses, with the share accompanied by a spouse ranging from just 5 percent in Peru and 7 percent in Guatemala to 20 percent in the Dominican Republic and 31 percent in Nicaragua. Mexico and Costa Rica were in between, at 14 percent each. Migration with children was even less common, ranging from single-digit percentages migrating from Mexico, Costa Rica, and Guatemala, to 10 percent in Peru and around 22 percent or 23 percent among migrants from Nicaragua and the Dominican Republic.

A key factor in determining the likelihood and amount of migradollars is obviously the amount of income at a migrant's disposal. For each migrant we computed net earnings by subtracting reported amounts spent on food and lodging from reported monthly earnings. According to this measure, Costa Ricans displayed the highest disposable income—an average of $1,685 per month—followed closely by Nicaraguans at $1,450 and Peruvians at $1,406. The other groups trailed further behind, led by Mexicans with $1,150 and followed by Guatemalans at $953 and Dominicans at $853. We include a dummy variable in our models to indicate whether taxes were withheld from the respondent's paycheck. Whereas 57–61 percent of Mexicans, Dominicans, and Nicaraguans had federal taxes withheld, only 54 percent of Guatemalans and 29 percent of Costa Ricans did. Among Peruvians, the rate was zero.

In early specifications of statistical models we introduced a variety of contextual variables to control for economic conditions at the community and national levels, but we encountered numerous statistical problems in estimation, with models failing to converge because of colinearity and cell size issues. In the end, we were able to include just two contextual indicators in the models: whether or not a community was connected to a major highway by a paved road, which is important in determining access to markets in Mexico, and whether or not there was a bank in the community, which proxies access to formal sources of capital and credit as well as access to basic pieces of financial infrastructure, such as automatic teller machines.

PATTERNS OF REMITTING AND SAVING

Before analyzing the determinants of remitting, saving, and investing, we describe the basic patterns that prevail in each country in Table 12.3. The top panel considers remittances and shows the percentage of migrants from each nation who remitted, the average monthly amount that was sent, and how these funds were spent. The spending categories are not mutually exclusive,

Table 12.3. Summary of Remittances and Savings Sent by Latin American Migrants on their Most Recent Trip to the United States (Amounts in Constant 2009 Dollars)

Variable	Mexico	Costa Rica	Dominican Republic	Guatemala	Nicaragua	Peru
Remittances						
Percent Remitted	76.4	73.4	68.7	80.3	68.0	62.1
Average Monthly Amount	$577	$966	$253	$320	$345	$626
How Remittances Spent						
Consumption	50.8	68.3	90.5	96.6	82.7	83.3
Savings or Debt	6.2	22.0	0.0	1.7	1.2	0.0
Housing	8.0	4.9	1.4	1.7	3.7	12.5
Human Capital	34.1	3.3	8.1	0.0	12.4	0.0
Business	0.9	1.6	0.0	0.0	0.0	4.2
Savings						
Percent with Savings	68.3	54.7	30.7	63.2	38.5	70.7
Average Amount Saved	$3,712	$9.148	$7,246	$3,684	$6,652	$7,909
How Savings Spent						
Consumption	41.9	24.7	30.0	51.4	60.0	33.3
Savings or Debt	11.6	11.8	5.0	0.0	5.0	11.1
Housing	21.7	41.2	45.0	37.8	15.0	18.5
Human Capital	17.7	3.5	0.0	0.0	10.0	14.8
Business	7.1	18.8	20.0	10.8	10.0	22.2
Annualized Migradollars						
% Remitted	85.0	82.7	82.8	70.6	83.5	73.7
% Saved	15.0	17.3	17.2	20.4	16.5	26.3
Total Amount	$8,142	$14,025	$3,672	$4,829	$4,950	$10,180
As Ratio GDP/ Capita	0.573	1.219	0.448	0.911	1.707	1.198
Number of Migrants	*6,162*	*192*	*163*	*76*	*156*	*58*

as respondents were told to report all uses to which the money was put. In each country, the vast majority of migrants reported sending money home on a regular basis, with the percentage remitting ranging from a low of 62 percent in Peru to a high of 80 percent in Guatemala. In Nicaragua and the Dominican Republic, around two-thirds remitted, whereas in Costa Rica and Mexico the figure was near three-quarters. The average amount of the monthly remittance ranged from $253 in the Dominican Republic to $966 in Costa Rica. Guatemala and Nicaragua were on the low side at $320 and $345, respectively, whereas Mexico and Peru were higher at $577 and $626.

As other studies have found, the bulk of the money sent home by migrants surveyed in the MMP and LAMP went to current consumption—mostly for family maintenance and support. The lowest share going to consumption was 51 percent in Mexico, and the highest was in Guatemala, where 97 percent of all migradollars were spent on family maintenance. Costa Rica was closer to Mexico at 68 percent, whereas the Dominican Republic, Nicaragua, and Peru were closer to Guatemala at 91 percent, 83 percent, and 83 percent, respectively. In most cases, relatively few migrants reported channeling remittances toward savings or the payment of debts, with the percentage ranging from 0 percent to 6 percent, except in Costa Rica where it was 22 percent. It is not clear a priori whether using remittances to save or pay down debts constitutes consumption or investment, because it depends on how the savings and debt were ultimately deployed. Between 1 percent (in the Dominican Republic) and 13 percent (in Peru) reported using remittances to obtain or improve housing, whereas between 0 percent (Dominican Republic) and 34 percent (Mexico) said remittances were channeled to human capital formation, which we defined as spending on education or health. Very few migrants said they used remittances for a business enterprise (including investments in agricultural production). The highest share devoted to business was in Peru (4 percent), followed by Costa Rica (2 percent), and Mexico (1 percent), with no such spending in the other countries.

Sending monthly remittances is predicted under the New Economics of Labor Migration for households seeking to diversify risks to household income by generating an alternative earnings stream, and it is therefore not surprising that most of the money is channeled into current consumption. Those seeking to overcome missing or failed markets for capital or credit, however, are more likely to accumulate funds through savings and then return home with money in one lump sum. Such behavior was least common for Dominican migrants, among whom only 31 percent returned with savings, and it was also infrequent for Nicaraguans, among whom the percentage was 39 percent. Saving was much more common among Peruvians (71 percent) and Mexicans

(68 percent), whereas Guatemalans and Costa Ricans were in-between with percentages saving of 63 percent and 55 percent, respectively. The amount saved ranged from around $3,700 among Guatemalans and Mexicans to around $9,100 among Costa Ricans, with figures of $7,900 among Peruvians, $7,200 among Dominicans, and $6,600 among Nicaraguans.

Consistent with our presumption that savings are more likely to be used to overcome deficiencies in capital and credit markets, larger shares of migradollars repatriated in this form are channeled into housing and business investments and less toward consumption. In only two cases, do a majority of migrants report using savings to fund current consumption: Nicaragua (60 percent) and Guatemala (51 percent). In contrast, only 42 percent of Mexican migrants reported using savings for consumption, with 33 percent in Peru, 30 percent in the Dominican Republic, and 25 percent in Costa Rica. The share of migrants who devoted savings to housing ranged from 15 percent in Nicaragua to 45 percent in the Dominican Republic. In Costa Rica and Guatemala the figures were 41 percent and 38 percent, respectively, whereas in Mexico 22 percent spent on housing, and the figure was19 percent among Peruvians. There was little or now use of savings to develop human capital in Costa Rica, the Dominican Republic, or Guatemala (where the share 4 percent or less), and not much more in Nicaragua (10 percent), Peru (15 percent), and Mexico (18 percent). Channeling foreign savings into business was relatively common in Peru (22 percent), the Dominican Republic (20 percent) and Costa Rica (19 percent), but less frequent Guatemala (11 percent), Nicaragua (10 percent), and Mexico (7 percent).

Given different trip durations in different settings, it is difficult to compare the economic potential latent in migrant remittances and savings across countries. The bottom panel therefore annualizes the amounts and combines them to determine the total number of migradollars that would be returned if a migrant remitted and saved for twelve months. To determine this quantity, we multiplied the reported monthly remittance by 12 and prorated total savings to a duration of twelve months.

This operation yields substantial variation in potential migradollars for a year's worth of work in the United States. The Dominican Republic lies at the low end of the continuum, as its migrants generally follow settled migration strategy that entails long-term residence in the United States, which yields relatively fewer ties and visits home and, hence, fewer savings and remittances compared with other countries—a total of just $3,700 for twelve months of work in the United States. The greatest earnings potential was evinced by Costa Rican migrants, whose potential migradollars totaled $14,000 per year, followed by Peru at $10,200, Mexico at $8,100 and Nicaragua at $5,000, and Guatemala at $4,800.

Although these amounts may seem modest by U.S. standards, they are quite large compared with average incomes in sending countries, which the bottom line of the table indicates by expressing annualized migradollars as a ratio of each country's per capita income. In three cases, the number of migradollars generated by a year's worth of work in the United States exceeds average national income, with a ratio of 1.70 in Nicaragua, 1.22 in Costa Rica, and 1.20 in Peru. In Guatemala, the number of migradollars almost equals annual income, with a ratio of 0.91. In Mexico, however, annual migradollars represent around 57 percent of per capita income compared with 45 percent in the Dominican Republic, figures that are lower but hardly insignificant. Migradollars thus have a very real potential to change a household's economic circumstances. On the basis of migradollars alone a household could easily move from the bottom to the median of the income distribution, or even higher.

DETERMINANTS OF REMITTING AND SAVING

Prior theory and research suggest that the propensity to remit and save is not uniform among migrants, but varies with personal, household, and trip characteristics as well as with structural economic conditions. In the left-hand columns of Table 12.4 we use a logit model to predict a dichotomous variable indicating whether or not the migrant remitted from the independent variables defined earlier, with dummy variables included to indicate country fixed effects. Whereas the unconditioned share remitting varied from 62 percent to 80 percent, the country coefficients indicate that this variation is largely explained by cross-national differences in the independent variables. Other things equal, only the Dominican Republic stands out from other nations, and whereas the unconditioned data put Dominicans in the middle of the pack with respect to remitting, the multivariate model reveals that, given their characteristics, migrants from the Dominican Republic actually display a much higher likelihood of remitting than those from other Latin American nations.

Life cycle factors generally operate as one would expect, with the odds of remitting rising as the number of minors increase and as migrants grow older, at least until the early 40s, after which the propensity to send funds peaks and begins to decline. Female household heads are less likely to remit than their male counterparts, and the odds of remitting decline with years of schooling. In contrast, the likelihood of sending money home increases with years of prior U.S. experience and with land and home ownership. Business ownership, however, decreases the odds of remitting, which could indicate that business owners have less need for capital to self-finance a business because they already own one.

Table 12.4. Logit Models Predicting Whether a Migrant Remitted or Saved During the Most Recent U.S. Trip

Independent Variables	Migrant Remitted β		SE	Returned with Savings β		SE
Life Cycle Characteristics						
Age	0.076	***	0.018	−0.023		0.018
Age Squared	−0.001	***	0.0002	0.000		0.000
Female	−1.088	***	0.143	−0.529	***	0.145
Number of Minors	0.103	***	0.023	0.002		0.019
Human Capital						
Years of Schooling	−0.021	**	0.010	−0.018	*	0.009
Prior U.S. Experience	0.259	***	0.086	−0.047		0.078
Physical Capital						
Land Owned	0.347	***	0.120	0.334	***	0.103
Business Owned	−0.361	***	0.108	0.041		0.101
Home Owned	0.248	***	0.084	0.133	*	0.075
Legal Status						
Undocumented	—					—
Temporary	0.025		0.262	0.146		0.236
Legal	−0.477	***	0.094	−0.348	***	0.086
Citizen	−0.751	*	0.441	−0.712	*	0.432
Trip Characteristics						
Duration of Trip (Years)	0.000		0.001	−0.008	***	0.001
Accompanied by Spouse	−1.237	***	0.095	−0.493	***	0.094
Accompanied by Children	−0.461	***	0.131	0.078		0.131
Net Monthly Earnings	0.126	***	0.038	0.178	***	0.037
Federal Taxes Withheld	0.166	***	0.082	−0.012		0.074
Community Infrastructure						
Paved Road to Highway	−0.287	***	0.104	0.274	***	0.093
Bank in Community	−0.401	***	0.103	−0.070		0.088
Country						
Mexico	—					—
Costa Rica	0.256		0.235	−0.628	***	0.204
Dominican Republic	1.244	***	0.253	−0.566	**	0.239
Guatemala	1.134		0.490	0.514		0.353
Nicaragua	0.474		0.236	−0.627	***	0.224
Peru	−0.410		0.590	0.068		0.624
Intercept	0.262		0.335	1.720	***	0.329
Likelihood Ratio	683.22	***		717.05	***	
Wald	584.62	***		555.66	***	
Number of migrants			*5,050*			*5,050*

+p=0.10; *p<0.05; **p<0.01; ***p<0.001

In terms of documentation, as one might expect, the stronger the attachment to the United States the less likely a migrant is to remit. Both legal residents and citizens are significantly less likely to send money home than undocumented migrants or temporary workers. Given that a primary motivation of remitting is family support, it is not surprising that migrants accompanied by a spouse or children are less likely to send money home, since their prime dependents are with them in the United States.

As expected, higher wages and more formal employment (indicated by tax withholding) are also associated a greater likelihood of remitting. For every additional $1,000 of income, the odds of remitting rise by 13 percent $(\exp(0.126)=1.13)$. Likewise holding a formal job where taxes are withheld raises the odds of remitting by around 18 percent $(\exp(0.166)=1.18)$. Finally, migrants from more developed communities—in the sense of having paved roads and bank branches—are less likely to send remittances home. In Mexico, having a paved link to a highway is associated with 25 percent lower odds of remitting $(\exp(-0.287)=0.75)$ and having a bank in the community reduces the odds by 33 percent $(\exp(-0.401)=0.67)$.

The right-hand columns present the results of a logit model estimated to predict whether or not the migrant returned from the last U.S. trip with accumulated savings. In contrast to remitting, returning with savings is unrelated to age, the number of minors, U.S. experience, business ownership, presence of children on the trip, formality of employment, or the presence of a bank in the sending community. Moreover, cross-national differences in the propensity to save remain even after controlling for independent variables. Compared with migrants from Mexico, those from Costa Rica, the Dominican Republic, and Nicaragua are less likely to return home with savings. In general, the propensity to save while working in the United States is reduced for females, legal immigrants, U.S. citizens, migrants traveling with spouses, and those coming from Mexican communities linked to a highway. The propensity to return with savings also falls with rising education and increasing trip duration, but positively predicted by greater monthly earnings and ownership of farmland and a home.

Deciding to save or remit is one thing, but choosing the amount to repatriate is another, and this facet of migrant decision-making is examined in Table 12.5, using Tobit models to predict the amount remitted and saved from the independent variables listed in Table 12.2. In terms of the amount remitted, it is Costa Rica that stands out, with its migrants sending around $271 per month more than those from other countries. Females send home $192 less than males, but the amount rises by around $8 for each year of age up to the age of 40 and increases by around $12 for each minor child who accompanies the migrant. Although the remittance amount is unrelated to education,

Table 12.5. Tobit Models Predicting Amounts Remitted and Sent During the most Recent U.S. Trip

Independent Variables	Amount Remitted β		SE	Amount Saved β		SE
Life Cycle Characteristics						
Age	7.96	*	4.81	−35.17		31.85
Age Squared	−0.14	**	0.06	0.27		0.40
Female	−192.03	***	40.67	65.94		257.21
Number of Minors	12.37	**	5.08	−56.03	*	32.64
Human Capital						
Years of Schooling	−0.86		2.51	33.35	**	15.93
Prior U.S. Experience	39.50	*	20.92	282.33	**	133.79
Physical Capital						
Land Owned	74.52	***	25.85	389.93	**	164.27
Business Owned	15.37		26.71	140.92		172.86
Home Owned	43.84	**	20.31	75.95		129.75
Legal Status						
Undocumented	—			—		
Temporary	−29.49		59.01	−253.57		386.83
Legal	−26.79		23.51	−402.50	***	150.57
Citizen	−214.04	*	126.40	−664.63		796.74
Trip Characteristics						
Duration of Trip (Years)	−0.35	**	0.154	0.03		0.97
Accompanied by Spouse	−170.02	***	26.58	−18.18		170.64
Accompanied by Children	−33.39		35.81	194.75		227.48
Net Monthly Earnings	104.11	***	8.97	458.70	***	59.06
Federal Taxes Withheld	24.99		19.74	548.13	***	127.20
Community Infrastructure						
Paved Road to Highway	−73.83	***	24.02	−605.81	***	154.62
Bank in Community	−30.86		23.02	69.86		150.08
Country						
Mexico	—			—		
Costa Rica	271.48	***	57.69	4116.19	***	386.11
Dominican Republic	−7.81		62.21	5929.29	***	386.08
Guatemala	−103.50		88.96	697.19		661.48
Nicaragua	−82.51		63.11	7208.14	***	388.71
Peru	−58.42		175.19	17.43	*	9.59
Intercept	263.23	***	87.52	1927.00	***	573.73
Sigma	598.82	***		3691.91	***	
Log Likelihood	−37538			−42876		
Mean Amount	422.36			2274.25		
Number of migrants		4,804			4,451	

+p=0.10; *p<0.05; **p<0.01; ***p<0.001

it increases by nearly $40 for each year of U.S. experience. The amount sent is unrelated to legal status except for the small number of U.S. citizens, who send home around $214 less per month than other migrants. Likewise, being accompanied by a spouse reduces the amount by $170 and each month spent in the United States lowers the amount sent by around $0.35, which works out to around $4.20 per year. With every additional $1,000 in net monthly earnings, the amount remitted rises by around $104; and in Mexico, coming from a community without a road link reduces remittances by $74 per month while owning land and a home in the sending community increase the amount remitted by $75 and $44 per month, respectively.

Savings accumulated on the trip are much greater than monthly remittances, of course, with a mean of $2,247 across all countries. Savings are raised by $33 for each year of schooling, by $282 for each year of prior U.S. experience, by $459 for each additional $1,000 of net income, and by $548 for holding a formal job in which taxes are withheld. Indeed, it is possible that a tax refund itself constitutes one method of saving in the United States. Surprisingly, the total amount saved is unrelated to the duration of the trip, but it is negatively related to holding legal status and being a U.S. citizen (though the latter effect is not significant owing to the small number of cases, despite the large size of the coefficient). Once again, country differences remain in the amount after controlling for other factors. Paradoxically, although migrants from Costa Rica, the Dominican Republic, and Nicaragua are less likely to return with savings, those who did return with savings came back with significantly more money—$4,116 in the case of Costa Rica, $5,929 in the case of the Dominican Republic, and $7,208 in the case of Peru. Thus, there appears to be some kind of a tradeoff between the likelihood of saving while abroad and the amount saved abroad.

DETERMINANTS OF SPENDING AND INVESTMENT

Finally, we consider the determinants of migrant spending decisions. Since the default use for migradollars is consumption, in Table 12.6 we estimate logit models to predict the likelihood of channeling funds to housing, human capital, and business enterprises. Given the small numbers involved, we combine spending on human capital and business enterprises into a single category of productive investment. The left-hand columns show coefficients for two models estimated to predict the use of remittances and savings on housing, and the right-hand columns show models predicting the use of savings and remittances for productive investments. All the models are highly significant statistically.

Table 12.6. Logit Models Predicting Investment in Housing and Human Capital or Business Enterprises

	Housing		Productive Investment	
	Remittances	Savings	Remittances	Savings
Independent Variables	β	β	β	β
Life Cycle Characteristics				
Age	−0.020	−0.027	−0.054 ***	−0.008
Age Squared	0.000	0.000	0.001 ***	−0.001
Female	0.583 **	0.176	0.643 ***	0.531 ***
Number of Minors	0.048 *	0.017	−0.084 ***	−0.016
Human Capital				
Years of Schooling	−0.042 ***	0.004	0.012	0.014
Prior U.S. Experience	−0.121	0.050	−0.162 **	−0.073
Physical Capital				
Land Owned	−0.222 *	−0.031	−0.256 ***	−0.283 ***
Business Owned	0.155	0.337 ***	−0.001	−0.021
Home Owned	−0.632 ***	−0.557 ***	−0.074	0.034
Legal Status				
Undocumented	—	—	—	—
Temporary	0.102	−0.230	0.155	0.139
Legal	0.467 ***	0.445 ***	0.055	0.243 ***
Citizen	0.661	0.684	0.666	0.840
Trip Characteristics				
Duration of Trip (Years)	−0.002 **	0.004 ***	0.001 **	0.007 ***
Accompanied by Spouse	0.659 ***	0.002	0.766 ***	0.308 ***
Accompanied by Children	0.197	0.160	0.054	−0.250 *
Net Monthly Earnings (000)	−0.006	−0.076 **	0.036	−0.014
Federal Taxes Withheld	−0.264 *	−0.216 ***	−0.394 ***	−0.269 ***
Community Infrastructure				
Paved Road to Highway	0.171	0.200 **	−0.099	0.122
Bank in Community	0.518 ***	0.210 **	−0.394 ***	−0.269 ***
Country				
Mexico	—	—	—	—
Costa Rica	0.371	−0.580 ***	0.123	0.148
Dominican Republic	0.916 *	0.406	0.950 ***	1.409 ***
Guatemala	−0.009	−0.683 **	0.417	0.520
Nicaragua	0.366	0.566 *	−0.657 **	0.352
Peru	0.527	0.872	0.718	−0.698
Intercept	2.230 ***	1.639 ***	1.460 ***	0.789 ***
Likelihood Ratio	176.46 ***	196.56 ***	421.32 ***	349.27 ***
Wald	163.66 ***	172.11 ***	364.72 ***	257.91 ***
Number of Migrants	5,050	5,050	5,050	5,050

+p=0.10; *p<0.05; **p<0.01; ***p<0.001

As can be seen, whereas the channeling of remittances to housing is more likely for females and to households with more dependents, these variables have no effect on the channeling of savings toward housing. In contrast, legal status increases the likelihood that both remittances and savings will be spent on housing, as does the presence of a bank in the community. As one would expect, migrants who already own their own homes are significantly less likely to spend remittances or savings on housing, but those who own a business are more likely than others to channel savings into housing, as are Mexicans whose community is connected to a major highway.

Rising levels of education and longer trip durations are associated with a lower likelihood of spending remittances for housing but a higher likelihood of channeling savings toward housing. Although net monthly earnings has no effect on the use of remittances for housing, it is negatively associated with the likelihood of using savings for housing. Finally, other things equal, migrants from the Dominican Republic are more likely to spend remittances on housing and those from Nicaragua are more likely to spending savings on housing, whereas those from Costa Rica, and Guatemala are less likely to spending savings on housing.

The use of remittances for productive investment is strongly connected to life cycle factors. As expected, the odds of productive investment drop with each additional child in the household and falls with age up to the early forties, when it begins to rise rapidly. In general, women are more likely to use remittances productively than men. The odds of using remittances for productive investment decline with each year of prior U.S. experience but rise with trip duration, rising by around 0.1 percent for each month or around 1.2 percent per year. Being accompanied by a spouse increases the odds of productive investment, as does coming from a community with a bank branch, but owning land and having taxes withheld are associated with a lower likelihood of investing remittances productively. Holding constant these factors, Dominicans are more likely than other migrants to use remittances productively, whereas those from Nicaragua are less likely.

The channeling of savings toward investment is not as closely tied to life cycle factors as the allocation of remittances for this purpose. Only gender is significant, and once again women are more likely than men to use savings productively. Other factors that positively predict the channeling of savings toward productive investments are legal status, the presence of a spouse on the trip, and coming from the Dominican Republic. The odds of using savings productively increase by around 0.7 percent for each month spent in the United States, or around 8.4 percent per year, but productive investment is less likely when children are present on the trip and when taxes are withheld.

CONCLUSION

In this analysis, we drew upon data from the Latin American and Mexican Migration Projects to study patterns of saving and remitting among international migrants from six countries—Mexico, Costa Rica, the Dominican Republic, Nicaragua, Costa Rica, and Peru. Although Peru and the Dominican Republic send a significant number of migrants to countries other than the United States, here we focus exclusively on U.S. migrants. The economic foundations of this migration are suggested by the fact that the large majority of migrants from each country regularly sent monthly remittances, with the percentage ranging from a low of 62 percent in Peru to a high of 80 percent in Guatemala. The amounts sent were significant, with the average remittance ranging from $253 per month in the Dominican Republic to $966 per month in Costa Rica.

The regular sending of remittances home is what one would expect to observe if households were acting to hedge risks to their income by diversifying earnings streams, as predicted by the New Economics of Labor Migration, and our data thus indicate the commonality of this motivation for migration to the United States. There is considerably more variation in the propensity to save in the course of migrating to the United States, with the share who returned with savings ranging from 31 percent in the Dominican Republic to 71 percent in Peru. The total amount saved likewise ranged widely, going from $3,712 in Mexico to $9,148 in Costa Rica. Given that savings behavior is what one would predict if migrants were motivated by a desire to overcome failures in capital and credit markets, these results suggest that this motivation for migration is not as universal as the wish to diversify earnings sources.

Whatever the motivation, the potential of migradollars to serve as an economic catalyst is suggested by annualized quantities of migradollars that we computed to estimate total amount potentially repatriated as a result of one year of labor in the United States. In several countries, we found that the likely financial return for a year of U.S. labor exceeded the country's per capita income, and even in the worst case it still constituted around 45 percent of per capita income. By sending country standards, therefore, international migration indeed offers poor and lower middle class households access to significant resources potentially able to help them overcome failures in insurance, capital, and credit markets.

The use of remittances as a means of income diversification and the commonality of his motivation is also suggested by our multivariate results. The person most likely to remit is a poorly educated, undocumented male with prior U.S. experience who is 20 to 40 years of age and who left a wife and multiple children behind in an owned home and tending farmland in a community that had a bank and was connected to the national highway network by a paved road. The same set of characteristics maximized the amount remitted, except that the monthly amount sent declined with duration of the U.S. trip. Once these individual, household, and contextual factors are held constant, we observe few international differences in either the likelihood of remitting or the amount sent.

In contrast, we observe more differences in both the likelihood of saving and the amount saved remain among migrants from different countries after independent variables are controlled, suggesting that failures in capital and credit markets vary systematically between countries in ways that are not fully captured in our models. Indeed, compared with the remittance models, fewer independent variables are significant in predicting savings behavior among migrants in our samples. Among all variables, we found that the likelihood of returning with savings was least for well-educated, documented females traveling with their husband on a trip of relatively long duration. The odds of returning with savings were greater, however, when migrants owned farmland land and a home. In terms of the amount saved, quantities were generally greatest for well-educated, undocumented migrants who have prior U.S. experience, and, not surprisingly, the amount saved is greater among migrants with higher earnings and more regular employment.

As other studies have found, we confirmed that most money earned in the United States is channeled into family support and maintenance. Nonetheless, models we estimated found that *remittances* were likely to be channeled into housing under certain circumstances, namely when migrants were documented but had not yet spent much time in the United States and did not own land or a home in the sending community. The use of *savings* for housing, in contrast, was likely when migrants were young, poorly educated, males with few dependents and no home owned in the community. The channeling of both savings and remittances toward housing was more likely in Mexican communities with a paved road to the nearest highway. Turning to the use of savings and remittances for productive investments in human capital formation or a business enterprise grows more likely as the trip duration increases and is greater for migrants that already own a home. In addition, the likelihood of spending remittances productively declines with age ands the likelihood of using savings productively declines with education.

Although our results are generally consistent with expectations derived from the new economics of labor migration and from a life course perspective on consumption and investment, they reveal several paradoxes. First, although women are less likely to remit or save and to send home less money than men, and when they do repatriate money they are more likely to channel the funds into productive investments. Second, although documented migrants and U.S. citizens are similarly less likely to remit and save and to repatriate fewer migradollars in either case, the money they do send home is again more likely to be spent productively. Third, regularized employment and higher monthly earnings predict a higher likelihood and greater quantities of both remitting and saving, but lower odds of productive investment. Finally, although long trip durations reduce the odds of returning with savings and lower the amount remitted, they increase the odds of channeling savings toward housing and both remittances and savings toward productive ends. In sum, those factors lower both the likelihood and quantity of funds repatriated appear simultaneously to increase the odds that whatever funds are remitted or sent will be spent on more productive ends. This paradox merits greater attention in future studies of remitting, saving, and investment.

References

Abel, L. K., and Kaufman, R. E. "Preserving Aliens' and Migrant Workers' Access to Civil Legal Services: Constitutional and Policy Considerations." *University of Pennsylvania Journal of Constitutional Law* 5, no. 3 (2003): 491–518.

Abel, L. K., et al. "Responses to Questions of the National Administrative Office of Mexico regarding Public Communication Mex 2005–1 (Rights of Migrant Workers with H2-B Visas) under the North American Agreement on Labor Cooperation," New York, Brennan Center for Justice at New York University School of Law, 2008.

Alarcón, R. "Migrants of the Information Age: Indian and Mexican Engineers and Regional Development in Silicon Valley." Working Paper Number 16, San Diego, California, Center for Comparative Immigration Studies, UCSD, 2000.

Amuedo-Dorantes, C., and Pozo, S. "Do Remittances Decay with Immigrants' Foreign Residencies? Evidence from Mexican Immigrants." *Well Being and Social Policy* 2 (2007): 49–66.

———. "Remittance Income Volatility and Labor Supply in Mexico." Mimeo, San Diego State University, 2009.

Amuedo-Dorantes, C., and Banzak, C. "Money Transfers among Banked and Unbanked Mexican Immigrants." *Southern Economic Journal* 73 (2006): 374–401.

Amuedo-Dorantes, C., Banzak, C., and Pozo, S. "On the Remitting Patterns of Immigrants: Evidence from Mexican Survey Data." *Economic Review* 90 (2005): 37–58.

Amuedo-Dorantes, C., Georges, A., and Pozo, S. 2010. "Migration, Remittances and Children's Schooling in Haiti." *Annals of the American Academy of Political and Social Science* 630 (2010): 224–244.

Arias, P., and Durand, J. "Las Remesas: ¿Continuidad o Cambio?" *Ciudades* 9 (1997): 3–11.

Attanasio, O. P., and Kaufmanny, K. M. "Educational Choices and Subjective Expectations of Returns: Evidence on Intra-Household Decisions and Gender Differences," presented to CES Ifo Area Conference on the Economics of Education, 2010.

Basch, L. G., Schiller, N. G., and Blanc, C. S. *Nations Unbound: Transnational Projects, Postcolonial Predicaments, and Deterritorialized Nation-States.* [S.l.]: Gordon and Breach, 1994.

Bassols-Batalla, A. *México, Formación De Regiones Económicas: Influencias, Factores y Sistemas.* México: UNAM, 1979.

Bean, F. D., King, A. G., and Passel, J. S. "The Number of Illegal Migrants of Mexican Origin in the United States: Sex Ratio-Based Estimates for 1980," *Demography* 20, no. 1 (1983): 99–109.

Bean, F., and Stevens, G. *America's Newcomers and the Dynamics of Diversity.* New York: Russell Sage Foundation, 2003.

Bencivenga, V., and Smith, B. "Unemployment, Migration and Growth." *Journal of Political Economy* 105, no. 3 (1997): 582–608.

Bilsborrow, R. E., Hugo, G., Oberai, A. S., and Zlotnik, H. *International Migration Statistics: Guidelines for Improving Data Collection Systems.* Geneva, Switzerland: International Labour Organization, 1997.

Blau, D. F., and Kahn, L. M. "Gender Assimilation among Mexican Americans." In Borjas, G. J. (ed), *Mexican Immigration to the United States.* Chicago: The University of Chicago Press, 2007.

Borges, M. J. "Migration Strategies, Networks, and Choice of Destination in the Algarve, Portugal, 1860s–1950s." paper presented in Fourth European Social Science History Conference. The Hague, 2002.

Borraz, F. "Assessing the Impact of Remittances on Schooling: The Mexican Experience." *Global Economy Journal* 5 (2005): 1–30.

Bratsberg, B., and Terrel, D. "Where Do Americans Live Abroad?" *International Migration Review* 30, no. 1 (1996): 788–802.

Brown, Stuart S. "Can Remittances Spur Development? A Critical Survey." *International Studies Review* 8, no. 1 (2006): 55–76.

Calderón-Madrid, A. "Job Stability and Labor Mobility in Urban Mexico: A Study Based on Duration Models and Transition Analysis." Analytical Studies Branch Research Paper Series. Research Network Working Paper R-419. Interamerican Development Bank, 2000.

Cano, A., and Nájar, A. (2004). De Braceros a "Trabajadores Huéspedes." Mexicanos en la Lista Negra. In *Masiosare*, no. 355, Mexico, October 10.

Cañas, J., Coronado, R., and Orrenius, P. "U.S.–Mexico Remittances: Recent Trends and Measurement Issues." In Hollifield, J. Orrenius, P. and Osang, T. (eds.), *Migration, Trade and Development: Conference Proceedings.* Dallas: Federal Reserve Bank of Dallas, 2007.

Card, D. "Is the New Immigration Really so Bad?" *the Economic Journal* 115 (2005): F300.

Card, D., and Lewis, E. "The Diffusion of Mexican Immigrants during the 1990S: Explanations and Impacts." In Borjas, G. J. (ed.), *Mexican Immigration to the United States.* Chicago: The University of Chicago Press, 2007.

Cardoso, F. H., and Faletto, E. *Dependencia y Desarrollo en América Latina.* México, D.F.: Siglo XXI, 1969.

Celikaksoy, A., Nielsen, H. S., and Verner, M. "Marriage Migration: Just Another Case of Positive Assortative Matching?" *Review of Economics of the Household* 3 (2006): 253–275.

Cerruti, M., and Massey, D. S. "On the Auspices of Female Migration from Mexico to the United States." *Demography* 38 (2001): 187–200.

———. "Trends in Mexican Migration to the United States 1965 to 1995." In: Durand, J. and Massey, D. S. (eds.) *Crossing the Border: Research from the Mexican Migration Project*, New York: Russell Sage, 2004.

Cervantes, J. "Improving Central Bank Reporting and Procedures on Remittances." Paper presented at the Federal Reserve Bank of Dallas Cross-Border Banking Conference, San Antonio, 2007.

Chávez, A. M. *La Nueva Dinámica de la Migración Interna en México, 1970–1990*. México: UNAM. Centro de Investigaciones Interdisciplinarias, 1999.

Chávez-Alvarado, M. A. "Reporte de la Encuesta Nacional a Hogares Rurales de México 2002," undergraduate thesis, Facultad de Ciencias, UNAM, México, 2007.

Chiquiar, D., and Hanson, G. "International Migration, Self Selection and the Distribution of Wages." *Journal of Political Economy* 113, no. 2 (2005): 239–281.

Chiswick, B. R., and Houseworth, C. "Ethnic Intermarriage among Immigrants: Human Capital and Assortative Mating," *Review of Economics of the Household* 9, no. 2 (2010): 149–180.

Choi, K., and Mare, R. D. "International Migration and Educational Assortative Mating in Mexico and the United States." Working Paper CCPR-004–08, California Center for Population Research, 2008.

Choldin, H. M. "Kinship Networks in the Migration Process." *International Migration Review* (1973*)*.

Coastworth, J. H. "Obstacles to Economic Growth in Nineteenth-Century Mexico." *The American Historical Review*. 83, no. 1 (1978): 80–100.

———. *El Impacto Económico de los Ferrocarriles en el Porfiriato: Crecimiento contra Desarrollo*. México: Ediciones Era, 1984.

Coello-Salazar, E. "El Comercio Interior." In Cosío Villegas, D., *Historia Moderna de México. El Porfiriato*. México: Editorial Hermes, 1965.

Cohen, J. H. "Transnational Migration in Rural Oaxaca, Mexico: Dependency, Development, and the Household." *American Anthropologist*, 103 (2001): 46–67.

Cohen, R. *The New Helots. Migrants in the International Division of Labor*. Asherlot, 1987.

Comisión para la Cooperación Laboral (NAALC) "La Protección de los Trabajadores Agrícolas Migratorios en Canadá, Estados Unidos y México," 2002.

Consejo Nacional de Población (CONAPO). "Estadísticas Sociodemográficas por Estado." México.

———. "Proyecciones de la Población en México, Estados, Municipios y Localidades 2000–2030." México.

Coughlin, C. C., Terza, J., and Arromdee, V. "States Characteristics and the Location of Foreign Direct Investment within the United States," *The Review of Economics and Statistics* 73 (1991): 675–683.

Cox-Edwards, A., and Rodríguez-Oreggia, E. "Remittances and Labor Force Participation in Mexico: An Analysis Using Propensity Score Matching." *World Development* 37 (2009): 1004–1014.

Creighton, M., and Park, H. "Closing the Gender Gap: Six Decades of Reform in
Mexican Education," *Comparative Education Review* 54 (2010): 513–537.

Cruz-Piñeiro, R., and Ruiz-Ochoa, W. "Migración Calificada de Mexicanos a Estados
Unidos Mediante Visado Preferencial," *Papeles de Población* 16, no. 66 (2010):
103–135.

Cuecuecha, A. *Mexican Migration to the U.S.: Theory and Eviden*ce. Berlin: Verlag
Dr. Müller, 2008.

Davies, P. S., Greenwood, M., and Li, H. "A Conditional Logit Approach to
U.S. State-to-State Migration." *Journal of Regional Science* 41, no. 2 (2001):
337–360.

Davis, B. Stecklov, G., and Winters, P. "Domestic and International Migration from
Rural Mexico: Disaggregating the Effects of Network Structure and Composition."
Population Studies 56 (2002): 291–309.

De Jong, G. "Choice Processes in Migration Behavior." In Kavita, P. and Davies
Whiters, S. *Migration and Restructuring in the United States*. Lanham, Boulder,
New York, Oxford: Rowman & Littlefield Publishers, Inc., 1999.

Delechat, C. "International Migration Dynamics: The Role of Experience and Social
Networks." *Labour* 15, no. 3 (2001): 457–486.

Demirgüç-Kunt, A., López-Córdova, E., Martinez-Pería, M., and Woodruff, C. "Remittances and Banking Services: Evidence from Mexico." Mimeo, University of
California, San Diego, 2007.

Docquier, F., Marfouk, A., Salomone, S., and Sekkat, K. "Are Skilled Women More
Migratory Than Skilled Men?" Universite Catholique de Louvain, Institut de Re-
cherches Economiques et Sociales, Discussion Paper 2009–21, 2008.

Docquier, F., and Rapoport, H. "The Economics of the Brain Drain," IRES, Univer-
sité Catholique de Louvain, 2009.

Docquier, F., Marfouk, A., Özden, C., and Parsons, C. "Geographic, Gender and Skill
Structure of International Migration," IRES, Universite Catholique de Louvain,
Belgium, 2010.

Donato, K. M., Hiskey, J., Durand, J., and Massey, D. S. "Migration in the Americas:
Mexico and Latin America in Comparative Context." *Annals of the American
Academy of Political and Social Science* 630 (2010): 6–19.

Duany, J. "To Send or Not to Send: Migrant Remittances in Puerto Rico, the Dominican Republic, and Mexico." *Annals of the American Academy of Political and
Social Science* 630 (2010): 205–223.

Duhau, E. *Mercado Interno y Urbanización en el México Colonial*. México D.F:
Universidad Autónoma Mexicana, 1988.

Dumont, J. C., Martin, J., and Spielvogel, G. "Women on the Move: The Neglected
Gender Dimension of the Brain Drain," IZA DP No. 2920, 2007.

Durand, J. "Los Migradólares: Cien Años de Inversión en el Medio Rural."
Argumentos: Estudios Críticos de la Sociedad 5 (1988): 7–21.

——. "Origen y Destino de Una Migración Centenaria." In Ariza, M. and Portes, A. (ed.), *El País Transnacional, Migración Mexicana y Cambio Social a Través de la Frontera*. México, D. F., México: Instituto de Investigaciones Sociales de la Universidad Nacional Autónoma de México, 2008.

Durand, J., Kandel, W., Parrado, E. A., and Massey, D. S. "International Migration and Development in Mexican Communities." *Demography* 33 (1996): 249–264.

Durand, J., and Massey, D. S. *Crossing the Border: Research from the Mexican Migration Project*. New York: Russell Sage Foundation, 2004.

Durand, J., Massey, D. S., and Capoferro, Ch. "The New Geography of Mexican Immigration." In Zúñiga, V. and Hernández-León, R. *New Destinations, Mexican Immigration in the United States*. New York: Russell Sage Foundation, 2005.

Durand, J., Parrado, E., and Massey, D. S. "Migradollars and Development: A Reconsideration of the Mexican Case." *International Migration Review* 30 (1996): 423–444.

Duryea, S., Galiani, S., Ñopo, H., and Piras, C. "The Educational Gender Gap in Latin America and the Caribbean," IADB, Research Department Working Paper Series No. 600, 2007.

Dustmann, Ch., and Kirchkamp, O. "The Optimal Migration Duration and Activity Choice after Re-Migration." Working Paper, IZA DP No. 266, Institute for the Study of Labor, 2001.

Escobar, A., Bean, F., and Weintraub, S. "The Dynamics of Mexican Emigration." In Reginald Appleyard. *Emigration Dynamics in Developing Countries*. England: Ashgate Publishing Ltd., 1999.

Esquivel, G., and Huerta-Pineda, A. "Remittances and Poverty in Mexico: A Propensity Score Matching Approach." *Integration and Trade Journal* 27 (2007): 45–71.

Eymann, A., and Ronning, G. "Microeconometric Models of Tourists' Destination Choice," *Regional Science and Urban Economics* 27, no. 6 (1997): 735–761.

Faist, T. *The Volume and Dynamics of International Migration and Transnational Social Spaces*. Oxford: Oxford University Press, 2000.

Fajnzylber, P., and López, H. "Close to Home: The Development Impact of Remittances in Latin America (Conference Edition)." The International Bank for Reconstruction and Development/The World Bank, 2007.

Fernández-Kelly, P., and Massey, D. S. "Borders for Whom? The Role of NAFTA in Mexico–U.S. Migration." *The ANNALS of the American Academy of Political and Social Science* 610 (2007): 98–118.

Fernández-Kelly, P. *For We Are Sold, I and My People: Women and Industry in Mexico's Frontier*. Albany: State University of New York Press, 1983.

Florescano, E., Toscano, A. M., Cisneros, A., Aguirre, C., and Terán, Y. *Atlas Histórico de México*. México: Siglo XXI, 1983.

Florini, A. (ed.), *The Third Force: The Rise of Transnational Civil Society*. Tokyo: Japan Center for International Exchange, Washington, D.C.: Carnegie Endowment for International Peace: Brookings Institution Press [distributor], 2000.

Frank, A. G. *Capitalism and Underdevelopment in Latin America*. New York: Monthly Review Press, 1969.

Frank, R., and Heuveline, P. "A Crossover in Mexican and Mexican-American Fertility Rates: Evidence and Explanations for an Emerging Paradox," *Demographic Research* 12, no. 4 (2005): 77–104.

Frenkel, R., and Ross, J. "Unemployment, Macroeconomic Policy and Labor Market Flexibility: Argentina and Mexico in the 1990s." Kellogg Institute for International Studies. Working Paper 309. University of Notre Dame, 2004.

Fry, R. *Gender and Migration*, Washington, D.C.: Pew Hispanic Center, 2006.

———. "Latino Settlement in the New Century." Report, Pew Hispanic Center, 2008.

Fox, J. "Unpacking Transnational Citizenship," *Annual Review of Political Science* 8, no. 1 (2005): 171–201.

Fussell, E., and Massey, D. S. "The Limits to Cumulative Causation: International Migration from Mexican Urban Areas." *Demography* 41 (2004): 151–171.

Furtado, C. *Economic Development of Latin America*. Cambridge, UK: Cambridge University Press, 1970.

Gamio, M. *Mexican Immigration to the United States*. Chicago: University of Chicago Press, 1930.

Gandini, L., and Castro, N. "La Salida de la Escuela y la Incorporación Al Mercado de Trabajo en los Años de Juventud. Análisis de Tres Cohortes de Hombres y Mujeres en México," Paper presented at the seminar Demographic Dynamics and Its Impact on the Youth Labor Market, Universidad Autónoma Metropolitana, Unidad Xochimilco, México City, Mexico, 2007.

Garip, F. "Social Capital and Migration: How Do Similar Resources Lead to Divergent Outcomes?" *Demography* 45, no. 3 (2008): 1–27.

Garza, G. "Tendencias de las Desigualdades Urbanas y Regionales en México, 1970–1996." *Estudios Demográficos y Urbanos* 15, no. 3 (2000): 489–532.

Goldring, L. "Family and Collective Remittances to Mexico: A Multi-dimensional Typology." *Development and Change* 35, no. 4 (2004): 799–840.

Gómez Quintero, N. "Amagan con Dar Revés a Empleo Temporal en Estados Unidos." *El Universal*, February 14, 2007.

González, M. V. "Nuevo Esclavismo en el *Sur Profundo*. Trabajadores Veracruzanos Relatan la Odisea Que Sufrieron en EU." *La Jornada*, July 18, 2007.

Goodman, G., and Hiskey, J. "Exit without Leaving: Political Disengagement in High Migration Municipalities in Mexico." *Comparative Politics* 40, no. 2 (2008): 169–188.

Government Accountability Office (GAO). "Human Trafficking. Better Data, Strategy, and Reporting Needed to Enhance U.S. Antitrafficking Efforts Abroad 2006." Report to the Chairman, Committee on the Judiciary and the Chairman, Committee on International Relations, House of Representatives United States, GAO-06-825, 2006.

Grant, M. J., and Behrman, J. R. "Gender Gaps in Educational Attainment in Less Developed Countries," *Population and Development Review* 36, no. 1 (2010): 71–89.

Greenhouse, S. "Migrants Plant Pine Trees but Often Pocket Peanuts." *New York Times*, February 14, 2001.

Greenwood, M. J. "Human Migration: Theory, Models and Empirical Studies." *Journal of Regional Science* 25 (1985): 521–544.

Greenwood, M. J., and Hunt, G. L. "The Early Story of Migration Research." *International Regional Science Review* 26, no. 1 (2003): 3–37.

Grieco, E. M. "Temporary Admissions of Nonimmigrants to the United States: 2005." Annual Flow Report, Office of Immigration Statistics, DHS, 2006.

Griffith, D. "El Avance del Capital y los Procesos Laborales Que No Dependen del Mercado." *Relaciones* 90 (2002): 16–53.

Grusky, D. "The Simple Virtues of Descriptive Modeling. Reply to Lin and Xie." *American Sociological Review* 63, no. 6 (1998): 907–913.

Guernsey, A. K. "Double Denial: How Both the DOL and Organized Labor Fail Domestic Agricultural Workers in the Face of H-2A," The National Agricultural Law Center, University of Arkansas School of Law, 2007.

Guy, C. "The Pilgrims of Palomas." *Baltimore Sun.* February and June, 2005.

Haber, S. *Industry and Underdevelopment: The Industrialization of Mexico, 1890–1940.* Stanford: Stanford University Press, 1989.

Hanson, G. "Increasing Returns, Trade and the Regional Structure of Wages." *The Economic Journal* 107 (1997): 113–133.

——. "Illegal Migration from Mexico to the United States." *Journal of Economic Literature*, 44 (2006): 869–924.

——. "Emigration, Remittances, and Labor Force Participation in Mexico." *Integration and Trade Journal* 27 (2007): 73–103.

Hanson, G., and Woodruff, C. "Emigration and Educational Attainment in Mexico." Mimeo, University of California, San Diego, 2003.

Hardoy, J. E. "The Building of Latin American Cities." In Gilbert, A., *Urbanization in Contemporary Latin America.* London: John Wiley Sons, 1983.

Harris, J. R., and Todaro, M. P. "Migration, Unemployment and Development: A Two-Sector Analysis." *The American Economic Review* 60, no. 1 (1970): 126–142.

Hauser, R. M. "Recent Developments in Longitudinal Studies of Aging." Paper presented at the IEAS Conference on Contemporary European and American Societies, Academia Sinica, Taipei, Taiwan, September 2009.

Heckman, J., and Pages-Serra, C. "The Cost of Job Security Regulation: Evidence from Latin American Labor Markets." *Economía* 1, no. 1 (2000): 109–154.

Hill, A. M., and King, E. M. *Women's Education in Developing Countries: An Overview.* Baltimore, Maryland: Johns Hopkins University Press, 1993.

Hill, K., and Wong, R. "Mexico–U.S. Migration: Views from Both Sides of the Border." *Population and Development Review* 31, no. 1 (2005): 1–18.

Hirschman, A. O. *Exit, Voice, and Loyalty: Responses to Decline in Firms, Organizations, and States.* Cambridge: Harvard University Press, 1970.

——. "Exit, Voice and the State." *World Politics* 31, no. 1 (1978): 90–107.

——. "Exit, Voice, and the Fate of the German Democratic Republic: An Essay in Conceptual History." *World Politics*, 45, no. 2 (1993): 173–202.

Hirschman, C., Kasinitz, P., and DeWind, J. *The Handbook of International Migration: The American Experience.* New York: Russell Sage Foundation, 1999.

Holley, M. "Disadvantaged by Design: How the Law Inhibits Agricultural Guest Workers from Enforcing Their Rights." *Labor and Employment Law Journal*, July 3, 2001.

Hunt, G. L. 2000. "Alternative Nested Logit Model Structures and the Special Case of Partial Degeneracy." *Journal of Regional Science* 40, no. 1 (2000): 89–113.

Ibarrarán, P., and Lubotsky, D. "Mexican Immigration and Self-Selection: New Evidence from the 2000 Mexican Census," *NBER Working Paper No. 11456*, JEL No. J6, F2 (2005).

Instituto Nacional de Estadística, Geografía e Informática (INEGI). "Conteo de Población 1995." México, 1995.

——. "XII Censo General de Población y Vivienda 2000: Resultados Preliminares," México, 2000.

——. "Encuesta Nacional de Empleo 2000." México. 2000.

——. "Censo de Población y Vivienda 2002." México. 2002.

——. *Cómo Se Hace la ENOE. Métodos y Procedimientos.* Aguascalientes, México: INEGI, 2007.

Inter-American Development Bank (IADB). "Sending Money Home: Remittance to Latin America and the Caribbean." Multilateral Investment Fund Inter-American Development Bank, 2004.

Jasso, G. "New Immigrant Survey." In Darity, W. A. J. (ed.), *International Encyclopedia of the Social Sciences*, Second Edition, Volume 5. Detroit: Macmillan Reference USA, 2008.

——. "Ethnicity and the Immigration of Highly Skilled Workers to the United States." *International Journal of Manpower* 30 (2009): 26–42.

——. "Migration and Stratification." *Social Science Research* Doi:10.1016/J.ssresearch.2011.03.007, 2011.

Jasso, G., Massey, D. S., Rosenzweig, M. R., and Smith, J. P. "The New Immigrant Survey Pilot (NIS-P): Overview and New Findings about Legal Immigrants at Admission." *Demography* 37 (2000): 127–138.

——. "Immigration, Health, and New York City: Early Results Based on the U.S. New-Immigrant Cohort of 2003." *Economic Policy Review* 11(2005): 127–151.

——. "From Illegal to Legal: Estimating Previous Illegal Experience among New Legal Immigrants to the United States." *International Migration Review* 42 (2008): 803–843.

Jasso, G., and Rosenzweig, M. "Estimating the Emigration Rates of Legal Immigrants Using Administrative and Survey Data: The 1971 Cohort of Immigrants to the United States." *Demography* 19, no. 3 (1982): 279–290.

——. "Characteristics of Immigrants to the United States: 1820–2003." In Reed Ueda (ed.), *A Companion to American Immigration*, 328–358, Blackwell Companions to American History. Malden, MA: Blackwell Publishing, 2006.

——. "Remit or Reunify? U.S. Immigrant Parents, Remittances, and the Sponsorship of Children." Presented at the Research Conference on Remittances and Immigration, Federal Reserve Bank of Atlanta, Atlanta, GA, November 2010.

Jones, R. "Remittances and Inequality: A Question of Migration Stage and Geographic Scale." *Economic Geography* 74, no. 1 (1998): 8–25.

Kanaiaupuni, S. M.. and Donato, K. M. "Migradollars and Mortality: The Effects of Migration on Infant Survival in Mexico." *Demography* 36 (1999): 339–353.

Kandel, W., and Massey, D. S. "The Culture of Mexican Migration: A Theoretical and Empirical Analysis." *Social Forces* 80, no. 3 (2002): 981–1004.

Kearney, M. "The Local and the Global: The Anthropology of Globalization and Transnationalism," *Annual Review of Anthropology*, 24 (1995): 547–556.

———. "From the Invisible Hand to the Visible Feet: Anthropological Studies of Migration and Development." *Annual Review of Anthropology* 15 (1986): 331–361.

Keely, C. B., and Tran, B. N. "Remittances from Labor Migration: Evaluations, Performance and Implications." *International Migration Review* 23, no. 3 (1989): 500–525.

Kelly, C. S., and Dalmia, S. "Marital Matching among Immigrants: A Multidimensional Approach," *International Business and Economics Research Journal* 9, No. 1 (2010): 71–82.

Kent, M. M., and Mather, M. "What Drives U.S. Population Growth?." *Population Bulletin* 57, no. 4 (2002).

Knodel, J. E., and Jones, G. W. "Post-Cairo Policy: Does Promoting Girls' Schooling Miss the Mark?" *Population and Development Review* 22, no. 4 (1996): 683–702.

Knudson, T. and Amezcua, H. "The Pineros Forest Workers Caught in Web of Exploitation." *The Sacramento Bee*, November 13–15, 2005.

Kochhar, R. "Unemployment Rises Sharply among Latino Immigrants in 2008." Report, Pew Hispanic Center, 2009.

Lafortune, J. "Making Yourself Attractive: Pre-Marital Investments and the Returns to Education in the Marriage Market," Unpublished manuscript, Department of Economics, University of Maryland, College Park, 2010.

Leite, P., Ramos, L. F., and Gaspar, S. "Tendencias Recientes de la Migración México–Estados Unidos." In *la Situación Demográfica de México 2003*. México, D. F., México: CONAPO, 2003.

Levine, D. B., Hill, K., and Warren, R. (eds.), *Immigration Statistics: A Story of Neglect*. Washington, D.C.: National Academies Press, 1985.

Levitt, P. "Social Remittances: Migration Driven Local-Level Forms of Cultural Diffusion." *International Migration Review*, 32(1998): 926–948.

———. *The Transnational Villagers*. Berkeley: University of California Press, 2001.

Liang, Z., and White, M. J. "Internal Migration in China, 1950–1988." *Demography* 33, no. 3 (1996): 375–384.

———. "Market Transition, Government Policies, and Interprovincial Migration in China: 1983–1988." *Economic Development and Cultural Change* 45, no. 2 (1997): 321–341.

Lin, G., and Xie, Y. "The Loglinear Modeling of Interstate Migration: Some Additional Considerations." *American Sociological Review* 63, no. 3 (1998): 900–906.

Longhi, S., Nijkamp, P., and Poot, J. "A Meta-Analytic Assessment of the Effect of Immigration on Wages." *Journal of Economic Surveys* 19, no. 3 (2005): 451–477.

López-Córdova, E. "Globalization, Migration and Development: The Role of Mexican Migrant Remittances." *Economía* 6 (2005): 217–256.

Lowell, B. L., Pederzini, C., and Passel, J. "The Demography of Mexico/U.S. Migration." In Escobar, A. and Martin, S. F. (eds.), *Mexico–U.S. Migration Management: A Binational Approach*, Lanham, MD: Lexington Books, 2008.

Lowell, B. L. "Trends in International Migration Flows and Stocks, 1975–2005," OECD Social, Employment and Migration Working Papers, No. 58, 2007.

Lowell, B. L., and Findlay, A. "Migration of Highly Skilled Persons from Developing Countries: Impact and Policy Responses." A Project Report for the International Labor Organization (IMP No. 44) and the United Kingdom's Department for International Development, Geneva, 2002.

Lozano, F., and Gandini, L. "La Emigración de Recursos Humanos Calificados Desde Países de América Latina y el Caribe Tendencias Contemporáneas y Perspectivas," SELA, SP/RR-ERHCPALC/DT N° 1–09, 2010.

Lucas, R. E. B. "Internal Migration in Developing Countries." In Rozensweig, M. R. and Stark, O., *Handbook of Population and Family Economics*. Amsterdam: Elsevier Science Publishers, 1997.

———. *International Migration and Economic Development: Lessons from Low-Income Countries*. Cheltenham, UK: Edward Elger, 2008.

Maimbo, S. M., and Ratha, D. (eds.) *Remittances: Development Impact and Future Prospects*. Washington, D.C.: World Bank Publications, 2005.

Maloney, W. *Are LDC Labor Markets Dualistic?* Washington D.C.: World Bank, 1997.

Marcelli, E. A., and Cornelius, W. A. "The Changing Profile of Mexican Migrants to the United States: New Evidence from California and Mexico," *Latin American Research Review* 36, no. 3 (2001): 105–131.

Martin, P. "Economic Integration and Migration: The Mexico–U.S. Experience." In Siddique, M. A. B., *International Migration into the 21st Century. Essays in Honour of Reginald Appleyard*. Cheltenham, UK: Edward Elgar, 2001.

———. "Farm Labor Shortages: How Real? What Response?" Center for Immigration Studies, 2007.

Martin, S. F. "Women, Migration and Development," Transatlantic Perspectives on Migration, Policy Brief #1. Institute for the Study of International Migration, 2007.

Mascaró, Y. "Development Impact of Remittances." Paper presented at the Federal Reserve Bank of Dallas Cross-Border Banking Conference, San Antonio, 2007.

Massey, D. S. "The Ethnosurvey in Theory and Practice." *International Migration Review*, 21 (1987): 1498–1522.

———. "Social Structure, Household Strategies, and the Cumulative Causation of Migration." *Population Index* 56 (1990): 3–26.

———. "The Social and Economic Origins of Immigration." *Annals of the American Academy of Political and Social Science* 510 (1990): 60–72.

———. *Worlds in Motion: Understanding International Migration at the End of the Millennium*. Edited by International Union for the Scientific Study of Population. Committee on South-North Migration., *International Studies in Demography*. Oxford; New York: Clarendon Press ;Oxford University Press, 1998.

———. *New Faces in New Places: The Changing Geography of American Immigration*. New York: Russell Sage Foundation, 2008.

Massey, D. S., Alarcón, R., Durand, J., and González, H. *Return to Aztlan: The Social Process of International Migration from Western Mexico*. Berkeley and Los Angeles: University of California Press, 1987.

Massey, D., Arango, J., Hugo, G., Kouaoci, A., Pellegrino, A., and Taylor, J. E. "Theories of International Migration: A Review and Appraisal." *Population and Development Review* 19, no. 4 (1993): 699–751.

——. *Worlds in Motion: Understanding International Migration at the End of the Millennium.* Oxford: Clarendon Press, 1998.

Massey, D., and Aysa, M. "Social Capital and International Migration from Latin America." Office of Population Research. Working Paper. Princeton University, 2005.

Massey, D. S., and Basem, L. "Determinants of Savings, Remittances, and Spending Patterns among Mexican Migrants to the United States." *Social Inquiry*, 62 (1992): 186–207.

Massey, D. S., and Capoferro, Ch. "Measuring Undocumented Migration." *International Migration Review*, 38 (2004): 1075–1102.

Massey, D. S., and Espinosa, K. "What's Driving Mexico–U.S. Migration? A Theoretical, Empirical and Policy Analysis." *American Journal of Sociology* 102 (1997): 939–999.

Massey, D. S., Fischer, M. J., and Capoferro, C. "Gender and Migration in Latin America: A Comparative Analysis." *International Migration* (2006): 44, 1–29.

Massey, D. S., and Garcia-España, F. "The Social Process of International Migration." *Science* 237 (1987): 733–738.

Massey, D. S., and Parrado, E. A. "Migradollars: The Remittances and Savings of Mexican Migrants to the United States." *Population Research and Policy Review* 13 (1994): 3–30.

——. "International Migration and Business Formation in Mexico." *Social Science Quarterly* 79(1997) 1–20.

Massey, D. S., and Sana, M. "Patterns of U.S. Migration from Mexico, the Caribbean, and Central America." *Migraciones Internacionales* 2 (2004): 1–39.

Massey, D. S., and Zenteno, R. "The Dynamics of Mass Migration." *Proceedings of the National Academy of Sciences,* 96, no. 8 (1999): 5325–5335.

Mehta, C. D. "U.S. Immigration Laws: Emerging Trends in Policies and Procedures." 2004. http://www.cyrusmehta.com/related/Powerpoint-Presentation.PPT.

McFadden, D. "Modelling the Choice of Residential Location." In Karlqvist, A., Lundqvist, L., Snickars, F. and Weibull, J. W., *Spatial Interaction Theory and Planning Models Vol. 3.* Amsterdam, New York, Oxford: North-Holland Publishing Company, 1978.

Mier y Terán, M., and Pederzini, C. "Cambio Sociodemográfico y Desigualdades Educativas." In Arnaut, A. and Giorguli, S. (eds.), *Los Grandes Problemas de México, Vol. VII Educación.* Ciudad de México: El Colegio de México, 2010.

Mora-Rivera, J. J. "The Impact of Migration and Remittances on Distribution and Source of Income: The Mexican Rural Case." Paper presented at United Nations Expert Group Meeting on International Migration and Development, United Nations Secretariat, New York, 2005.

Mora-Rivera, J. J. "Essays on Migration and Development in Rural Mexico," Ph.D. dissertation, El Colegio de México, 2007.

Moreno-Toscano, A. "Cambios en los Patrones de Urbanización en México, 1810–1910." *Historia Mexicana* 22, no. 2 (1972): 160–187.

———. "Economía Regional y Urbanización. Ciudades y Regiones en Nueva España." In Silva-Riquer, J. and Lopez- Martinez, J., *Mercado Interno en México. Siglos XVIII–XIX*. México: Instituto Mora, El Colegio de Michoacán, El Colegio de México, Instituto de Investigaciones Históricas—UNAM, 1998.

Moreno Toscano, A., and Florescano, E. *El Sector Externo y la Organización Espacial y Regional de México (1521–1910)*. Puebla, Mexico, 1977.

Moretti, M. J. "Social Networks and Migrations: Italy 1876–1913." In *International Migration Review* 33, no. 3 (1999): 640–657.

Munshi, K. "Networks in the Modern Economy: Mexican Migrants in the U.S. Labor Market." *Quarterly Journal of Economics* 118, no. 2 (2003): 549–599.

National Administrative Office (NAO). "Responses to Questions of the National Administrative Office of Mexico. Regarding Public Communication MEX 2005–1 (Rights of Migrant Workers with H2-B Visas) under the North American Agreement on Labor Cooperation." October 12, 2007.

Olson, G. "Liberan en EU a 25 Esclavos Mexicanos." *Excélsior*, December 14, 2008.

Orozco, Manuel. "Globalization and Migration: The Impact of Family Remittances in Latin America." *Latin American Politics and Society* 44, no. 2 (2002a): 41.

———. "Latino Hometown Associations as Agents of Development in Latin America." In Rodolfo O. De la Garza and Briant Lindsay Lowell (eds.), *Sending Money Home: Hispanic Remittances and Community Development*, viii, 235 p. Lanham, MD: Rowman & Littlefield Publishers, 2002b.

———. "Between Hardship and Hope: Remittances and the Local Economy in Latin America." Multilateral Investment Fund and the Inter-American Development Bank, 2006.

———. "Migraciones y Remesas en América Latina y el Caribe: Los Flujos Intrarregionales y las Determinantes Macroecónomicas." SP/DI No. 4–06, Sistema Económico Latinoamericano y del Caribe, 2006a.

Orozco, M., and Rouse, R. "Migrant Hometown Associations and Opportunities for Development: A Global Perspective." Washington, D.C.: Migration Information Source. February, 2007.

Orrenius, P. M. "The Effect of U.S. Border Enforcement on the Crossing Behavior of Mexican Migrants." In Durand, J. and Massey, D. S. (eds.), *Crossing the Border: Research from the Mexican Migration Project*. New York: Russell Sage Foundation, 2004.

Orrenius, P. M., Zavodny, M., Cañas, J., and Coronado, R. "Do Remittances Boost Economic Development? Evidence from Mexican States." Mimeo, Federal Reserve Bank of Dallas, 2009.

Ortíz-Hernán, S. *Caminos y Transportes en México: Una Aproximación Socioeconómica: Fines de la Colonia y Principios de la Vida Independiente*. México: Fondo de Cultura Económica, 1994.

Özden, C., Rapoport, H., and Schiff, M. "Five Questions on International Migration and Development," *World Bank Econ Rev* 25, no. 1 (2011): 1–11.

Özden, Ç., and Schiff, M. W. *International Migration, Economic Development, and Policy*. Washington, D.C.: World Bank, 2005.

Palloni, A., Massey, D. S., Ceballos, M., Espinosa, K., and Spittel, M. "Social Capital and International Migration: A Test Using Information on Family Networks." *American Journal of Sociology* 106(2001): 1262–1298.

Parker, S., and Pederzini, C. "Gender Differences in Education in Mexico." In Katz, E. and Correia, M. (eds.), *The Economics of Gender in Mexico: Work, Family, State, and Market*. Washington, D.C.: World Bank, 2001.

Parnreiter, C. "Mexico City: The Making of a Global City?" In Sassen, S. (ed.), *Global Networks, Linked Cities*. New York, London: Routledge, 2002.

Parrado, E. A. "U.S. Migration, Home Ownership, and Housing Quality." In J. Durand and D.S. Massey (eds.), *Crossing the Border: Research from the Mexican Migration Project*. New York: Russell Sage Foundation, 2004.

Passel, J. S. "The Size and Characteristics of the Unauthorized Migrant Population in the U.S." Report, Pew Hispanic Center, 2006.

Passel, J. S., Capps, R., and Fix, M. "Undocumented Immigrants: Facts and Figures." Report, Urban Institute Immigration Studies Program, 2004.

Passel, J., and Suro, R. "Rise, Peak and Decline: Trends in U.S. Immigration 1992–2004." Report, Pew Hispanic Center, 2005.

Pérez-Armendáriz, C., and Crow, D. "Do Migrants Remit Democracy? International Migration, Political Beliefs, and Behavior in Mexico." *Comparative Political Studies* 43, no. 1 (2010): 119–148.

Petras, E. M. "The Global Market in the Modern World-Economy." In Kritz, M. M. and Tomasi, S. M., *Global Trends in Migration: Theory and Research on International Population Movements*. New York: The Center for Migration Studies of New York, 1981.

Pew Hispanic Center. "Survey of Mexican Migrants (Part Two)." *Pew Hispanic Center Project*, Washington, D.C.: March 14, 2005.

——. "Mexican Immigrants in the United States, 2008." Report, 2009. http://pewhispanic.org/files/factsheets/47.pdf.

Piore, M. *Birds of Passage*. New York: Cambridge University Press, 1979.

Portes, A. "Migration and Underdevelopment." *Politics and Society* 1 (1978): 1–48.

——. "Conclusion: Theoretical Convergencies and Empirical Evidence in the Study of Immigrant Transnationalism." *The International Migration Review* 37, no. 3 (2003): 874.

Portes, A., Itzingsohn, J., and Dore-Cabral, C. "Urbanization in the Caribbean Basin. Social Change during the Years of the Crisis." In Portes, A., Dore-Cabral, C. and Landolt, P. *The Urban Caribbean. Transition to the New Global Economy*. Baltimore: Johns Hopkins University Press, 1997.

Portes, A., and Rumbaut, R. G. "Children of Immigrants Longitudinal Study (CILS), 1991–2006." Computer file ICPSR20520-v1, Inter-University Consortium for Political and Social Research, 2008.

Poston, D. L. J., and Mao, M. X. "Interprovincial Migration in China, 1985–1990." *Research in Rural Sociology and Development* 7 (1998): 227–250.

Programa de las Naciones Unidas para el Desarrollo (PNUD). "Informe Sobre Desarrollo Humano México 2002." 2002.

———. "Informe Sobre Desarrollo Humano México 2004." 2004.

Quinn, M. A. "Remittances, Savings and Relative Rates of Return." *Journal of Developing Areas* 38 (2005): 1–23.

———. "Estimating the Impact of Migration and Remittances on Agricultural Technology." *Journal of Developing Areas* 43 (2009): 199–216.

Rallu, J. L. "One-Way or Both-Ways Migration Surveys." In Bonifazi, C. , Okólski, M. , Schoorl, J. and Patrick Simon, *International Migration in Europe: New Trends and New Methods of Analysis.* Amsterdam: Amsterdam University Press, 2004.

Rangan, Kasturi, V., and Lee, K. "Repositioning CARE USA." Harvard Business School Case 509–005. First published 12 August 2008, revised 30 July 2009.

Ratha, D., and Xu, Z. *Migration and Remittances Factbook 2008.* Washington, D.C.: World Bank, 2008.

Reichert, J. S. "The Migrant Syndrome: Seasonal U.S. Wage Labor and Rural Development in Central Mexico." *Human Organization* 40 (1981): 56–66.

———. "Social Stratification in a Mexican Sending Community: The Effect of Migration to the United States." *Social Problems* 29 (1982): 422–433.

Rendall, M. S., Aguila, E., Basurto-Dávila, R., and Handcock, M. S. "Migration between Mexico and the U.S. Estimated from a Border Survey," prepared for presentation at the 2009 Annual Meeting of the Population Association of America, Detroit, and the 2009 Metropolis British Columbia and Center for Research and Analysis of Migration Workshop on the Economics of Immigration, 2009. http:// mbc.metropolis.net/assets/uploads/files/Rendallnew.pdf.

Rendon, S., and Cuecuecha, A. "International Job Search: Mexicans in and out of the U.S." *Review of Economics of the Household* 7, no. 4 (2009): 1–30.

Reyes, B. *Dynamics of Immigration: Return Migration to Western Mexico.* San Francisco: Public Policy Institute of California, 1997.

Riosmena, F. "Policy Shocks: On the Legal Auspices of Latin American Migration to the United States." *Annals of the American Academy of Political and Social Science* 630 (2010): 270–293.

Roberts, K. D., and Morris, M. "Fortune, Risk and Remittances: An Application of Option Theory to Participation in Village-Based Migration Networks." *International Migration Review* 37 (2004): 1252–1281.

Rubalcava, L., Teruel, G., Goldman, N., and Thomas, D. "The Healthy Migrant Effect: New Findings from the Mexican Family Life Survey." *American Journal of Public Health* 2007.

Rural Migration News. "Midwest, Northeast, Northwest." January, 2005.

Sana, M. "Growth of Migrant Remittances from the United States to Mexico, 1990–2004." *Social Forces* 86 (2008): 995–1025.

Sana, M., and Massey, D. S. "Household Composition, Family Migration, and Community Context: Migrant Remittances in Four Countries." *Social Science Quarterly* 86 (2005): 509–528.

Sassen, S. *The Mobility of Labor and Capital. A Study of International Investment and Labor Flow.* Cambridge: Cambridge University Press, 1988.

Sastry, N., Ghosh-Dastidar, B., Adams, J., and Pebley, A. R. "The Design of a Multilevel Survey of Children, Families, and Communities: The Los Angeles Family and Neighborhood Survey." Working Paper No. 2003–06, Office of Population Research Princeton University, 2003.

Schiller, N. G. "Transmigrants and Nation-States: Something Old and Something New in the U.S. Immigrant Experience." In Hirschman, C., Kasinitz, P. and DeWind, J. (eds.), *The Handbook of International Migration: The American Experience*. New York: Russell Sage Foundation, 1999.

Schultz, T. P. "Investments in the Schooling and Health of Women and Men: Quantities and Returns." *The Journal of Human Resources* 28, no. 4 (1993): 694–734.

Secretaría de Comunicaciones y Transportes. "Encuestas de Origen-Destino." México, 2002.

Singer, A., and Massey, D. S. "The Social Process of Undocumented Border Crossing among Mexican Migrants." *International Migration Review*. 32 (1998): 561–592.

Sjaastad, L. "The Costs and Returns of Human Migration." *Journal of Political Economy* 70, no. 5 (1962): 80–93.

Smith, R. C. *Mexican New York: Transnational Lives of New Immigrants*. Berkeley: University of California Press, 2006.

Somoza, J. L. "El Método de Encuesta Demográfica de CELADE." Systems of Demographic Measurement Data Collection Systems. Laboratories for Population Statistics, Scientific Report Series No. 18. February 1975.

Southern Poverty Law Center (SPLC). "Cercano a la Esclavitud. Programas de Trabajadores Huéspedes en los Estados Unidos," 2007.

Stark, Oded . *The Migration of Labor*. Cambridge: Basil Blackwell, 1991.

Stark, O., and Bloom, D. E. "The New Economics of Labor Migration." *American Economic Review* 75 (1985): 173–178.

Strom, Stephanie. (2011) "CARE, in Return to Roots, Will Offer Virtual Packages." *The New York Times*, 7 March 2011.

Suárez-Orozco, C., and Suárez-Orozco, M. M. *Children of Immigration*. USA: Harvard University Press, 2001.

Taylor, J. E. "Differential Migration, Networks, Information, and Risk." In Stark, O. (ed.), *Migration Theory, Human Capital, and Development*. Greenwich, CT: JAI Press, 1986.

———. "The New Economics of Labour Migration and the Role of Remittances in the Migration Process," *International Migration* 37, no. 1 (1999): 63–87.

Taylor, J. E., and Wyatt, T. J. "The Shadow Value of Migrant Remittances, Income and Inequality in a Household-Farm Economy." *Journal of Development Studies* 32 (1996): 899–912.

Terry, D. F., and Wilson, S. R. *Beyond Small Change: Making Migrant Remittances Count*. Washington, D.C.: Inter-American Development Bank, 2005.

Thomas, D., Frankenberg, E., and Smith, J. P. "Lost but Not Forgotten: Attrition and Follow-up in the Indonesia Family Life Survey." *The Journal of Human Resources* 36, no. 3 (2000): 556–592.

Thomas, W. I., and Znaniecki, F. *The Polish Peasant in Europe and America*. Boston: William Badger (1918–1919).

Todaro, M. "A Model of Urban Migration and Urban Unemployment in Less Developed Countries." *The American Economic Review* 59, no. 1 (1969): 138–148.

Torres, G., and Pelham, B. "Is All the Talent Leaving Latin America? Perhaps, but the Highly Educated Wish to Stay," GALLUP, 2008.

Unikel, L. "Políticas de Desarrollo Regional en México." *Demografía y Economía* 9, no. 2 (1975): 143–181.

United Nations Population Division. *Trends in Total Migrant Stock: The 2005 Revision*. New York: UN Population Division, 2005.

U.S. Bureau of the Census. *Historical Statistics of the United States: Colonial Times to 1970*. Two volumes. Washington, D.C.: Government Printing Office, 1975.

U.S. Department of Homeland Security. *Yearbook of Immigration Statistics*. Washington, D.C.: Government Printing Office, 2002–2010.

U.S. Department of Labor. "Findings from the National Agricultural Workers Survey (NAWS) 2001–2002. A Demographic and Employment Profile of United States Farm Workers." Research Report No. 9, 2005. http://www.doleta.gov/agworker/naws.cfm.

U.S. Department of State. Various Issues. *Visa Bulletin*. Posted Online.

U.S. Immigration and Naturalization Service. *Annual Report of the Immigration and Naturalization Service*. Washington, D.C.: U.S. Government Printing Office, 1943–1978.

———. *Statistical Yearbook of the Immigration and Naturalization Service*. Washington, D.C.: U.S. Government Printing Office, 1979–2001.

U.S. Immigration Commission. *Reports of the Immigration Commission*. 42 Volumes. Washington, D.C.: U.S. Government Printing Office. Also known as the Dillingham Commission Report, 1911.

Valencia-Lomelí, E. "Conditional Cash Transfers as Social Policy in Latin America: An Assessment of Their Contributions and Limitations." *Annual Review of Sociology* 34 (2008): 475–499.

Van Hook, J., Zhang, W., Bean, F. D., and Passel, J. S. "Foreign-Born Emigration: A New Approach and Estimates Based on Matched CPS Files." *Demography*, 43 (2006): 361–382.

Vertovec, S. "Migration and Other Modes of Transnationalism: Towards Conceptual Cross-Fertilization." *The International Migration Review* 37, no. 3 (2003): 641.

Waldinger, R. S., and Fitzgerald, D. "Transnationalism in Question." *American Journal of Sociology* 109, no. 5 (2004): 1177–1195.

Waller Meyers, D. "Temporary Worker Programs: A Patchwork Policy Response." Migration Policy Institute, Insight # 12, January, 2006.

Wassem, R. E., and Collver, G. "Immigration of Agricultural Guest Workers: Policy, Trends and Legislative Issues." Report prepared for the Congressional Research Service (CRS), United States, 2001.

Warren, R. Estimates of the Unauthorized Immigrant Population Residing in the United States: 1990 to 2000. Department of Homeland Security, 2003.

Warren, R. "Detailed Methodology for Annual Estimates of the Unauthorized Immigrant Population Residing in the United States: 1990–2000 (Unpubl.).

Wong, R., Resano, E., and Martínez, L. *Una Constante Cambiante: La Migración de la Población Mexicana Hacia los Estados Unidos de Norteamérica*. Zapopan,

Jalisco, México: Universidad del Estado de México, Universidad de Guadalajara y University of Maryland, 2006.

Woodruff, C., and Zenteno, R. "Migration Networks and Microenterprises in Mexico." *Journal of Development Economics* 82 (2007): 509–528.

Yang, D. "Why Do Migrants Return to Poor Countries? Evidence from Phillipine Migrants' Responses to Exchange Rate Shocks." *Review of Economics and Statistics* 88, no. 4 (2006): 715–735.

Yeoman, B. "Silence in the Fields." *Mother Jones News*, January/February, 2001.

Yúnez-Naude, A., Taylor, J. E., and García, J. Becerril. "Los Pequeños Productores Rurales en México: Características y Análisis de Impactos." In A. Yúnez-Naude (Comp.) *Los Pequeños Productores Rurales en México: Las Reformas y las Opciones*. México: El Colegio de México, 2000.

Zuñiga, V., and Hernández-León, R. "Introduction." In V. Zúñiga and R. Hernández-León *New Destinations, Mexican Immigration in the United States*. New York: Russell Sage Foundation, 2005.

Zhou, M. "Contemporary Female Immigration to the United States: A Demographic Profile." In *Women Immigrants in the United States*. Washington, D.C.: Woodrow Wilson International Center for Scholars, 2002.

Zhu, J. "Rural Out-Migration in China: A Multilevel Model." In Bilsborrow, R., *Migration, Urbanization, and Development: New Directions and Issues*. Kluwer Publishing, 1998.

Index

Italicized numbers indicate a figure or a table.

283